SUPERMAN BATMAN
PUBLIC ENEMIES

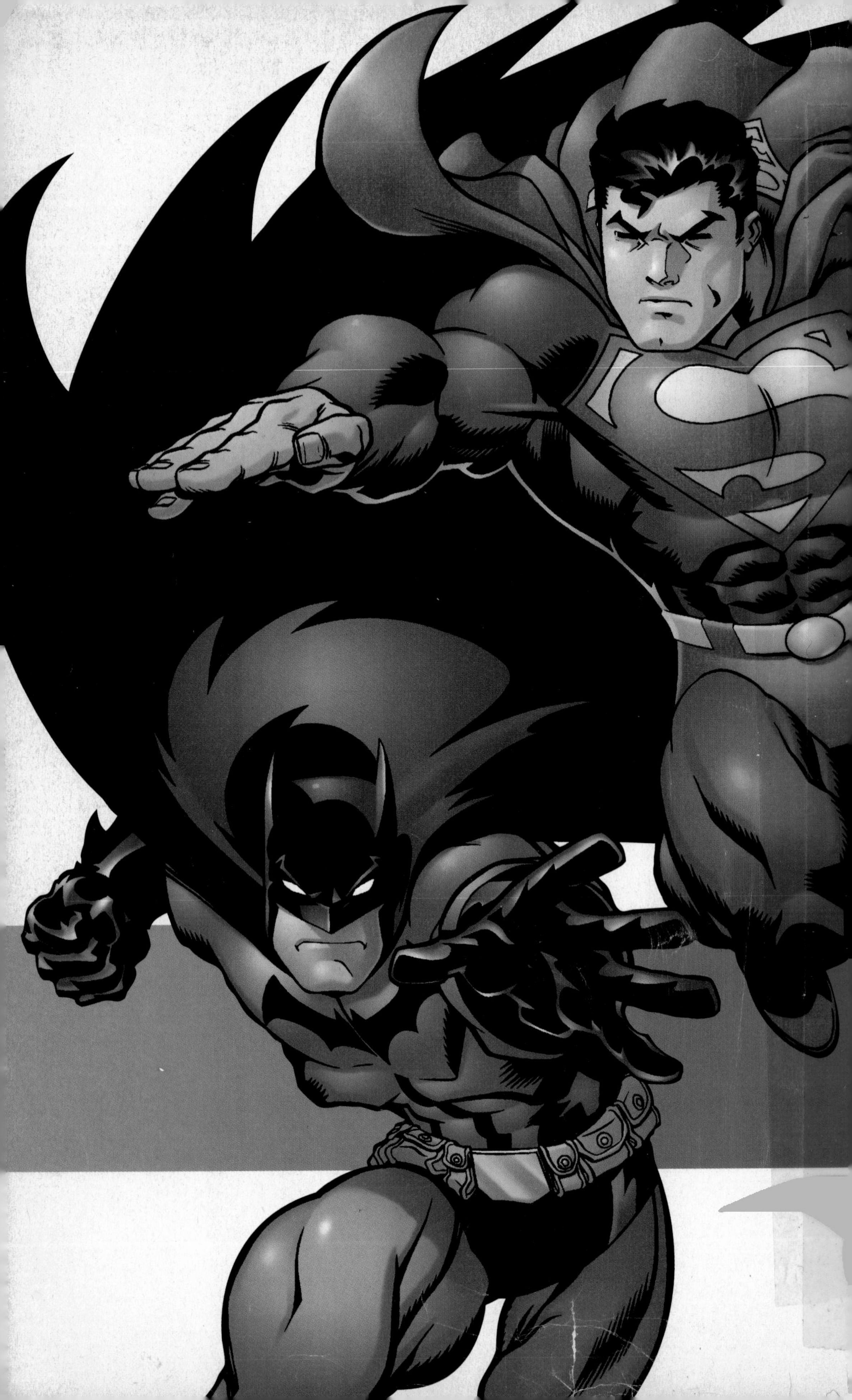

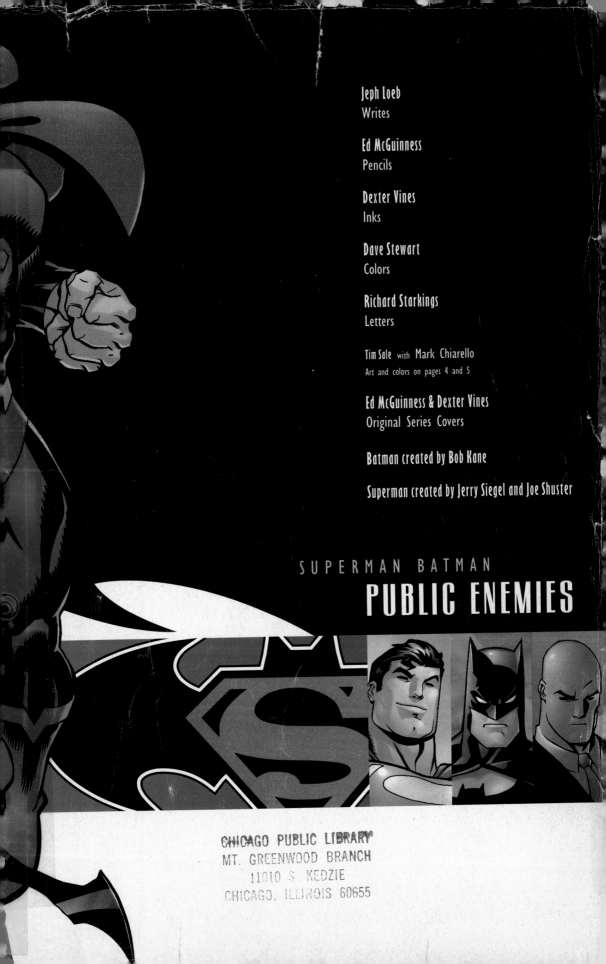

Jeph Loeb
Writes

Ed McGuinness
Pencils

Dexter Vines
Inks

Dave Stewart
Colors

Richard Starkings
Letters

Tim Sale with **Mark Chiarello**
Art and colors on pages 4 and 5

Ed McGuinness & Dexter Vines
Original Series Covers

Batman created by Bob Kane

Superman created by Jerry Siegel and Joe Shuster

SUPERMAN BATMAN
PUBLIC ENEMIES

When Clark met Bruce

A TALE FROM THE DAYS OF SMALLVILLE

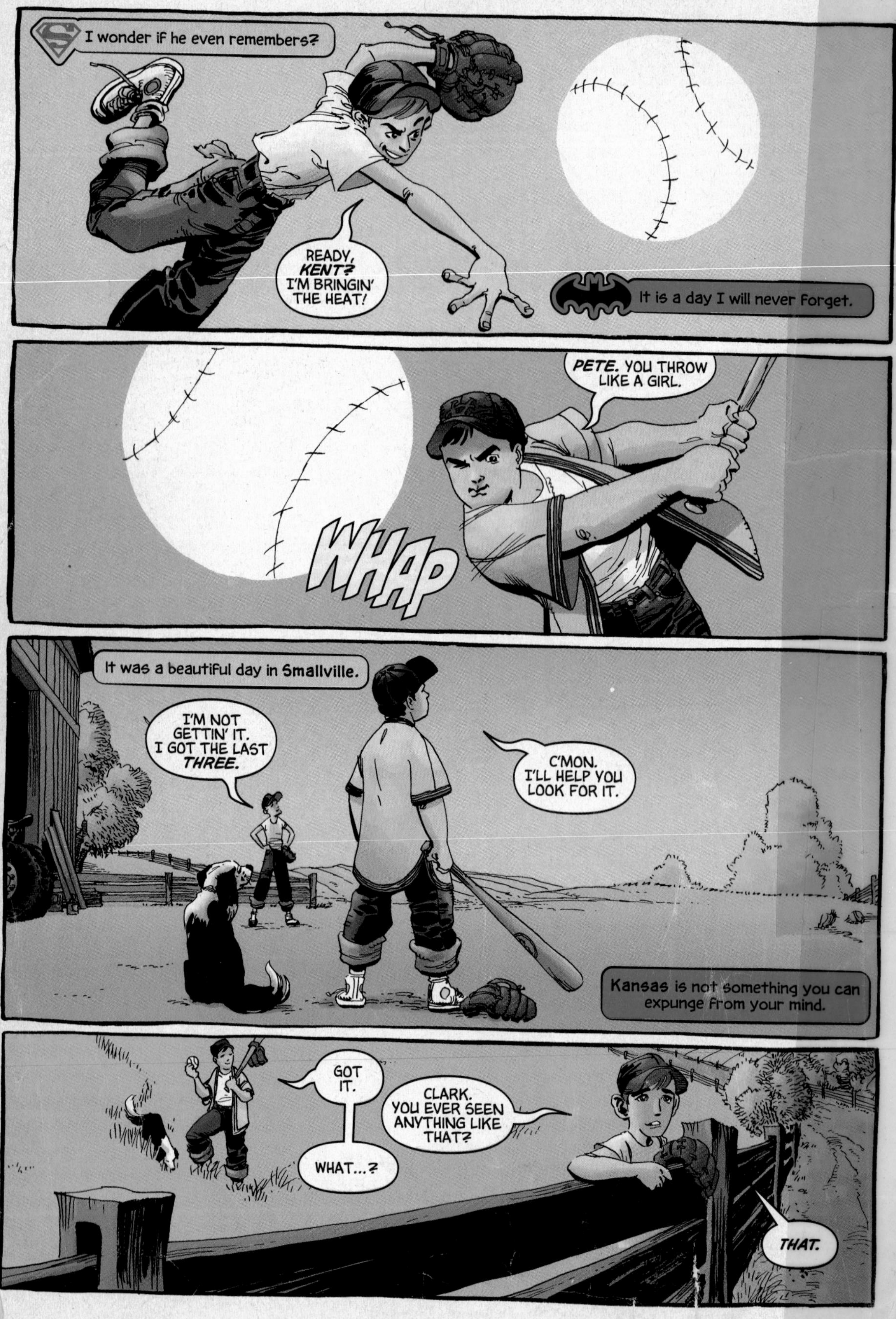
I wonder if he even remembers?
READY, KENT? I'M BRINGIN' THE HEAT!
It is a day I will never forget.
PETE. YOU THROW LIKE A GIRL.
WHAP
It was a beautiful day in Smallville.
I'M NOT GETTIN' IT. I GOT THE LAST THREE.
C'MON. I'LL HELP YOU LOOK FOR IT.
Kansas is not something you can expunge from your mind.
GOT IT.
CLARK. YOU EVER SEEN ANYTHING LIKE THAT?
WHAT...?
THAT.

Pete was right. No one in Smallville had that kind of wealth.

After my parents died, Alfred thought that I needed to get out of Gotham City. We drove to California.

THINK WE SHOULD ASK THAT KID TO PLAY BALL?

CLARK. LOOK AT HIM. THAT KID HAS NEVER PLAYED *ANYTHING*.

By the time we reached the West Coast, I had convinced Alfred we should fly back home.

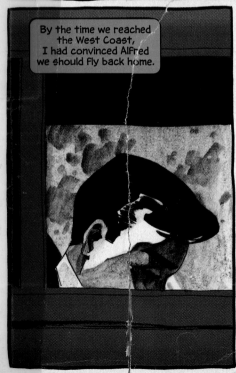

WONDER WHO THAT WAS...?

WHO CARES? RACE YA. LAST ONE IN HAS TO KISS *LANA!*

I still wonder if we should've asked him to play. If it would've made a difference.

Sometimes, I wish they had asked me to play. But, by then, my life had changed. I had no time for games.

LOEB
SALE
2002

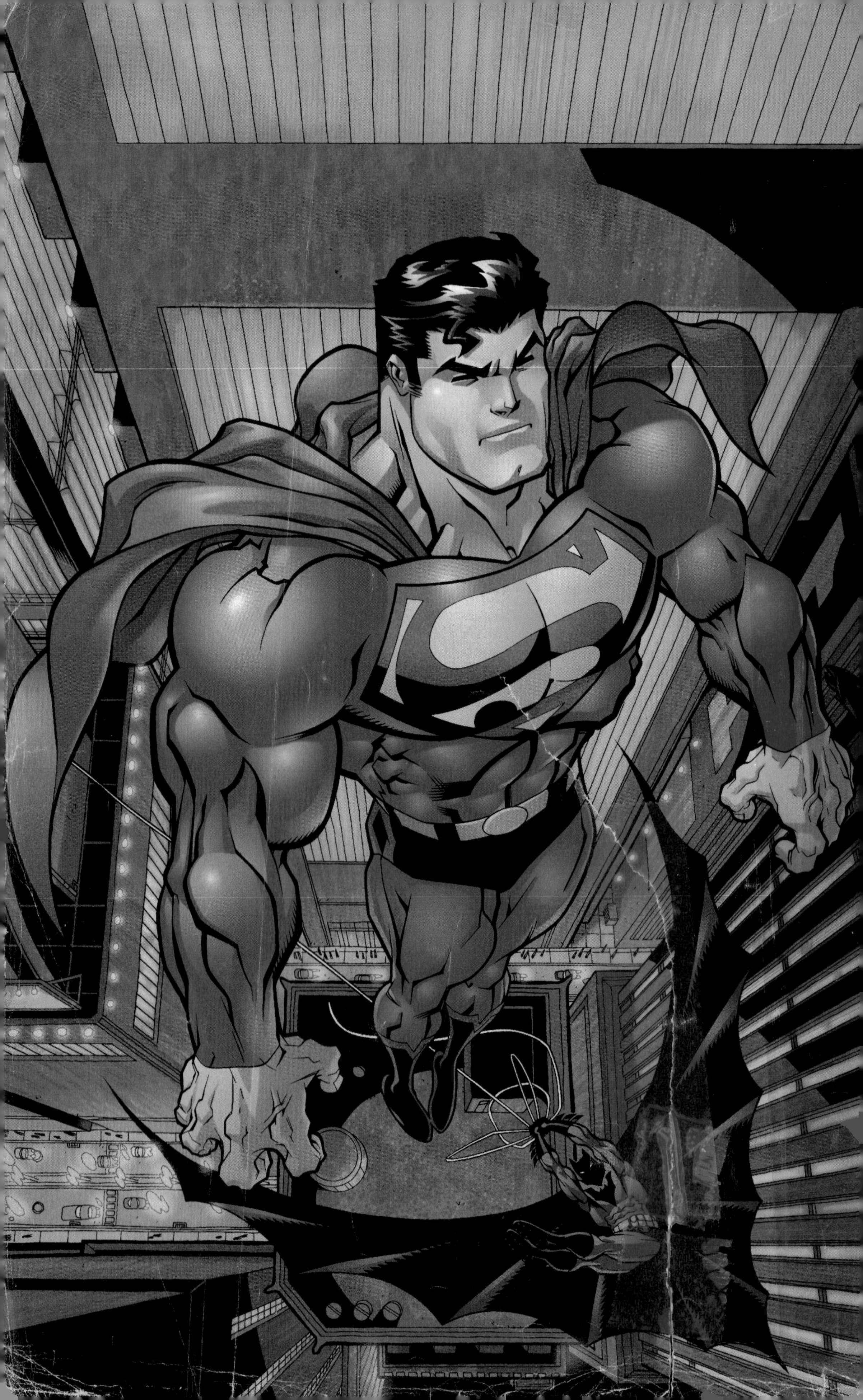

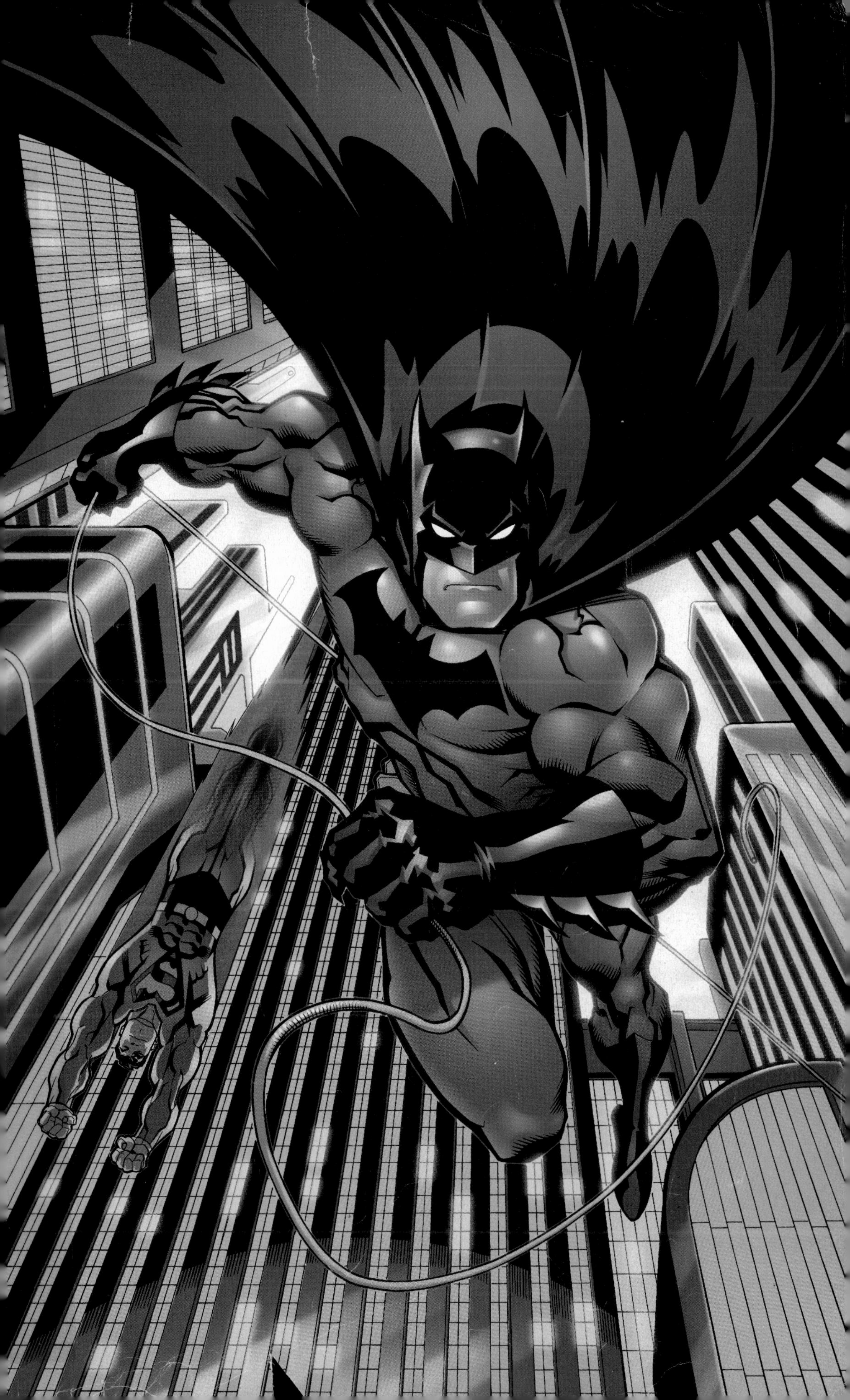

"Clark, sometimes you can be a fool."

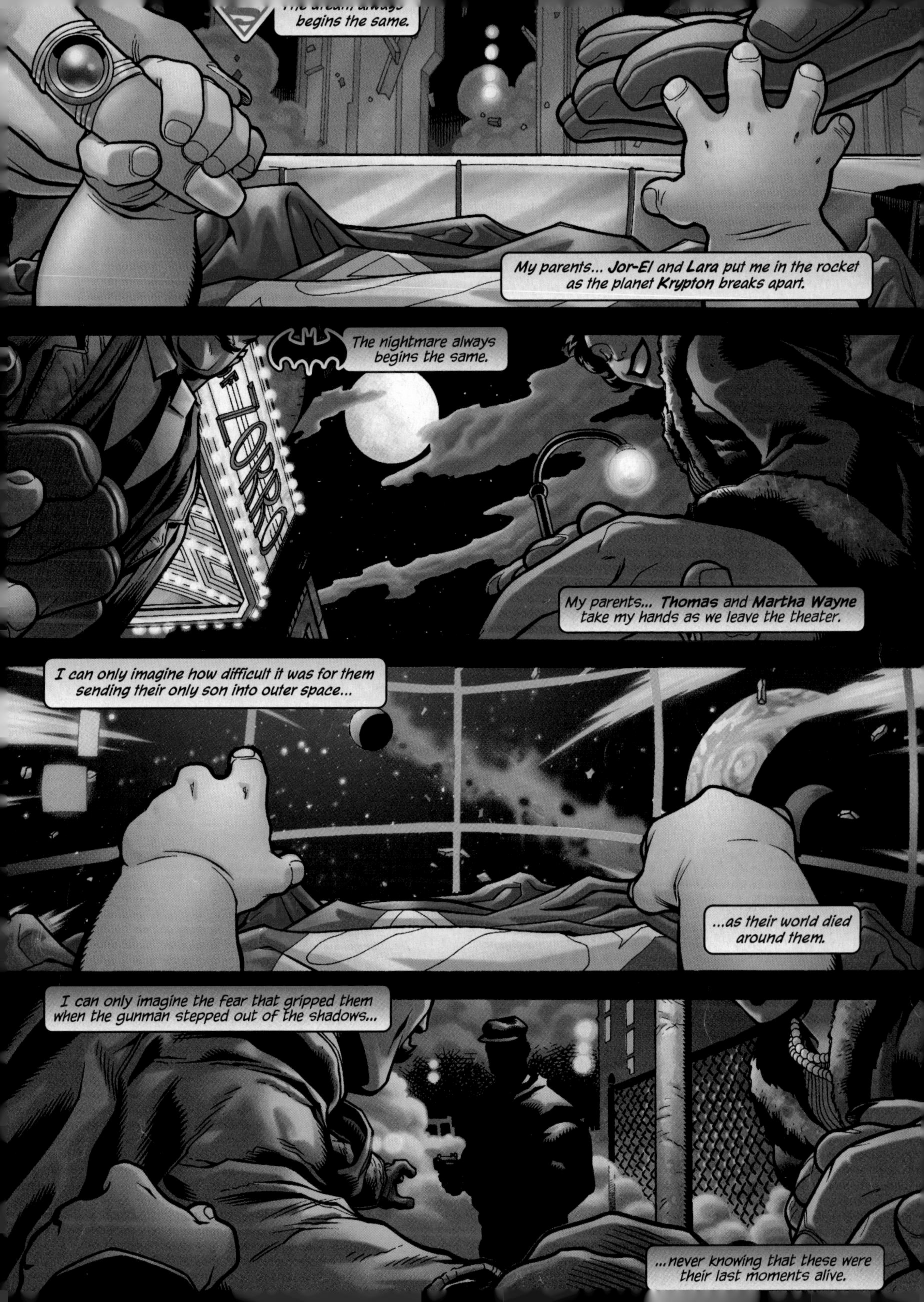
begins the same.
My parents... Jor-El and Lara put me in the rocket as the planet Krypton breaks apart.
The nightmare always begins the same.
ZORRO
My parents... Thomas and Martha Wayne take my hands as we leave the theater.
I can only imagine how difficult it was for them sending their only son into outer space...
...as their world died around them.
I can only imagine the fear that gripped them when the gunman stepped out of the shadows...
...never knowing that these were their last moments alive.

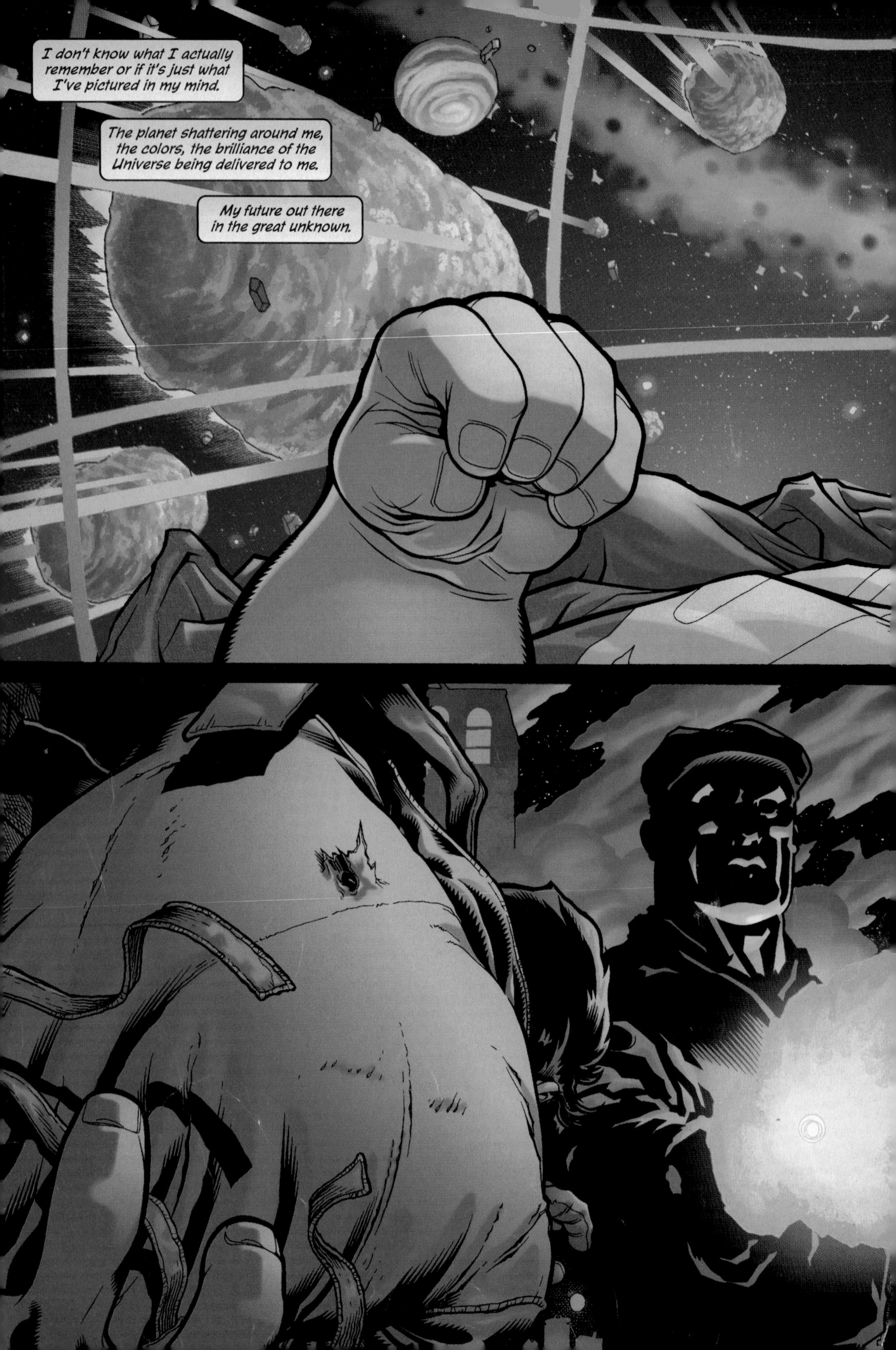
I don't know what I actually remember or if it's just what I've pictured in my mind.
The planet shattering around me, the colors, the brilliance of the Universe being delivered to me.
My future out there in the great unknown.

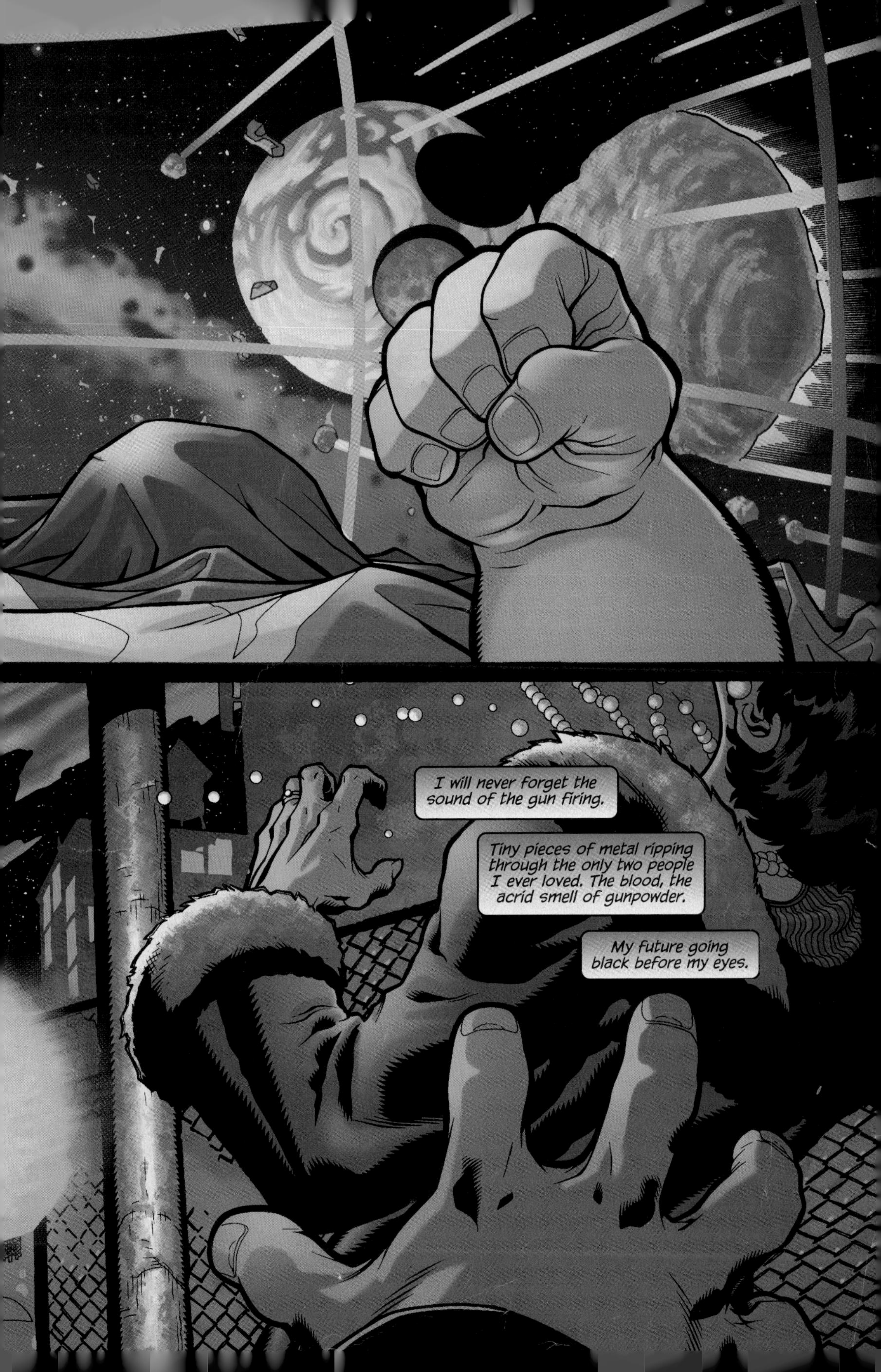
I will never forget the sound of the gun firing.
Tiny pieces of metal ripping through the only two people I ever loved. The blood, the acrid smell of gunpowder.
My future going black before my eyes.

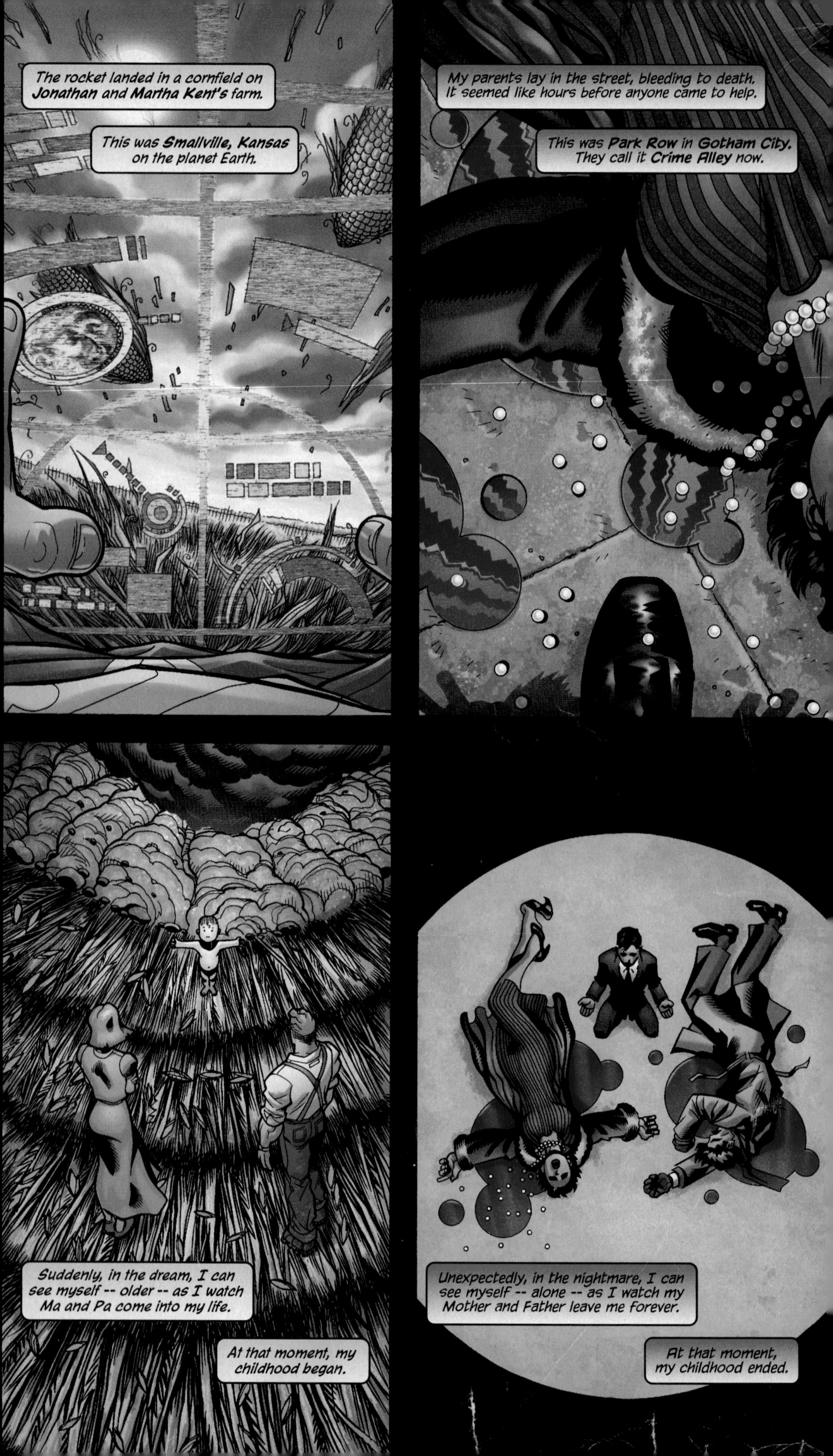

The rocket landed in a cornfield on Jonathan and Martha Kent's farm.
This was Smallville, Kansas on the planet Earth.
My parents lay in the street, bleeding to death. It seemed like hours before anyone came to help.
This was Park Row in Gotham City. They call it Crime Alley now.
Suddenly, in the dream, I can see myself -- older -- as I watch Ma and Pa come into my life.
At that moment, my childhood began.
Unexpectedly, in the nightmare, I can see myself -- alone -- as I watch my Mother and Father leave me forever.
At that moment, my childhood ended.

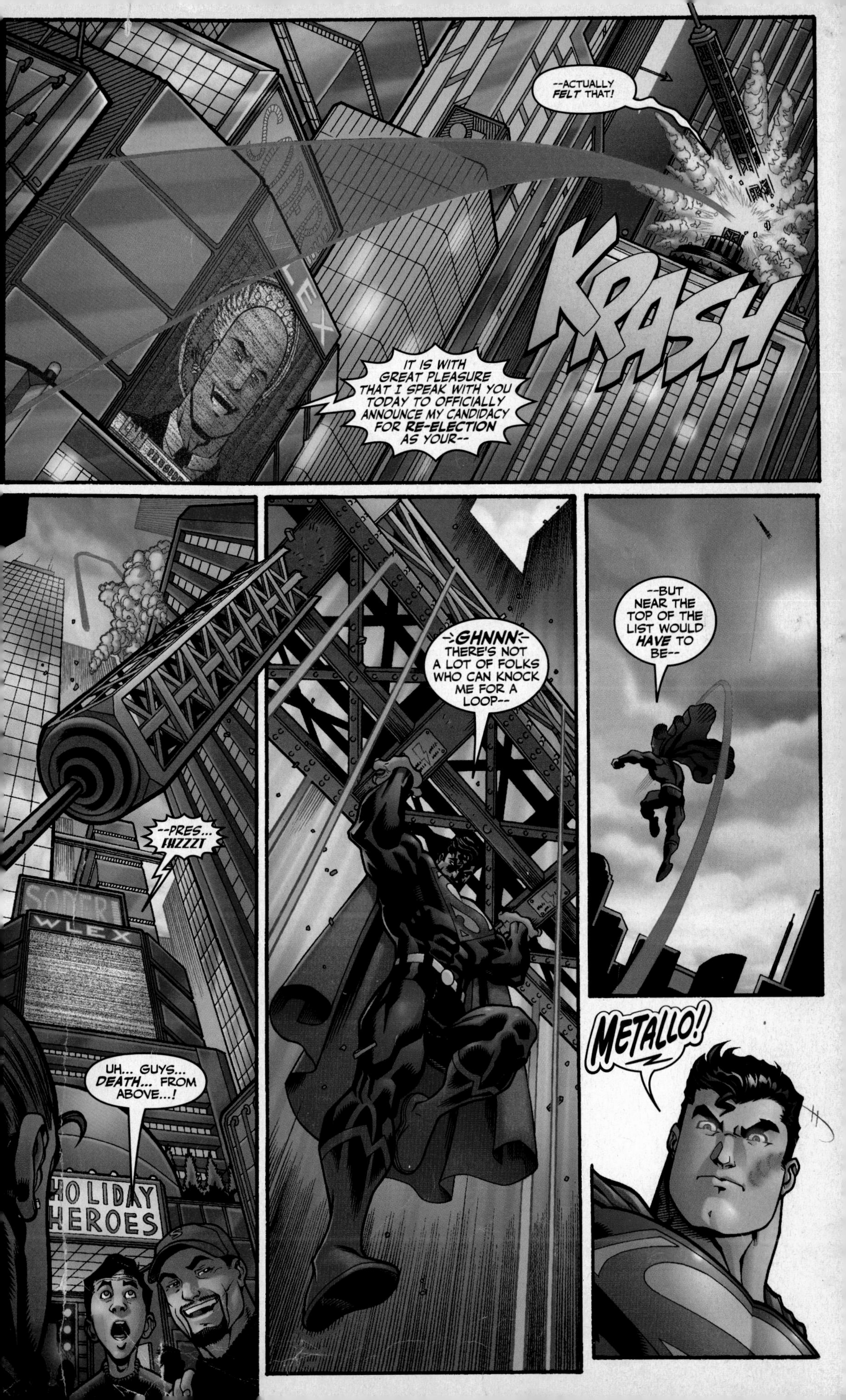
--ACTUALLY FELT THAT!
KRASH
IT IS WITH GREAT PLEASURE THAT I SPEAK WITH YOU TODAY TO OFFICIALLY ANNOUNCE MY CANDIDACY FOR RE-ELECTION AS YOUR--
WLEX
--PRES... FHZZZT
WLEX
HOLIDAY HEROES
UH... GUYS... DEATH... FROM ABOVE...!
--GHNNN-- THERE'S NOT A LOT OF FOLKS WHO CAN KNOCK ME FOR A LOOP--
--BUT NEAR THE TOP OF THE LIST WOULD HAVE TO BE--
METALLO!

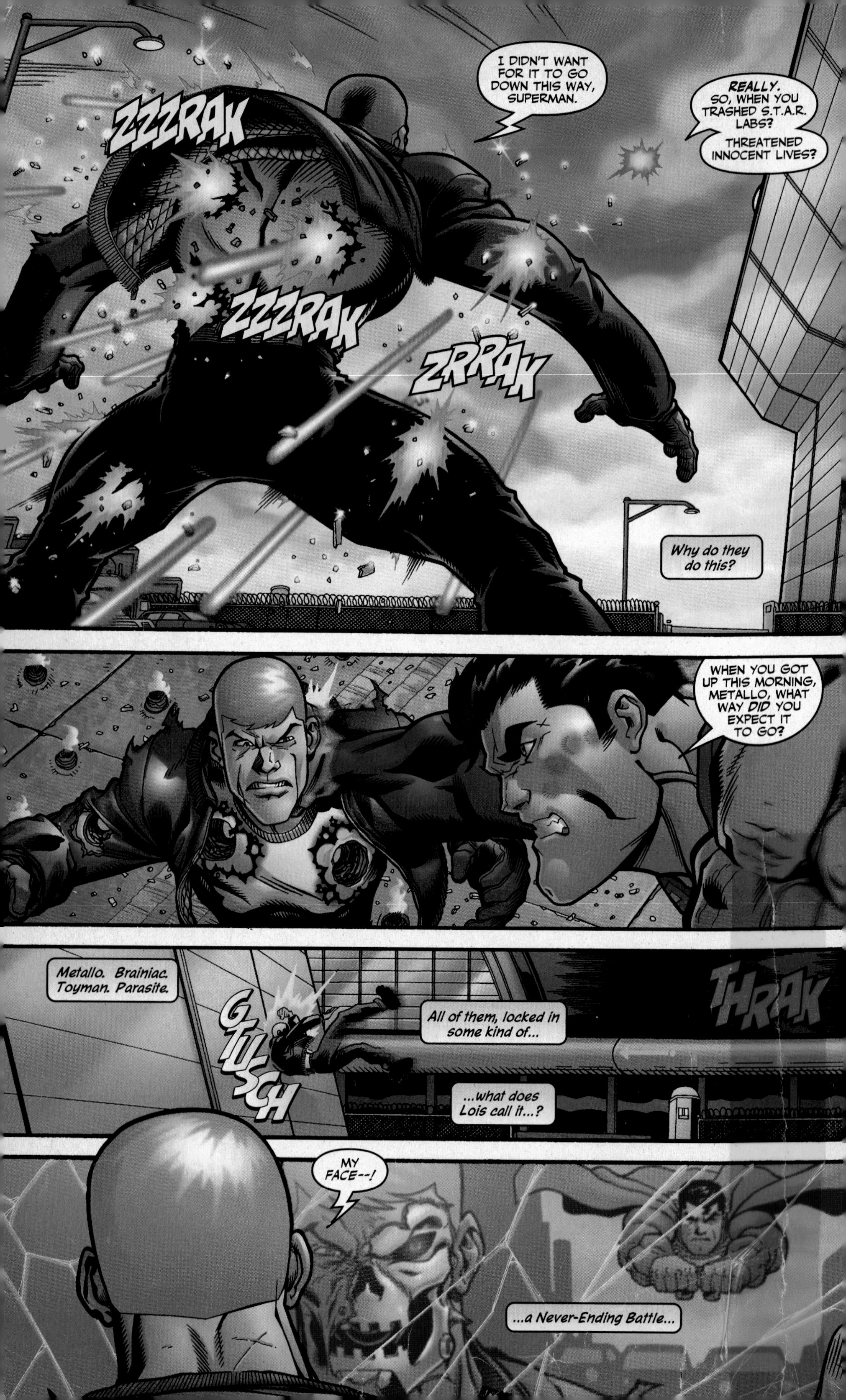
ZZZRAK
I DIDN'T WANT FOR IT TO GO DOWN THIS WAY, SUPERMAN.
REALLY. SO, WHEN YOU TRASHED S.T.A.R. LABS?
THREATENED INNOCENT LIVES?
ZZZRAK
ZRRAK
Why do they do this?
WHEN YOU GOT UP THIS MORNING, METALLO, WHAT WAY DID YOU EXPECT IT TO GO?
Metallo. Brainiac. Toyman. Parasite.
GTUSCH
All of them, locked in some kind of...
THRAK
...what does Lois call it...?
MY FACE--!
...a Never-Ending Battle...

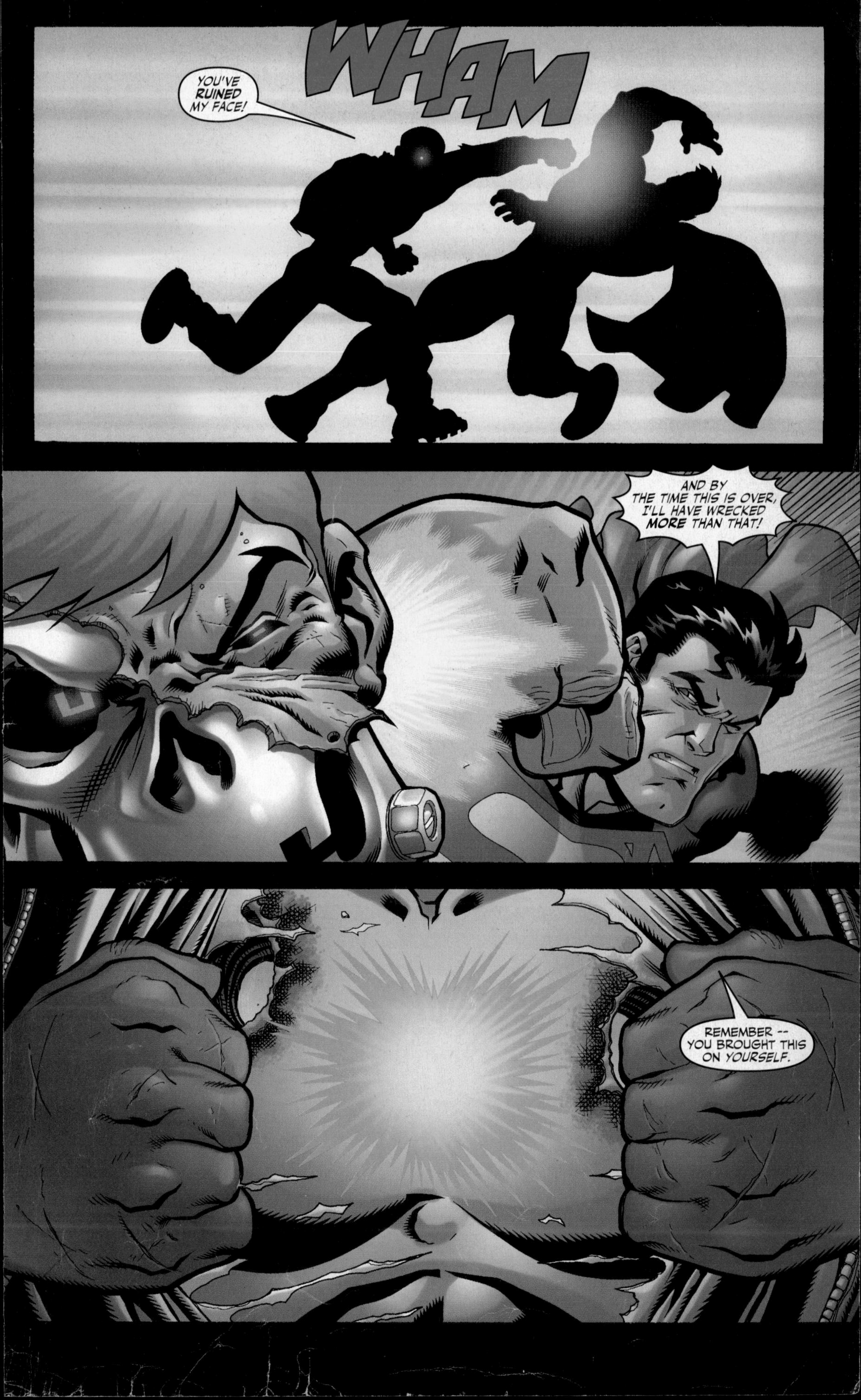
WHAM
YOU'VE RUINED MY FACE!
AND BY THE TIME THIS IS OVER, I'LL HAVE WRECKED MORE THAN THAT!
REMEMBER -- YOU BROUGHT THIS ON YOURSELF.

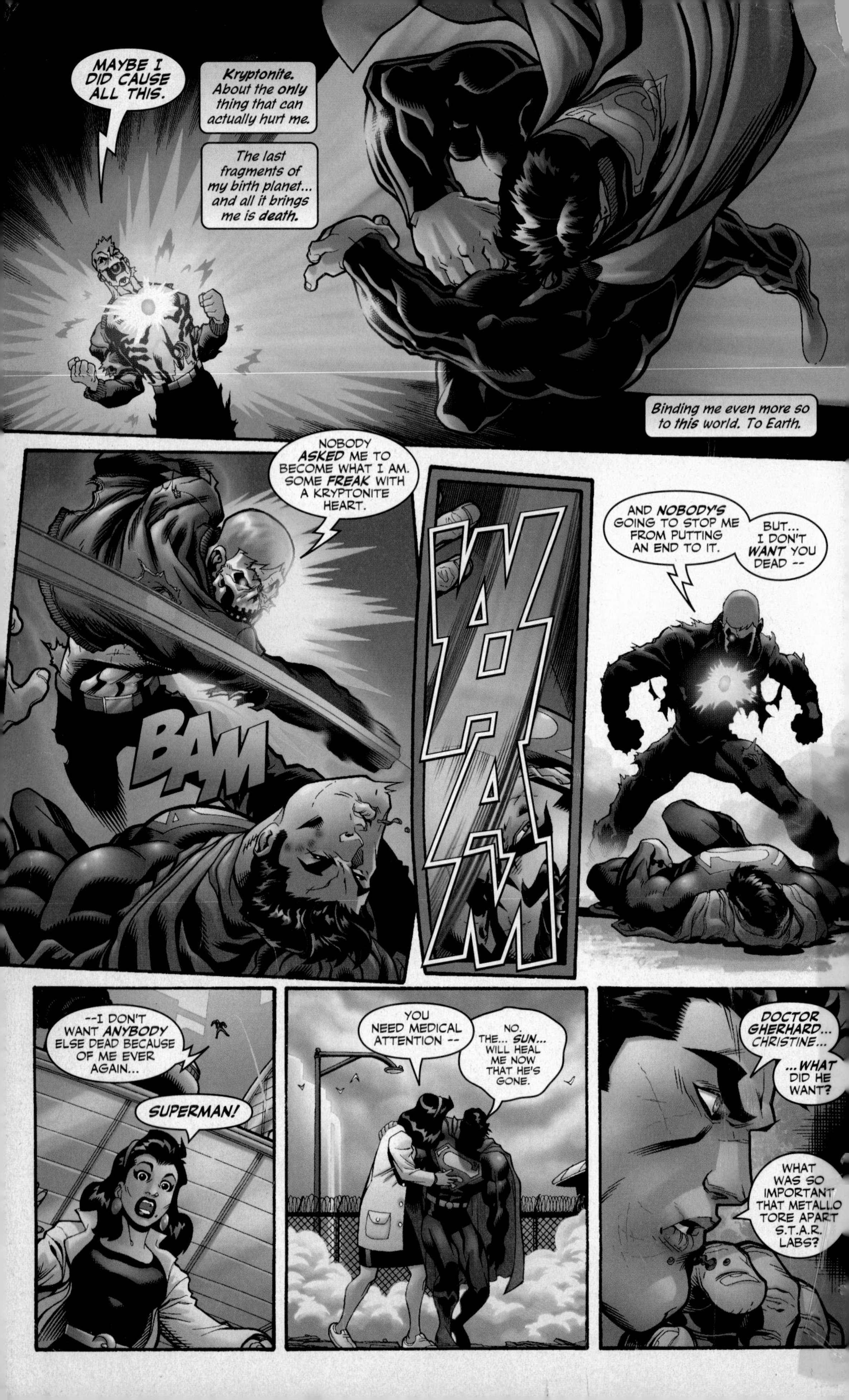

MAYBE I DID CAUSE ALL THIS.
Kryptonite. About the only thing that can actually hurt me.
The last fragments of my birth planet... and all it brings me is death.
Binding me even more so to this world. To Earth.
NOBODY ASKED ME TO BECOME WHAT I AM. SOME FREAK WITH A KRYPTONITE HEART.
BAM
WHAM
AND NOBODY'S GOING TO STOP ME FROM PUTTING AN END TO IT.
BUT... I DON'T WANT YOU DEAD --
--I DON'T WANT ANYBODY ELSE DEAD BECAUSE OF ME EVER AGAIN...
SUPERMAN!
YOU NEED MEDICAL ATTENTION --
NO. THE... SUN... WILL HEAL ME NOW THAT HE'S GONE.
DOCTOR GHERHARD... CHRISTINE...
...WHAT DID HE WANT?
WHAT WAS SO IMPORTANT THAT METALLO TORE APART S.T.A.R. LABS?

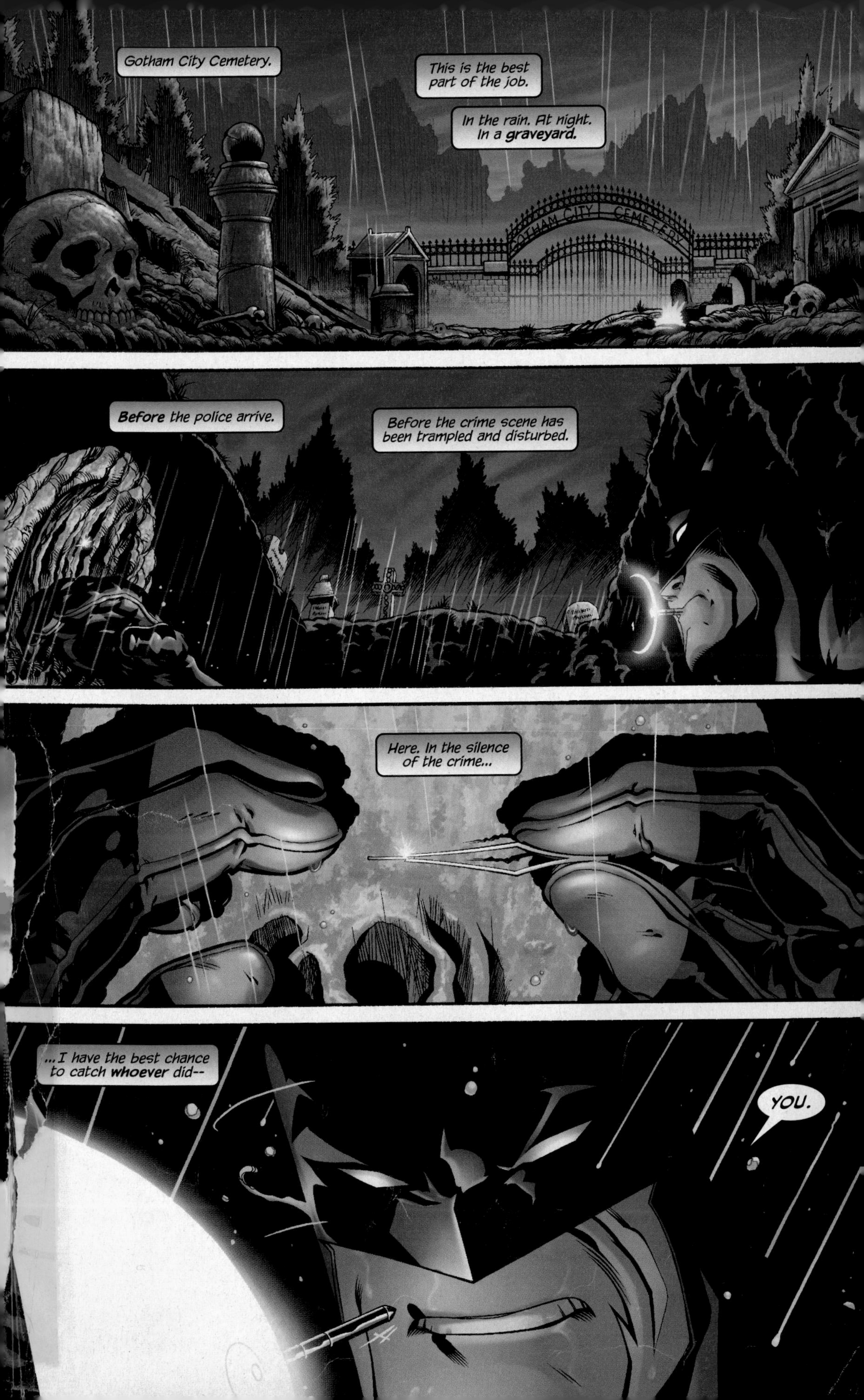

Gotham City Cemetery.
This is the best part of the job.
In the rain. At night. In a **graveyard.**
GOTHAM CITY CEMETERY
Before the police arrive.
Before the crime scene has been trampled and disturbed.
Here. In the silence of the crime...
...I have the best chance to catch ***whoever*** did--
YOU.

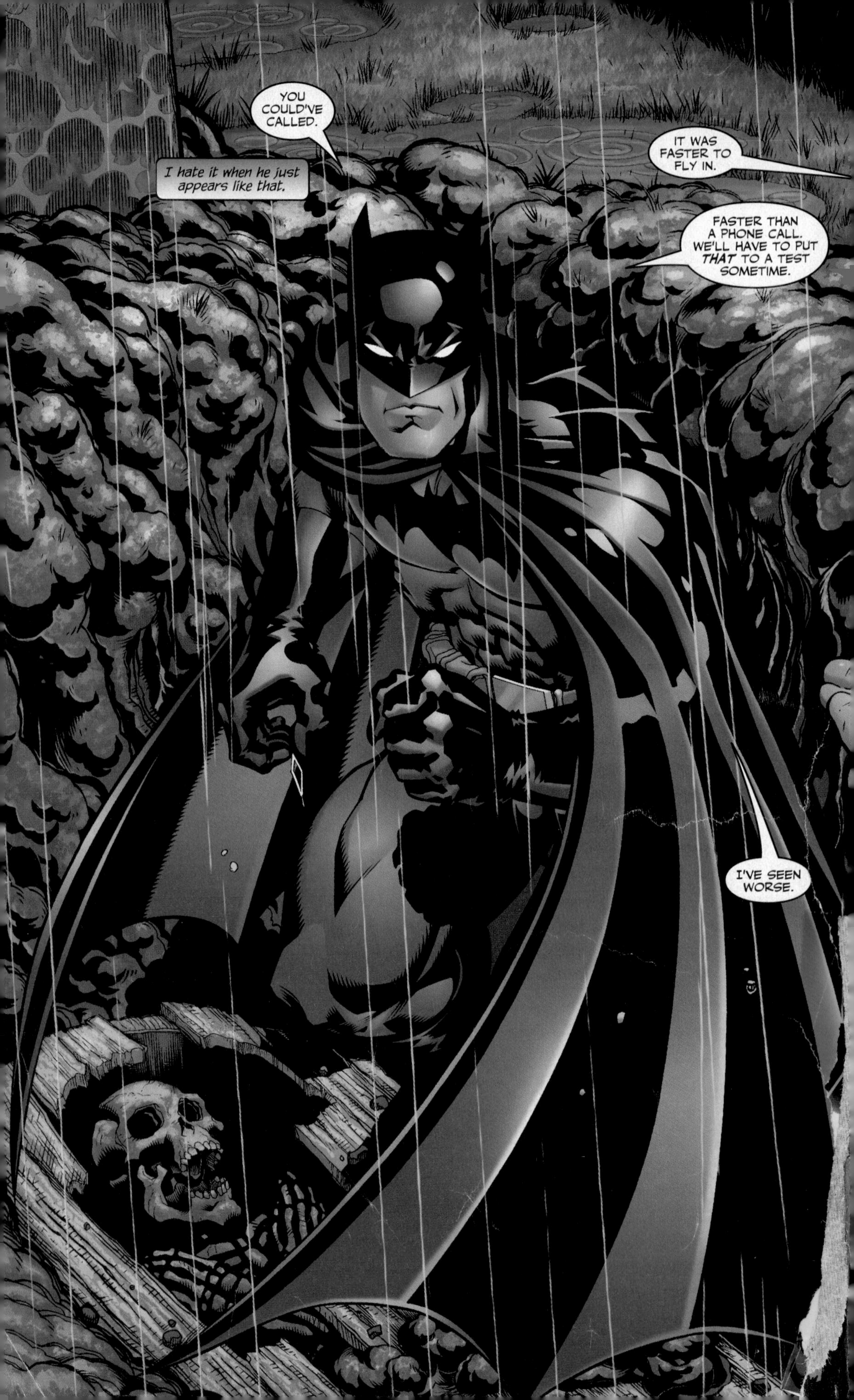
YOU COULD'VE CALLED.
I hate it when he just appears like that.
IT WAS FASTER TO FLY IN.
FASTER THAN A PHONE CALL. WE'LL HAVE TO PUT THAT TO A TEST SOMETIME.
I'VE SEEN WORSE.

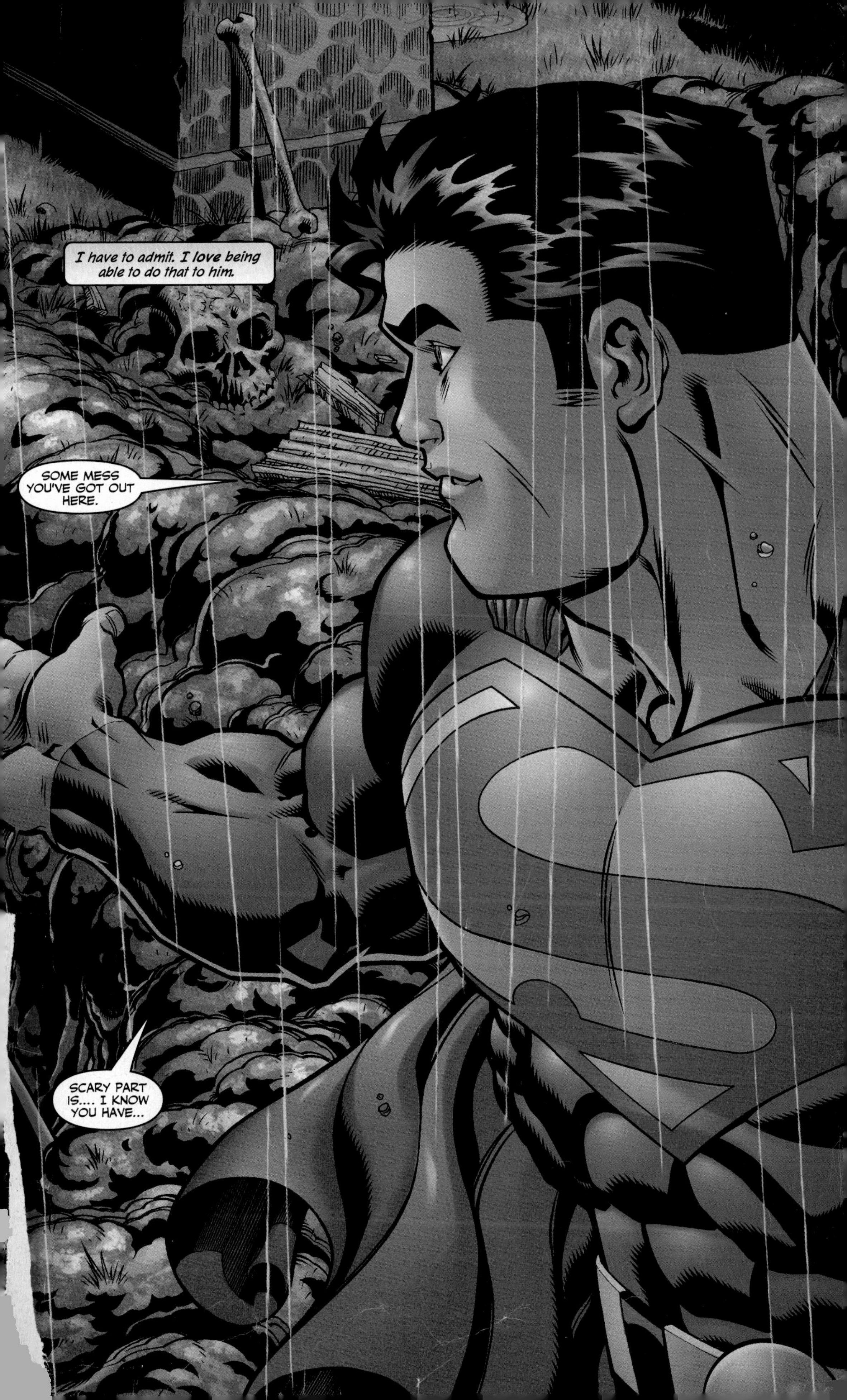
I have to admit. I love being able to do that to him.
SOME MESS YOU'VE GOT OUT HERE.
SCARY PART IS.... I KNOW YOU HAVE...

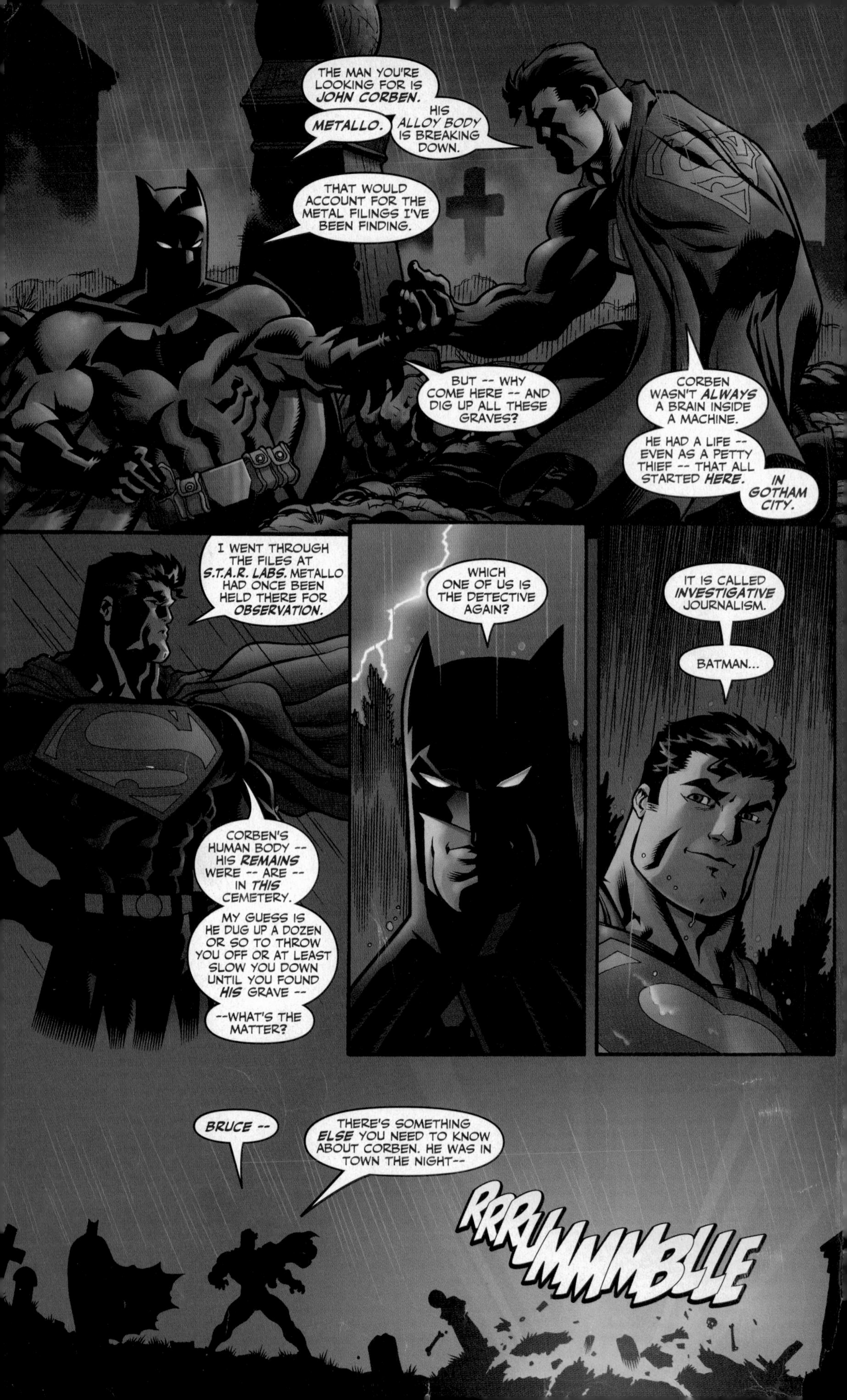
THE MAN YOU'RE LOOKING FOR IS JOHN CORBEN.
METALLO.
HIS ALLOY BODY IS BREAKING DOWN.
THAT WOULD ACCOUNT FOR THE METAL FILINGS I'VE BEEN FINDING.
BUT -- WHY COME HERE -- AND DIG UP ALL THESE GRAVES?
CORBEN WASN'T ALWAYS A BRAIN INSIDE A MACHINE.
HE HAD A LIFE -- EVEN AS A PETTY THIEF -- THAT ALL STARTED HERE.
IN GOTHAM CITY.
I WENT THROUGH THE FILES AT S.T.A.R. LABS. METALLO HAD ONCE BEEN HELD THERE FOR OBSERVATION.
CORBEN'S HUMAN BODY -- HIS REMAINS WERE -- ARE -- IN THIS CEMETERY.
MY GUESS IS HE DUG UP A DOZEN OR SO TO THROW YOU OFF OR AT LEAST SLOW YOU DOWN UNTIL YOU FOUND HIS GRAVE --
--WHAT'S THE MATTER?
WHICH ONE OF US IS THE DETECTIVE AGAIN?
IT IS CALLED INVESTIGATIVE JOURNALISM.
BATMAN...
BRUCE --
THERE'S SOMETHING ELSE YOU NEED TO KNOW ABOUT CORBEN. HE WAS IN TOWN THE NIGHT--
RRRUMMMBLLE

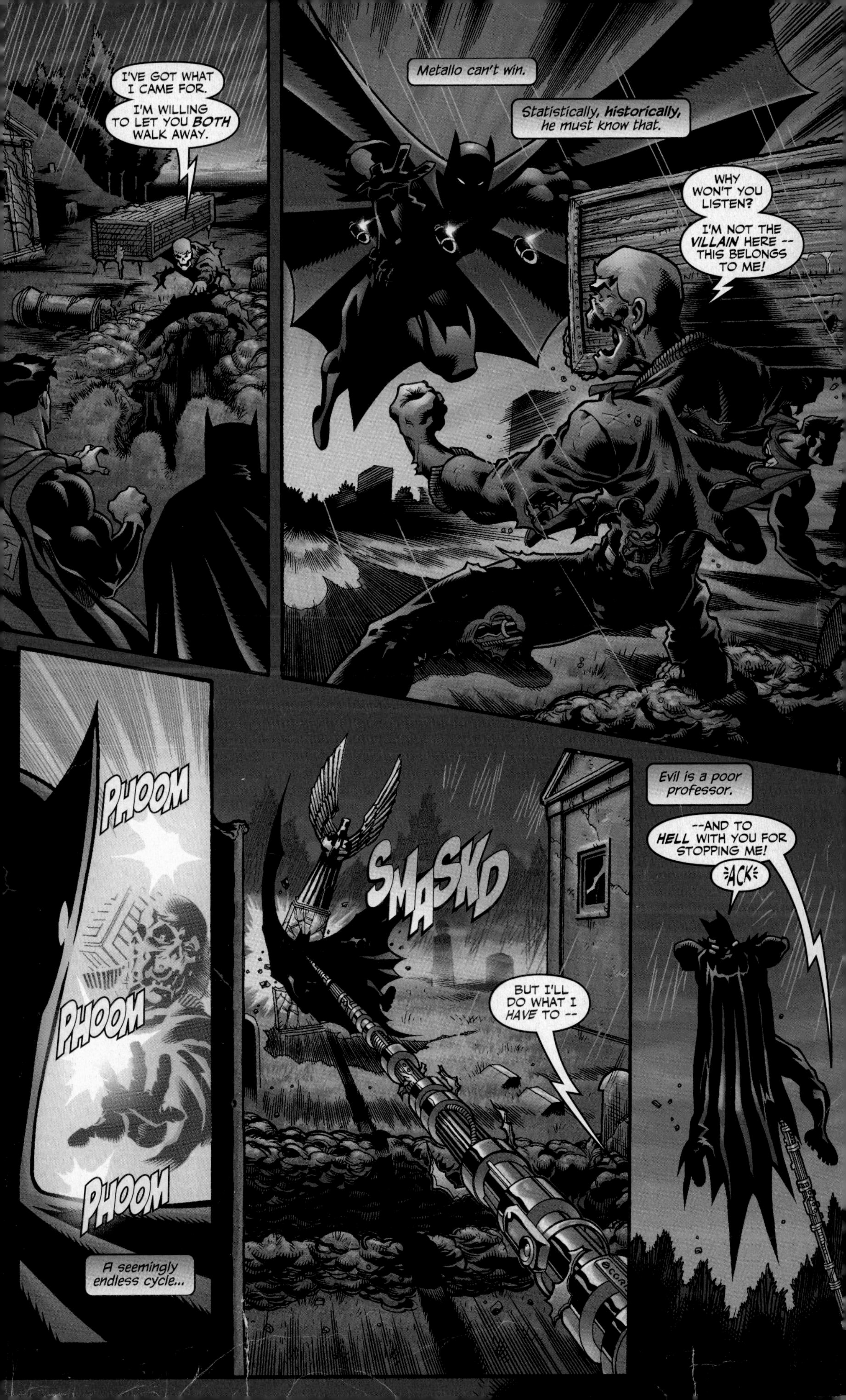
I'VE GOT WHAT I CAME FOR.
I'M WILLING TO LET YOU BOTH WALK AWAY.
Metallo can't win.
Statistically, historically, he must know that.
WHY WON'T YOU LISTEN?
I'M NOT THE VILLAIN HERE -- THIS BELONGS TO ME!
PHOOM
PHOOM
PHOOM
A seemingly endless cycle...
SMASKD
BUT I'LL DO WHAT I HAVE TO --
Evil is a poor professor.
--AND TO HELL WITH YOU FOR STOPPING ME!
ACK

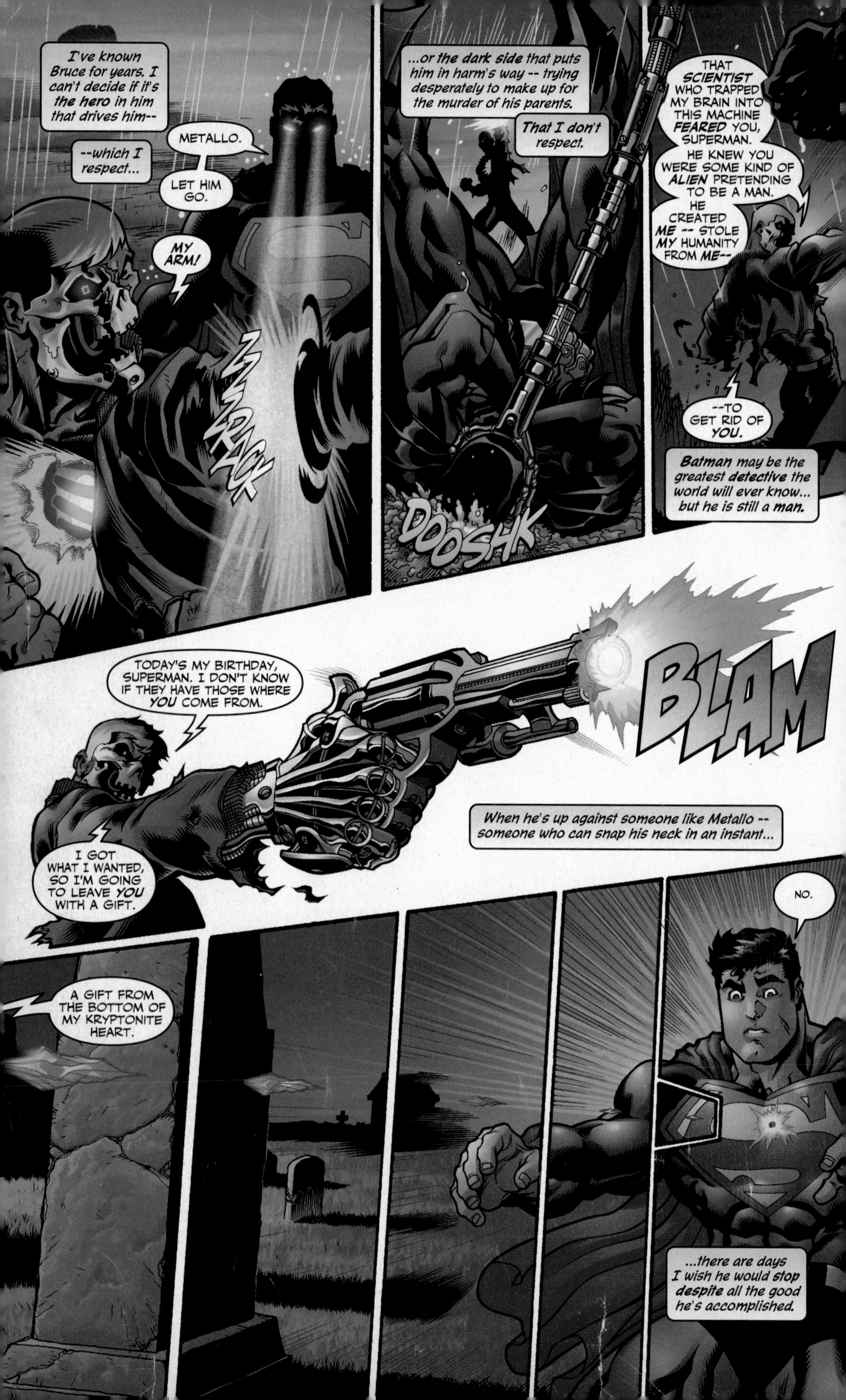
I've known Bruce for years. I can't decide if it's the hero in him that drives him--
--which I respect...
METALLO.
LET HIM GO.
MY ARM!
ZZZRACK
...or the dark side that puts him in harm's way -- trying desperately to make up for the murder of his parents.
That I don't respect.
DOOSHK
THAT SCIENTIST WHO TRAPPED MY BRAIN INTO THIS MACHINE FEARED YOU, SUPERMAN.
HE KNEW YOU WERE SOME KIND OF ALIEN PRETENDING TO BE A MAN.
HE CREATED ME -- STOLE MY HUMANITY FROM ME--
--TO GET RID OF YOU.
Batman may be the greatest detective the world will ever know... but he is still a man.
TODAY'S MY BIRTHDAY, SUPERMAN. I DON'T KNOW IF THEY HAVE THOSE WHERE YOU COME FROM.
BLAM
I GOT WHAT I WANTED, SO I'M GOING TO LEAVE YOU WITH A GIFT.
When he's up against someone like Metallo -- someone who can snap his neck in an instant...
A GIFT FROM THE BOTTOM OF MY KRYPTONITE HEART.
NO.
...there are days I wish he would stop despite all the good he's accomplished.

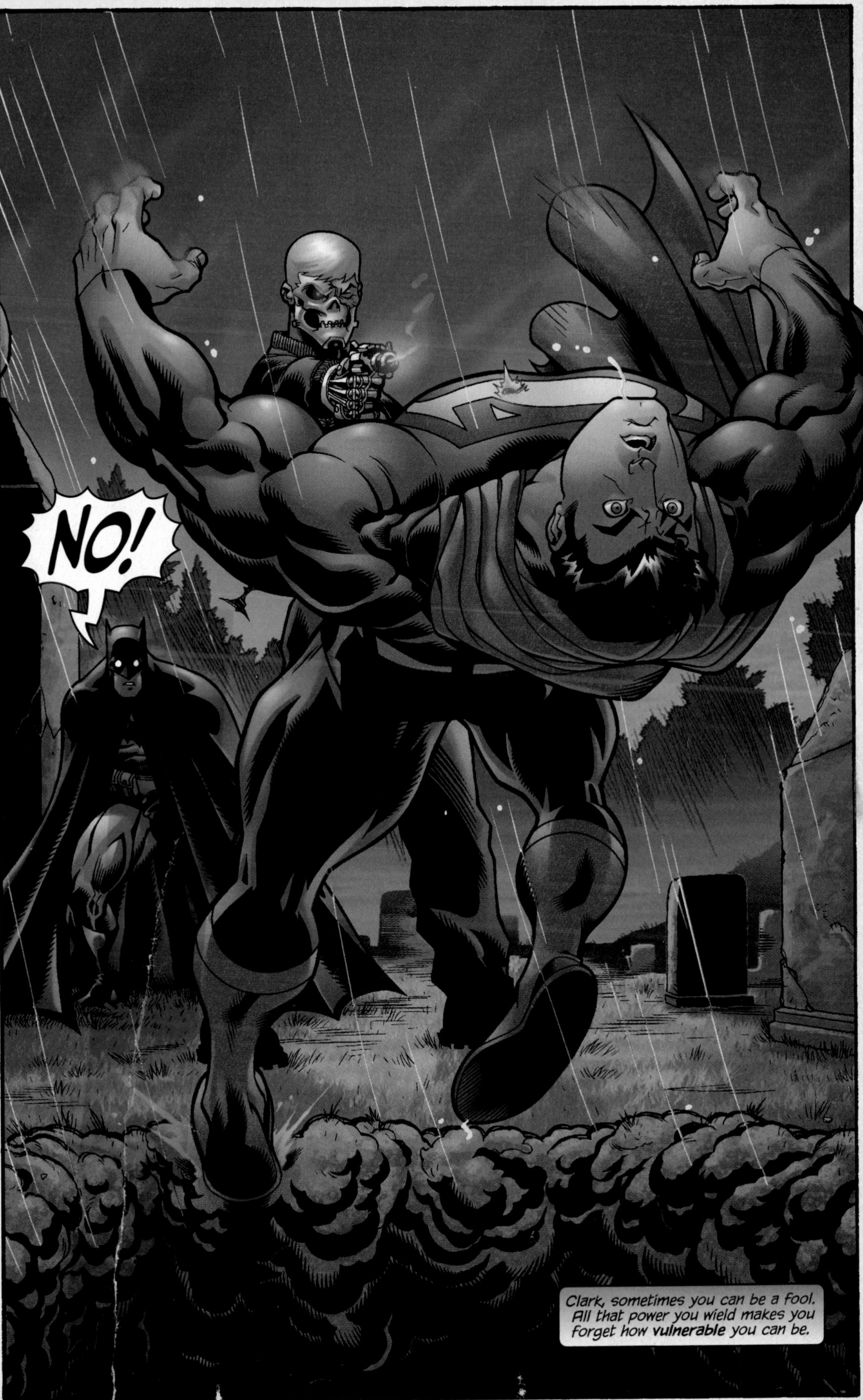
NO!
Clark, sometimes you can be a fool. All that power you wield makes you forget how **vulnerable** you can be.

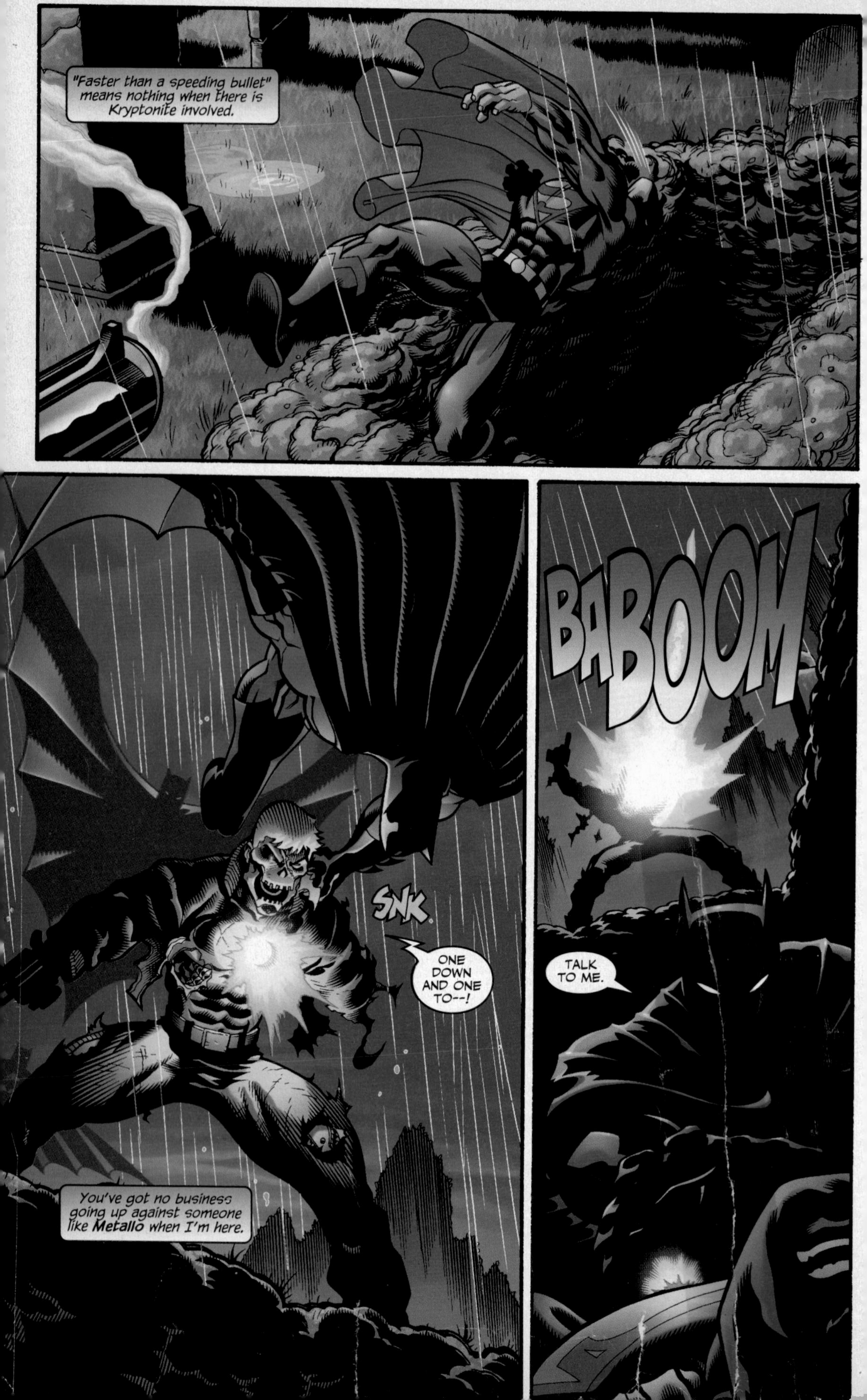
"Faster than a speeding bullet" means nothing when there is Kryptonite involved.
SNK
ONE DOWN AND ONE TO--!
You've got no business going up against someone like Metallo when I'm here.
BABOOM
TALK TO ME.

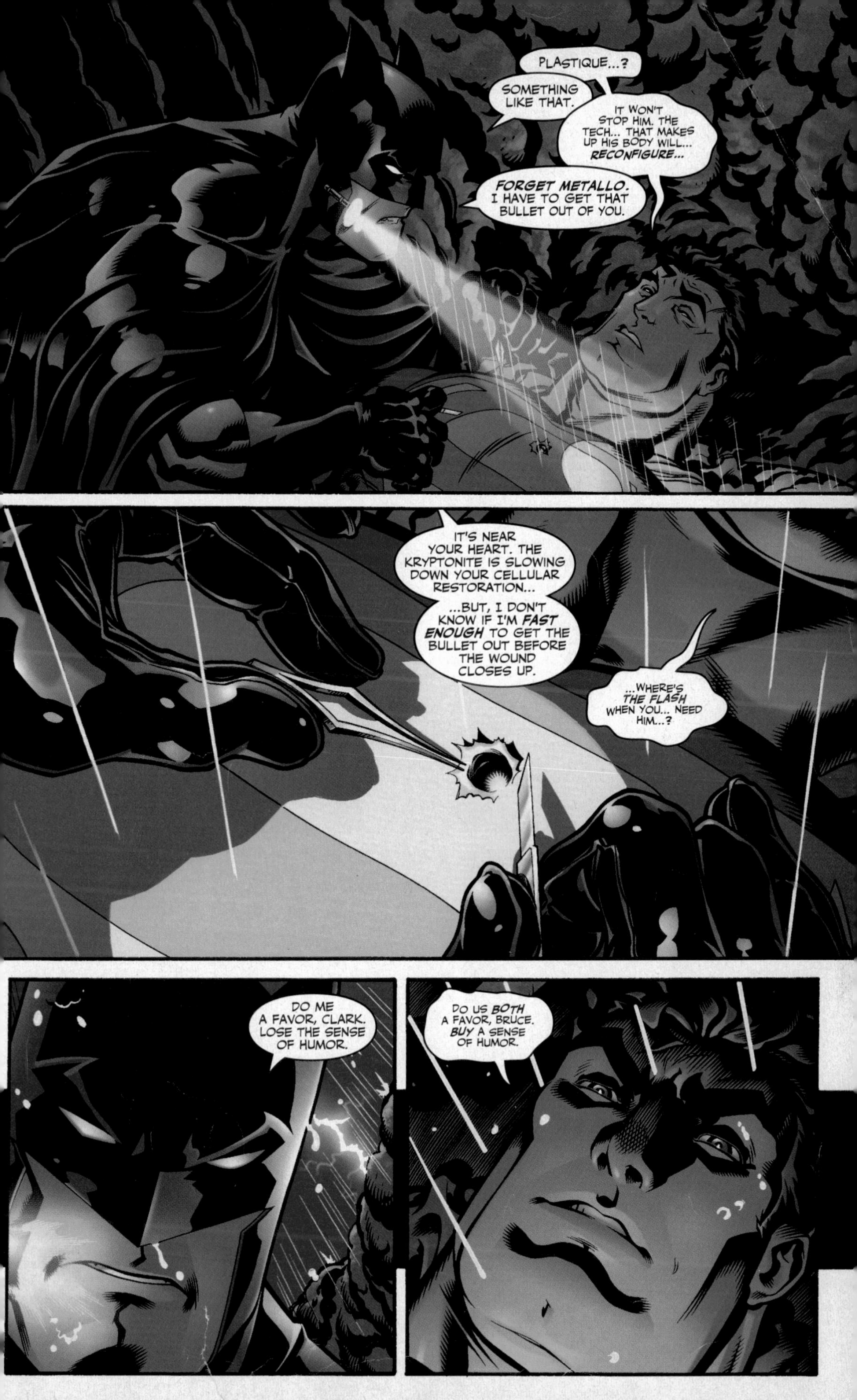
PLASTIQUE...?
SOMETHING LIKE THAT.
IT WON'T STOP HIM. THE TECH... THAT MAKES UP HIS BODY WILL... RECONFIGURE...
FORGET METALLO. I HAVE TO GET THAT BULLET OUT OF YOU.
IT'S NEAR YOUR HEART. THE KRYPTONITE IS SLOWING DOWN YOUR CELLULAR RESTORATION...
...BUT, I DON'T KNOW IF I'M FAST ENOUGH TO GET THE BULLET OUT BEFORE THE WOUND CLOSES UP.
...WHERE'S THE FLASH WHEN YOU... NEED HIM...?
DO ME A FAVOR, CLARK. LOSE THE SENSE OF HUMOR.
DO US BOTH A FAVOR, BRUCE. BUY A SENSE OF HUMOR.

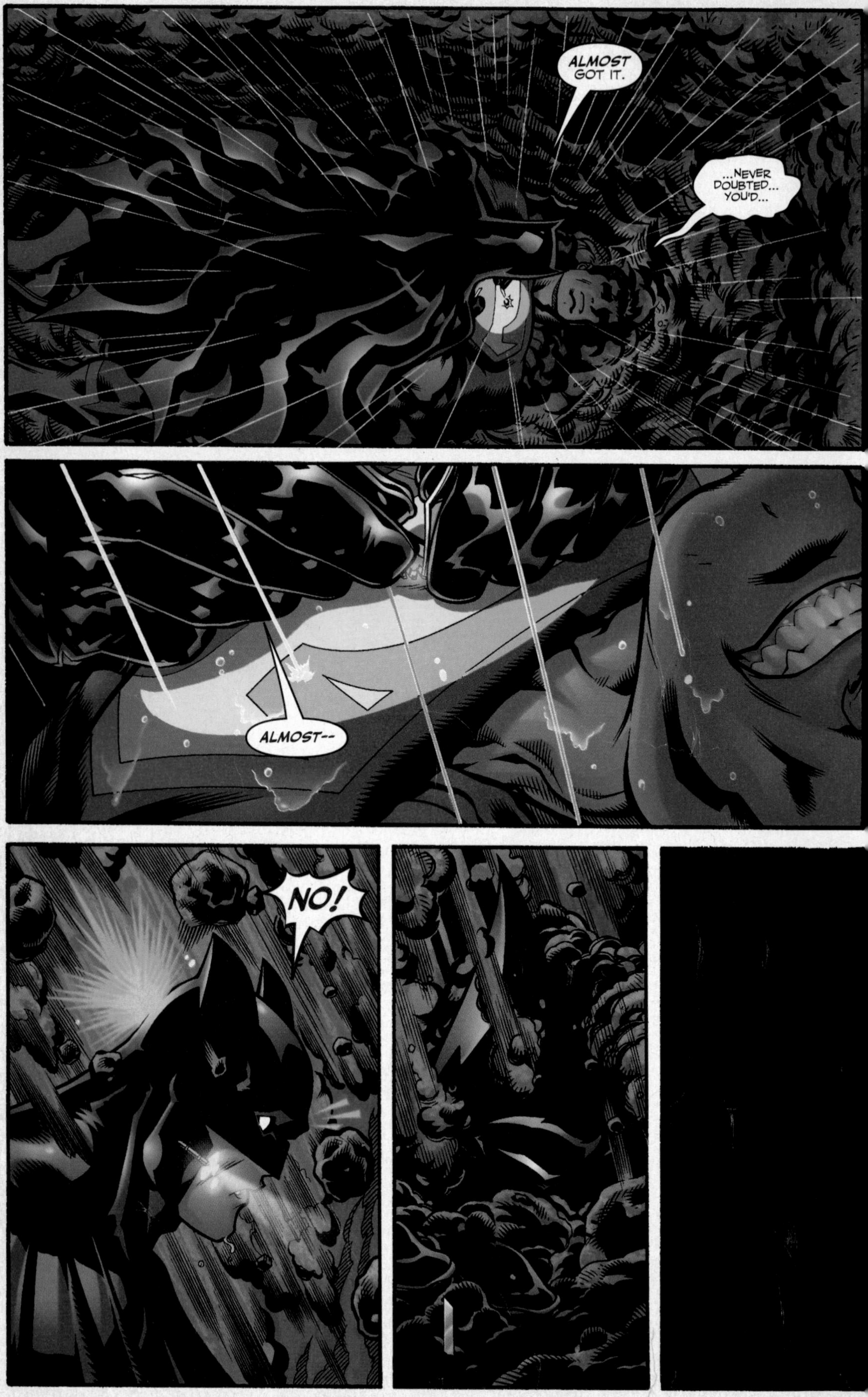
ALMOST GOT IT.
...NEVER DOUBTED... YOU'D...
ALMOST--
NO!

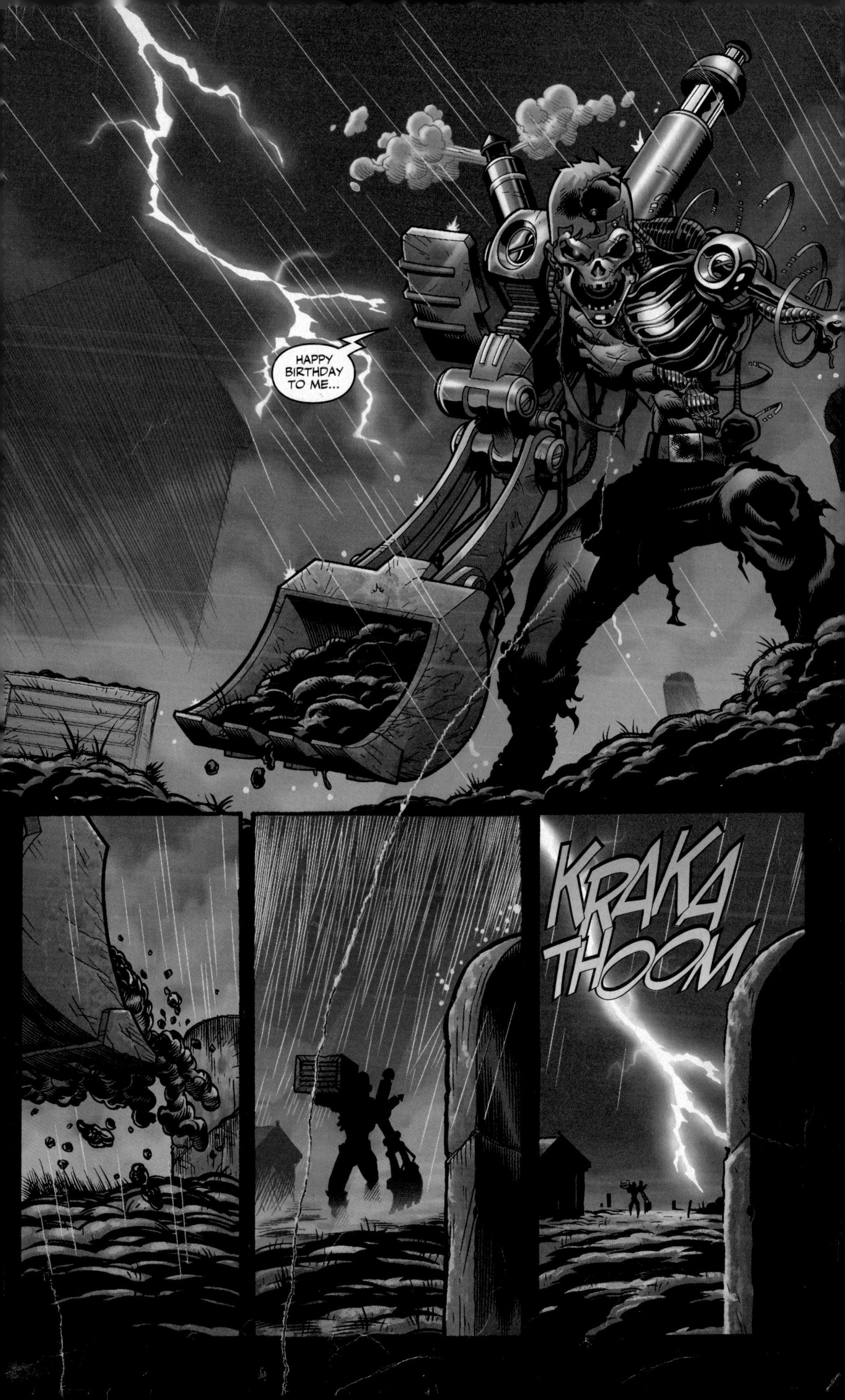
HAPPY BIRTHDAY TO ME...
KRAKA THOOM

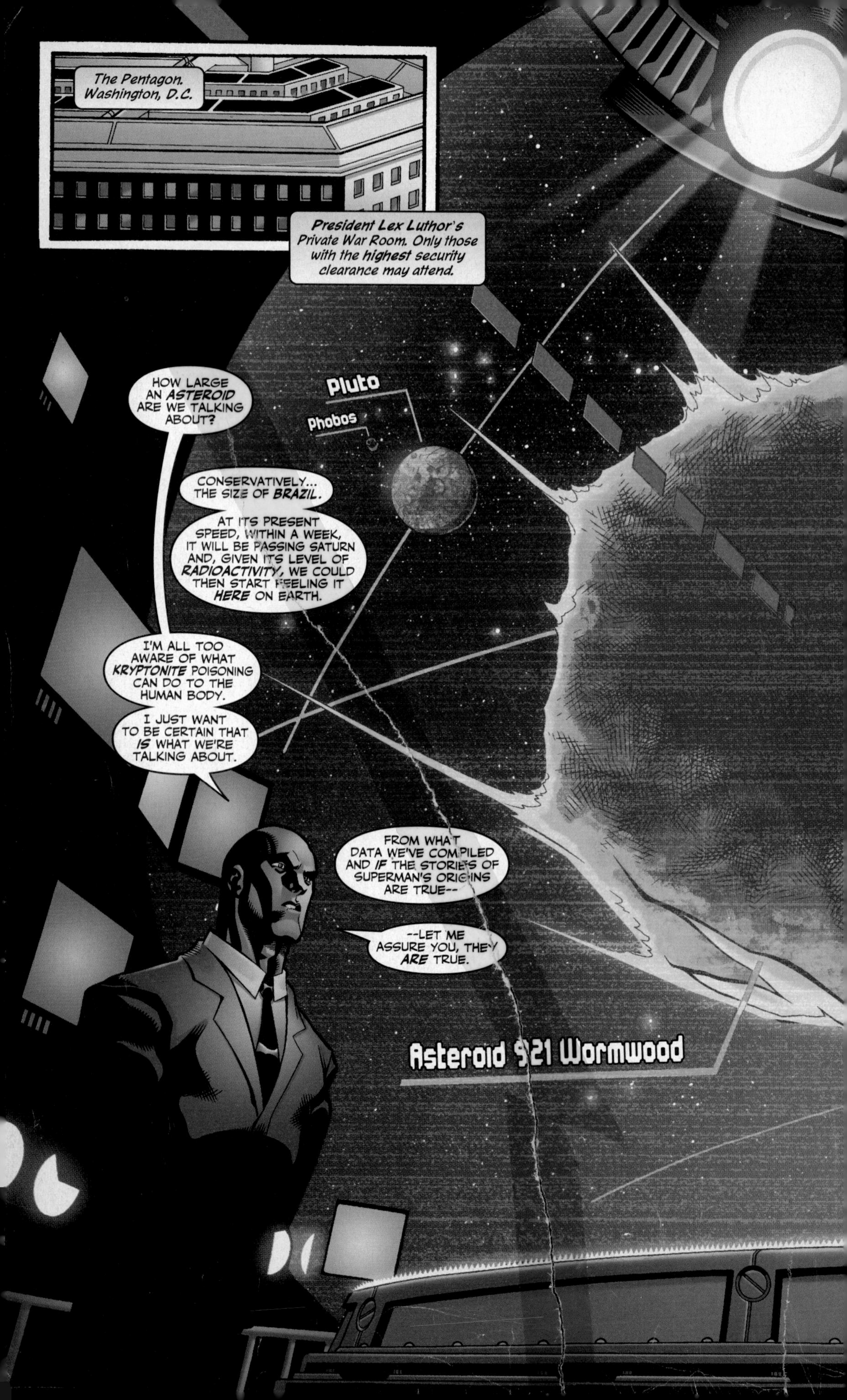
The Pentagon. Washington, D.C.
President Lex Luthor's Private War Room. Only those with the highest security clearance may attend.
HOW LARGE AN ASTEROID ARE WE TALKING ABOUT?
Pluto
Phobos
CONSERVATIVELY... THE SIZE OF BRAZIL.
AT ITS PRESENT SPEED, WITHIN A WEEK, IT WILL BE PASSING SATURN AND, GIVEN ITS LEVEL OF RADIOACTIVITY, WE COULD THEN START FEELING IT HERE ON EARTH.
I'M ALL TOO AWARE OF WHAT KRYPTONITE POISONING CAN DO TO THE HUMAN BODY.
I JUST WANT TO BE CERTAIN THAT IS WHAT WE'RE TALKING ABOUT.
FROM WHAT DATA WE'VE COMPILED AND IF THE STORIES OF SUPERMAN'S ORIGINS ARE TRUE--
--LET ME ASSURE YOU, THEY ARE TRUE.
Asteroid 921 Wormwood

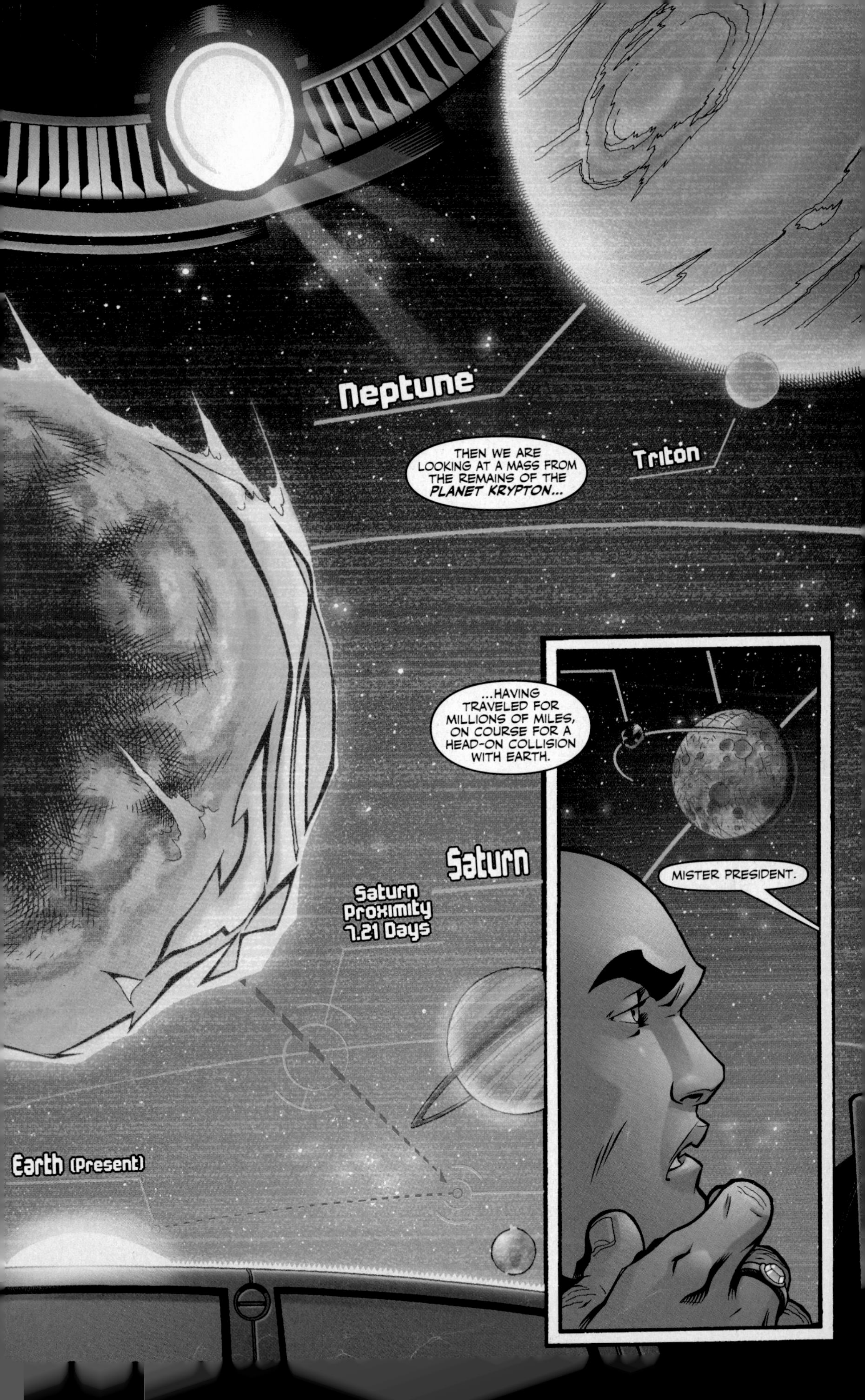
Neptune
Triton
THEN WE ARE LOOKING AT A MASS FROM THE REMAINS OF THE *PLANET KRYPTON*...
...HAVING TRAVELED FOR MILLIONS OF MILES, ON COURSE FOR A HEAD-ON COLLISION WITH EARTH.
Saturn
MISTER PRESIDENT.
Saturn Proximity 7.21 Days
Earth (Present)

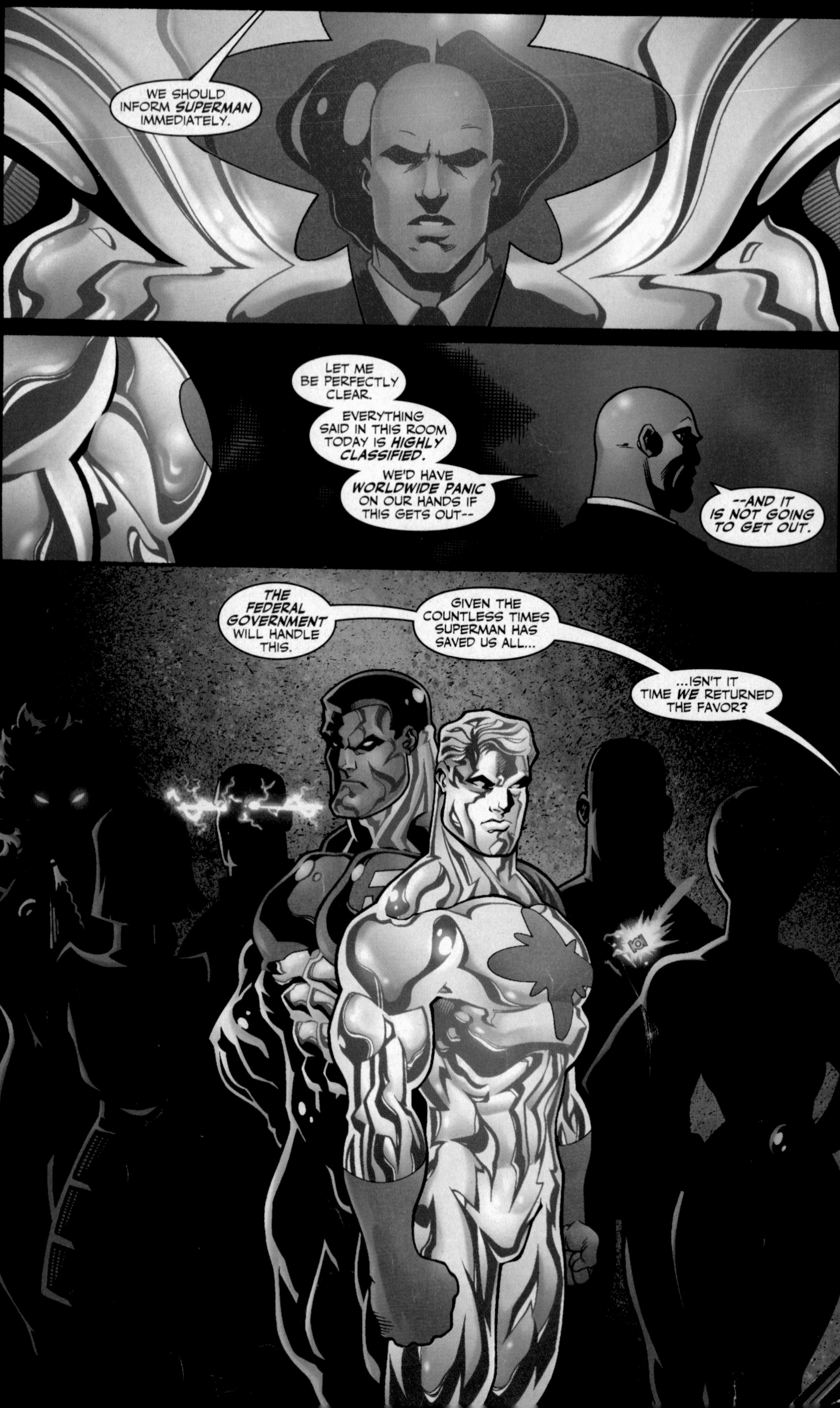
WE SHOULD INFORM SUPERMAN IMMEDIATELY.
LET ME BE PERFECTLY CLEAR.
EVERYTHING SAID IN THIS ROOM TODAY IS HIGHLY CLASSIFIED.
WE'D HAVE WORLDWIDE PANIC ON OUR HANDS IF THIS GETS OUT--
--AND IT IS NOT GOING TO GET OUT.
THE FEDERAL GOVERNMENT WILL HANDLE THIS.
GIVEN THE COUNTLESS TIMES SUPERMAN HAS SAVED US ALL...
...ISN'T IT TIME WE RETURNED THE FAVOR?

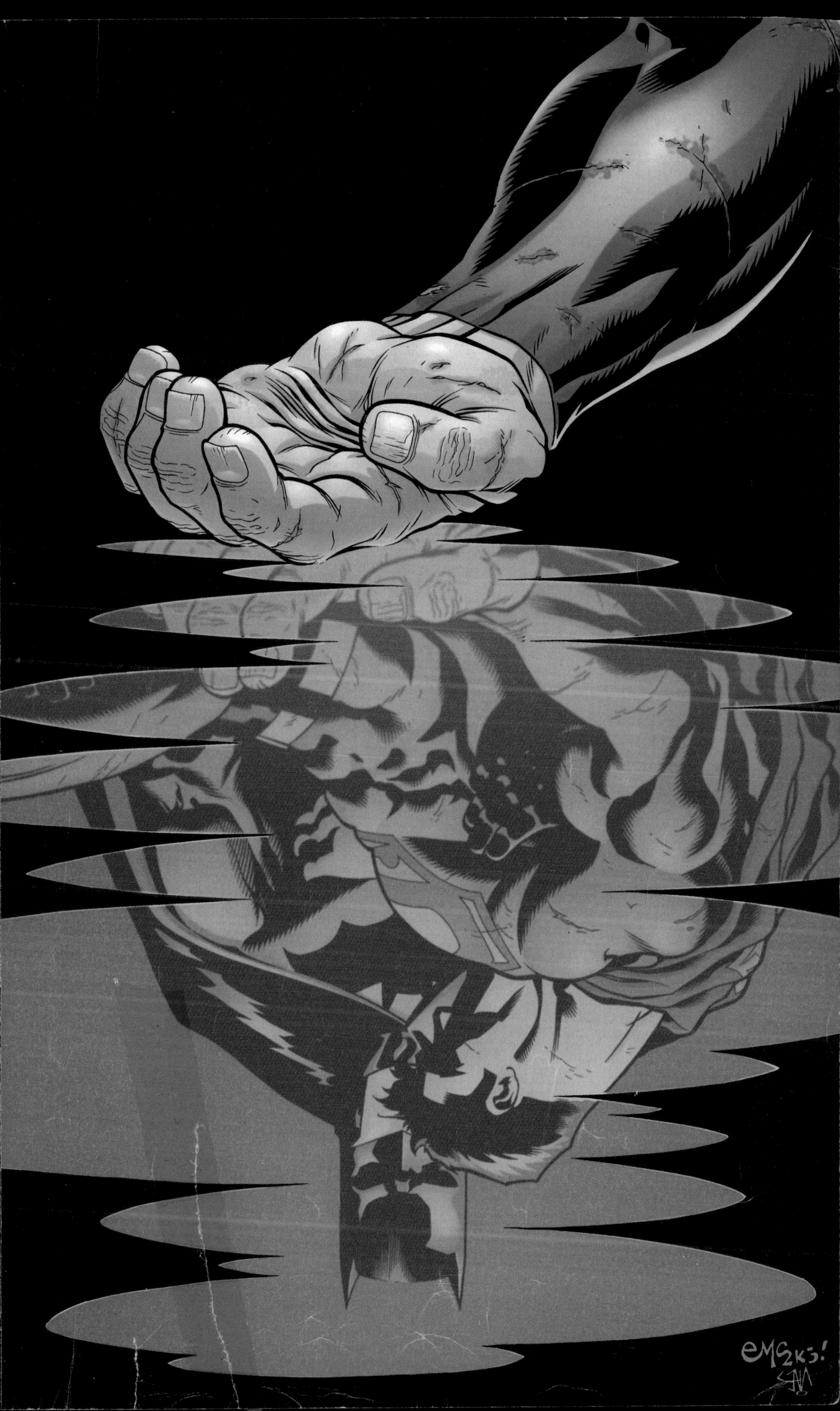

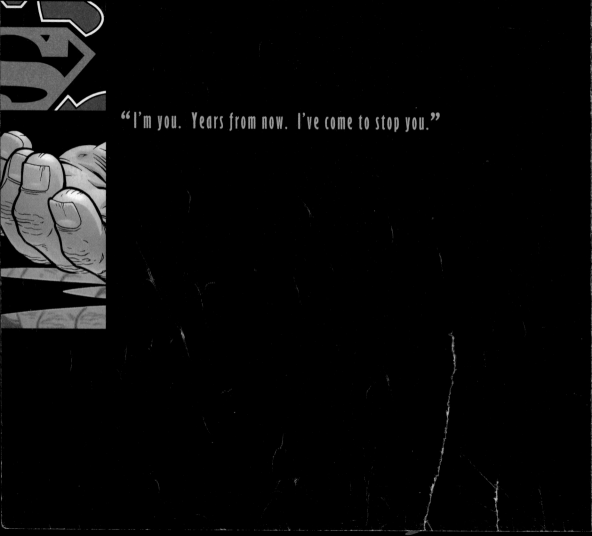

"I'm you. Years from now. I've come to stop you."

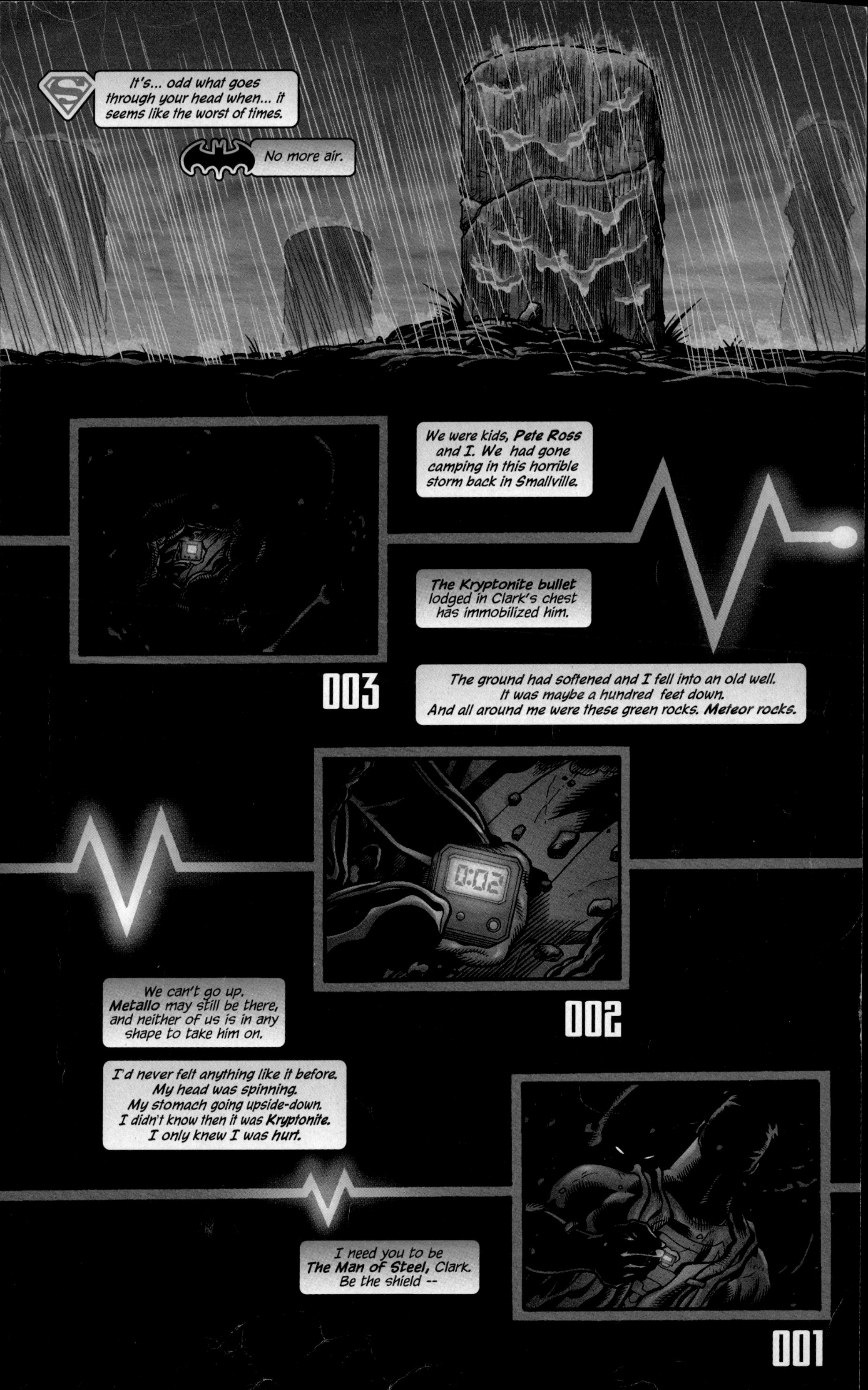
It's... odd what goes through your head when... it seems like the worst of times.
No more air.
We were kids, Pete Ross and I. We had gone camping in this horrible storm back in Smallville.
The Kryptonite bullet lodged in Clark's chest has immobilized him.
003
The ground had softened and I fell into an old well. It was maybe a hundred feet down. And all around me were these green rocks. Meteor rocks.
0:02
We can't go up. Metallo may still be there, and neither of us is in any shape to take him on.
002
I'd never felt anything like it before. My head was spinning. My stomach going upside-down. I didn't know then it was Kryptonite. I only knew I was hurt.
I need you to be The Man of Steel, Clark. Be the shield --
001

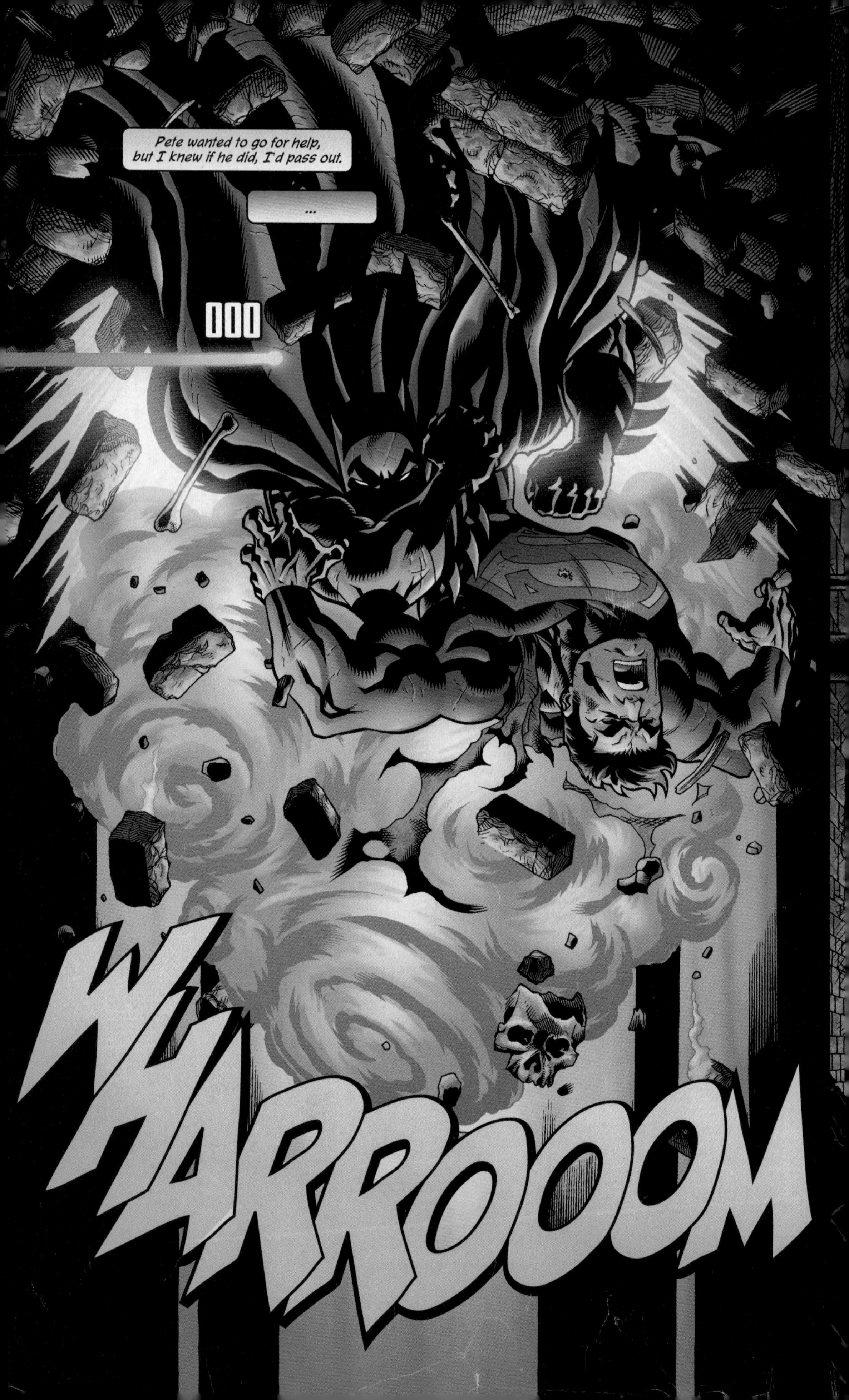
Pete wanted to go for help, but I knew if he did, I'd pass out.
...
OOO
WHARROOOM

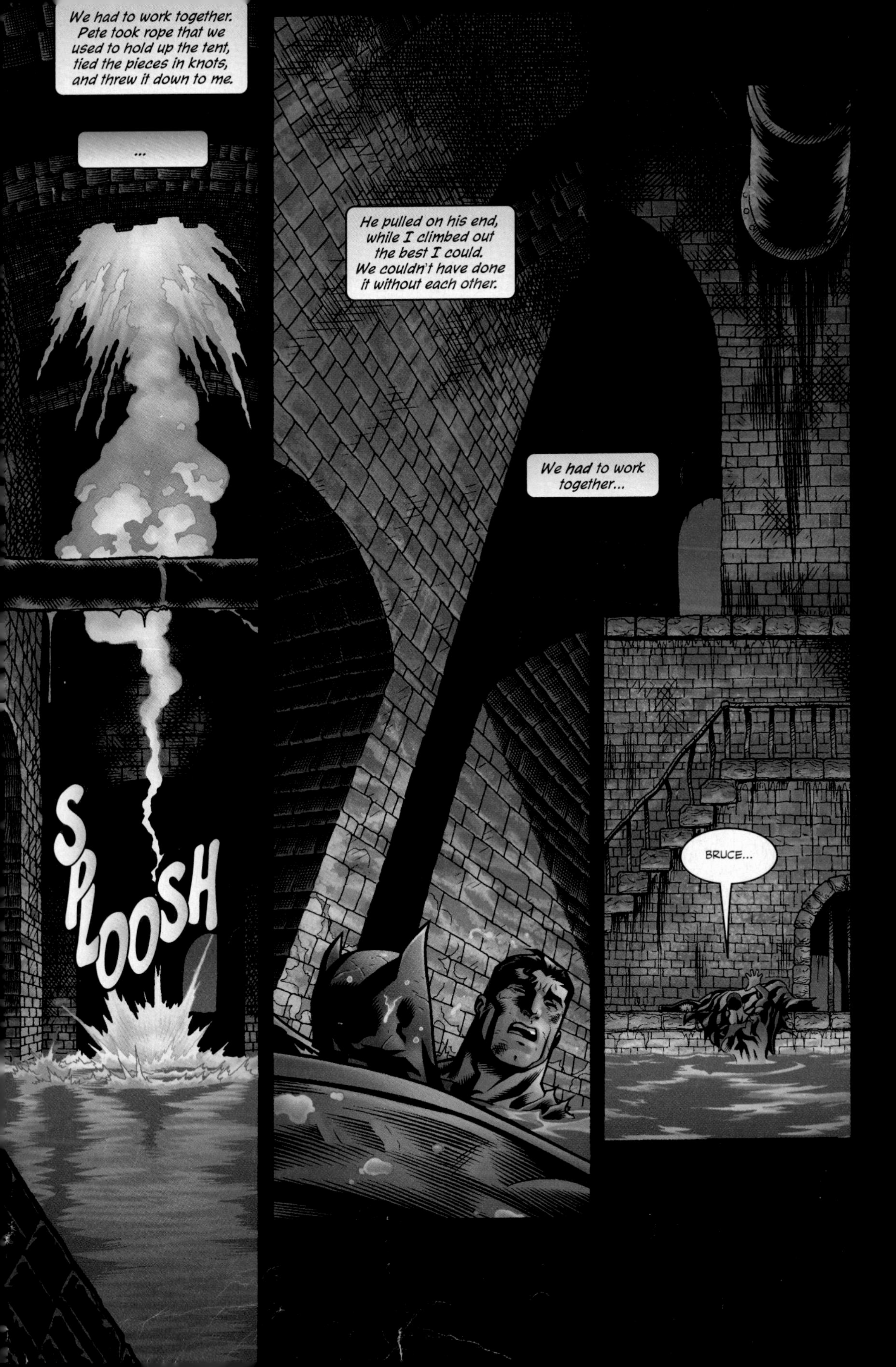
We had to work together. Pete took rope that we used to hold up the tent, tied the pieces in knots, and threw it down to me.
...
SPLOOSH
He pulled on his end, while I climbed out the best I could. We couldn't have done it without each other.
We had to work together...
BRUCE...

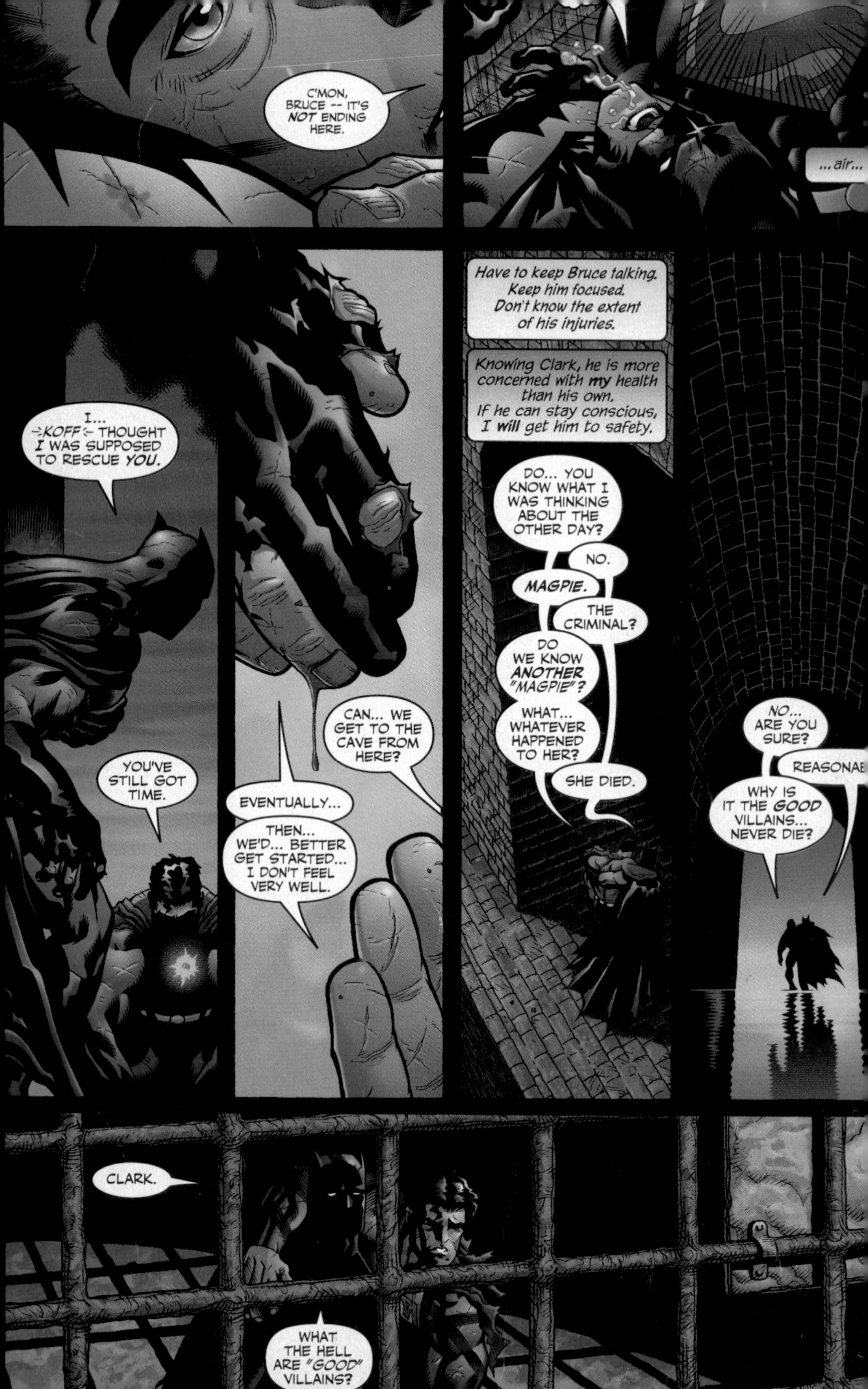
C'MON, BRUCE -- IT'S NOT ENDING HERE.
...air...
I... KOFF THOUGHT I WAS SUPPOSED TO RESCUE YOU.
YOU'VE STILL GOT TIME.
CAN... WE GET TO THE CAVE FROM HERE?
EVENTUALLY...
THEN... WE'D... BETTER GET STARTED... I DON'T FEEL VERY WELL.
Have to keep Bruce talking. Keep him focused. Don't know the extent of his injuries.
Knowing Clark, he is more concerned with my health than his own. If he can stay conscious, I will get him to safety.
DO... YOU KNOW WHAT I WAS THINKING ABOUT THE OTHER DAY?
NO.
MAGPIE.
THE CRIMINAL?
DO WE KNOW ANOTHER "MAGPIE"?
WHAT... WHATEVER HAPPENED TO HER?
SHE DIED.
NO... ARE YOU SURE?
REASONAB
WHY IS IT THE GOOD VILLAINS... NEVER DIE?
CLARK.
WHAT THE HELL ARE "GOOD" VILLAINS?

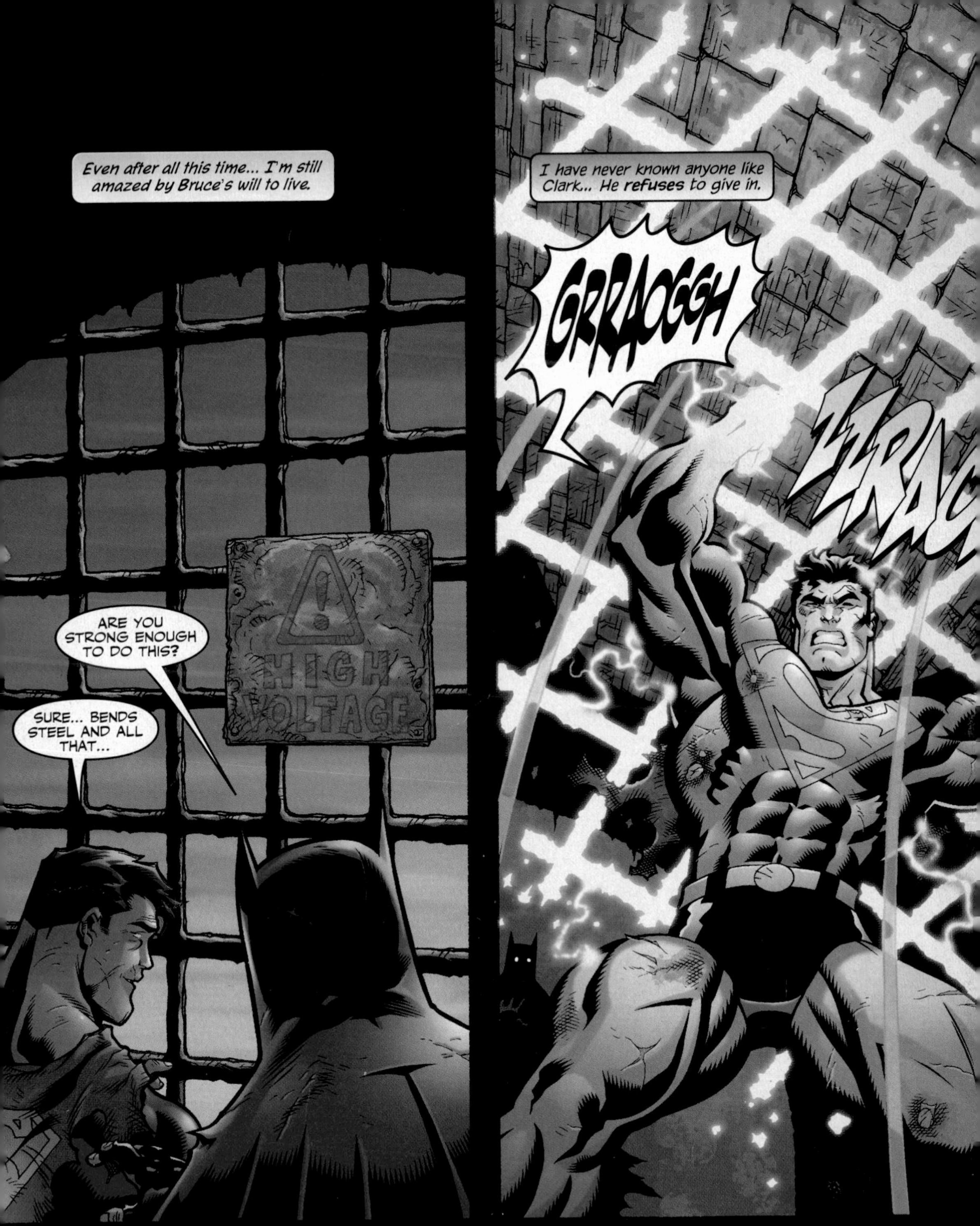

Even after all this time... I'm still amazed by Bruce's will to live.
HIGH VOLTAGE
ARE YOU STRONG ENOUGH TO DO THIS?
SURE... BENDS STEEL AND ALL THAT...
I have never known anyone like Clark... He refuses to give in.
GRRAOGGH

PART TWO: EARLY WARNING

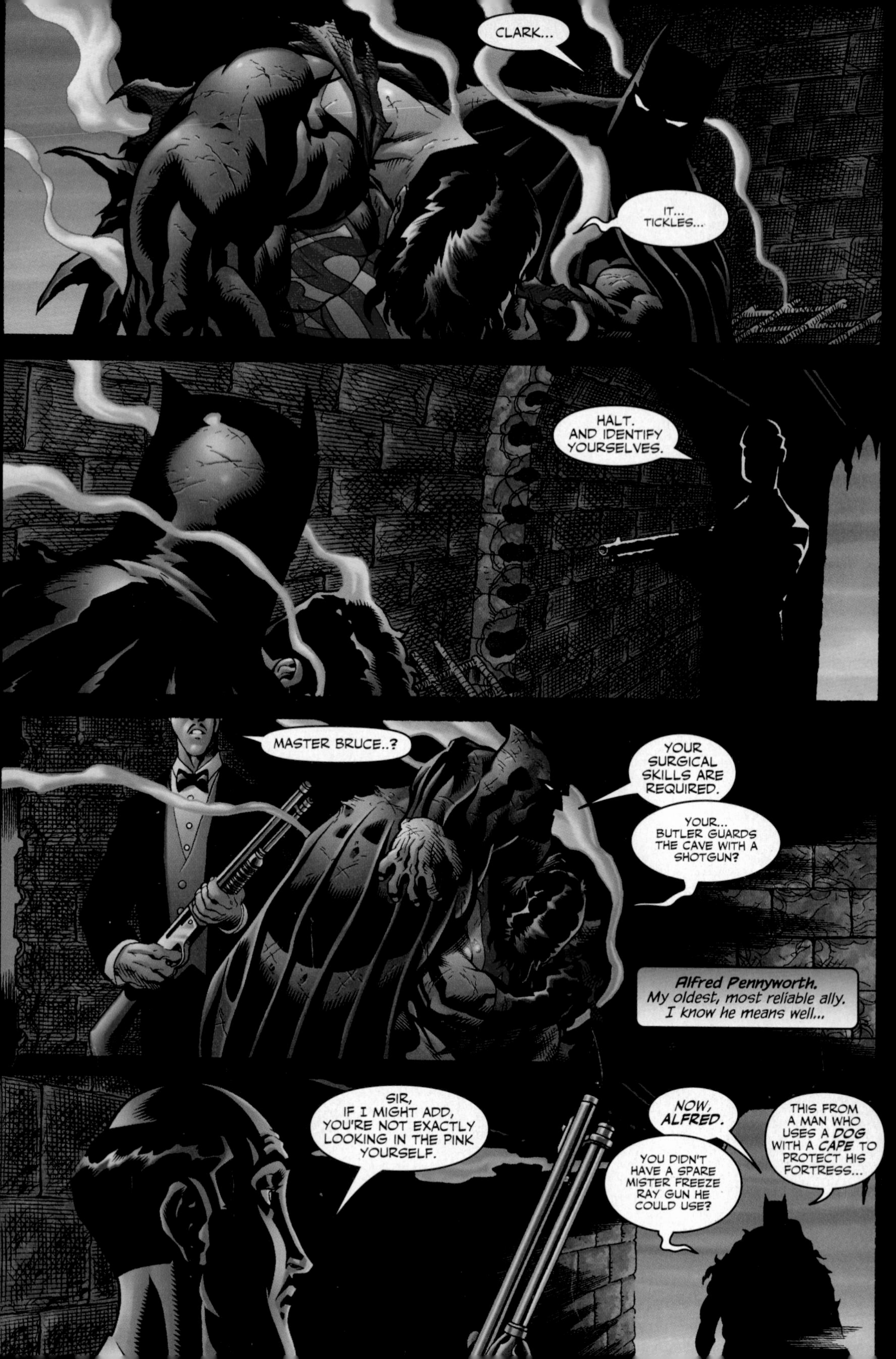
CLARK...
IT... TICKLES...
HALT. AND IDENTIFY YOURSELVES.
MASTER BRUCE..?
YOUR SURGICAL SKILLS ARE REQUIRED.
YOUR... BUTLER GUARDS THE CAVE WITH A SHOTGUN?
Alfred Pennyworth. My oldest, most reliable ally. I know he means well...
SIR, IF I MIGHT ADD, YOU'RE NOT EXACTLY LOOKING IN THE PINK YOURSELF.
NOW, ALFRED.
YOU DIDN'T HAVE A SPARE MISTER FREEZE RAY GUN HE COULD USE?
THIS FROM A MAN WHO USES A DOG WITH A CAPE TO PROTECT HIS FORTRESS...

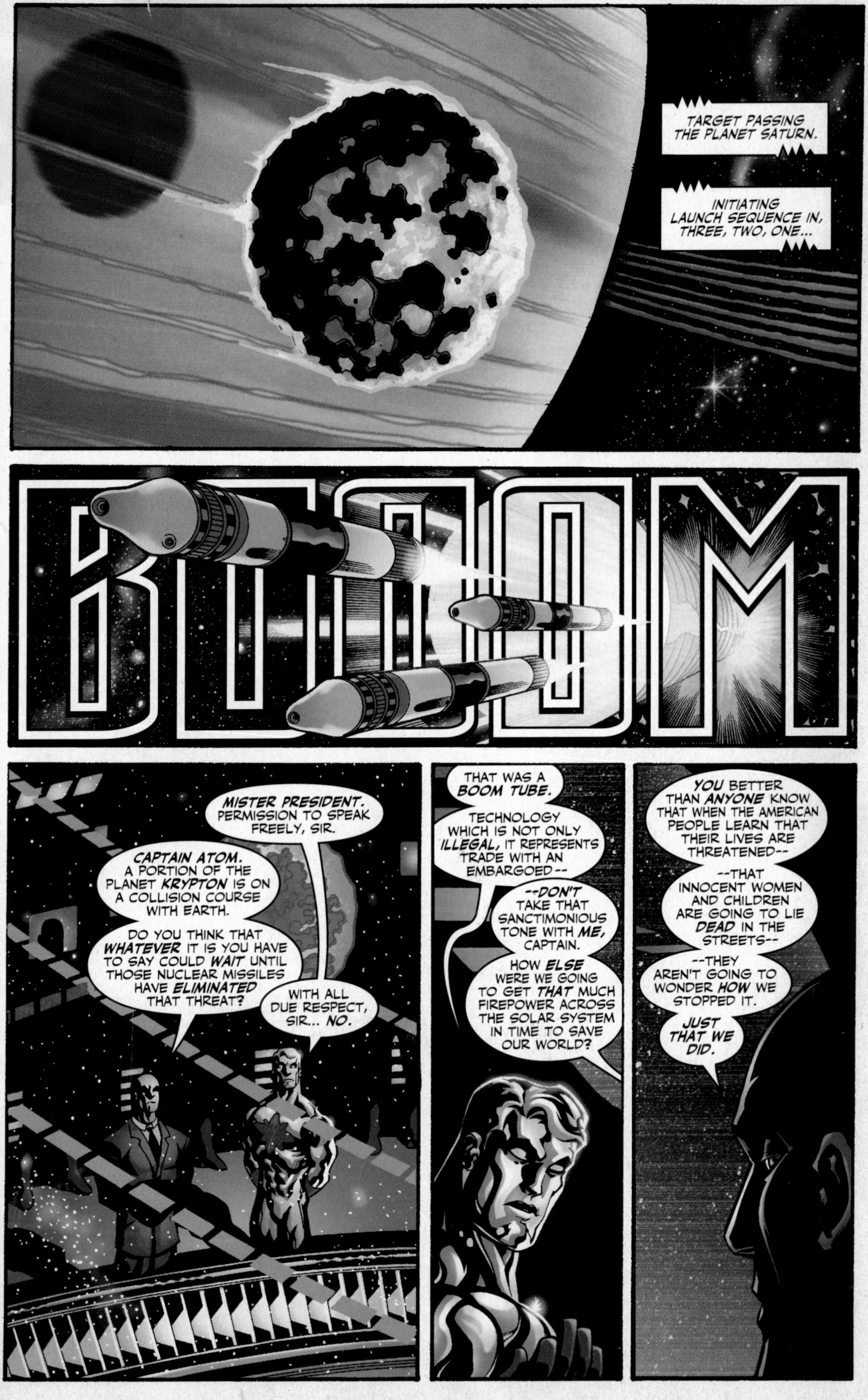
TARGET PASSING THE PLANET SATURN.
INITIATING LAUNCH SEQUENCE IN, THREE, TWO, ONE...
BOOOOM
MISTER PRESIDENT. PERMISSION TO SPEAK FREELY, SIR.
CAPTAIN ATOM. A PORTION OF THE PLANET KRYPTON IS ON A COLLISION COURSE WITH EARTH.
DO YOU THINK THAT WHATEVER IT IS YOU HAVE TO SAY COULD WAIT UNTIL THOSE NUCLEAR MISSILES HAVE ELIMINATED THAT THREAT?
WITH ALL DUE RESPECT, SIR... NO.
THAT WAS A BOOM TUBE.
TECHNOLOGY WHICH IS NOT ONLY ILLEGAL, IT REPRESENTS TRADE WITH AN EMBARGOED--
--DON'T TAKE THAT SANCTIMONIOUS TONE WITH ME, CAPTAIN.
HOW ELSE WERE WE GOING TO GET THAT MUCH FIREPOWER ACROSS THE SOLAR SYSTEM IN TIME TO SAVE OUR WORLD?
YOU BETTER THAN ANYONE KNOW THAT WHEN THE AMERICAN PEOPLE LEARN THAT THEIR LIVES ARE THREATENED--
--THAT INNOCENT WOMEN AND CHILDREN ARE GOING TO LIE DEAD IN THE STREETS--
--THEY AREN'T GOING TO WONDER HOW WE STOPPED IT.
JUST THAT WE DID.

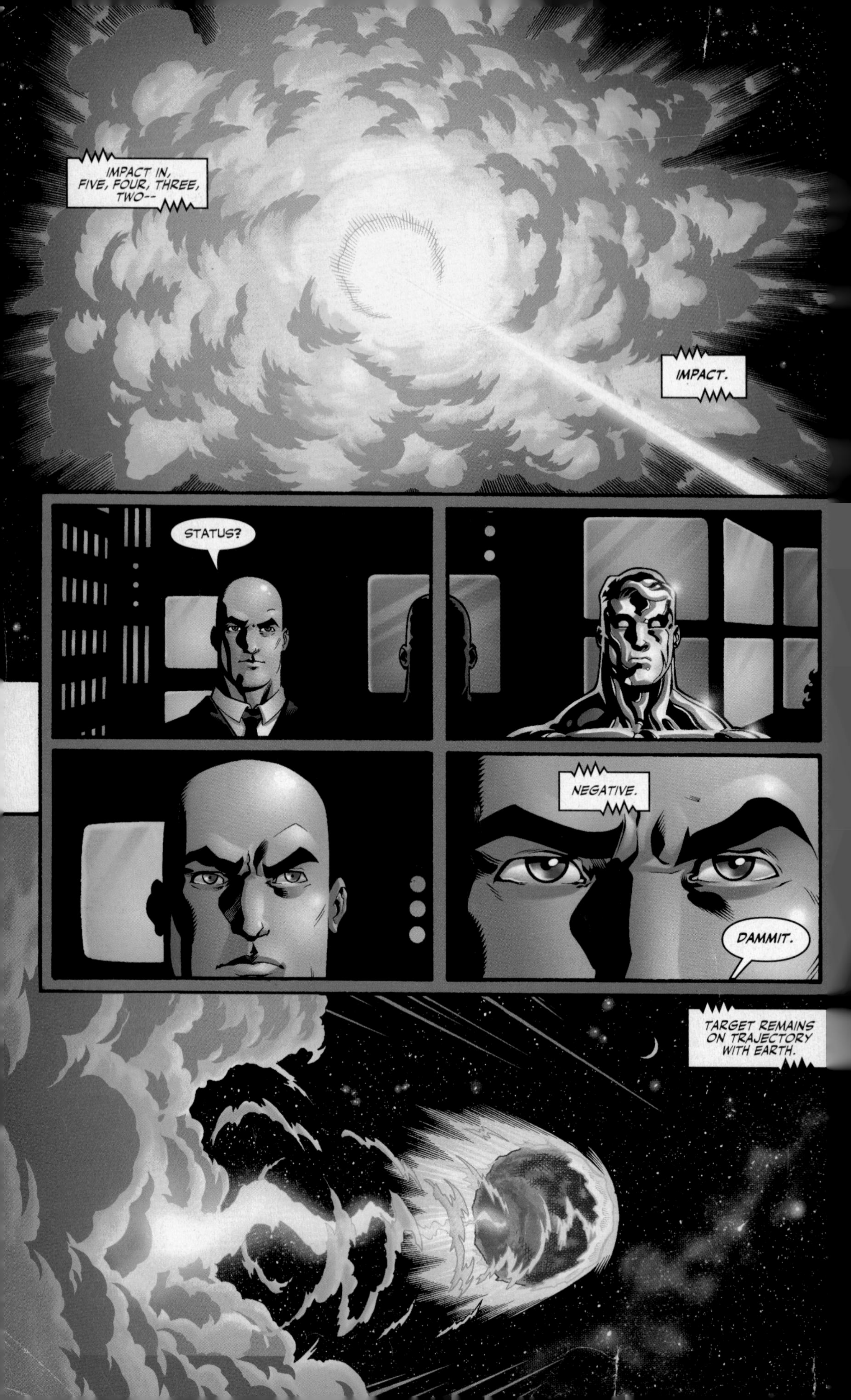
IMPACT IN, FIVE, FOUR, THREE, TWO--
IMPACT.
STATUS?
NEGATIVE.
DAMMIT.
TARGET REMAINS ON TRAJECTORY WITH EARTH.

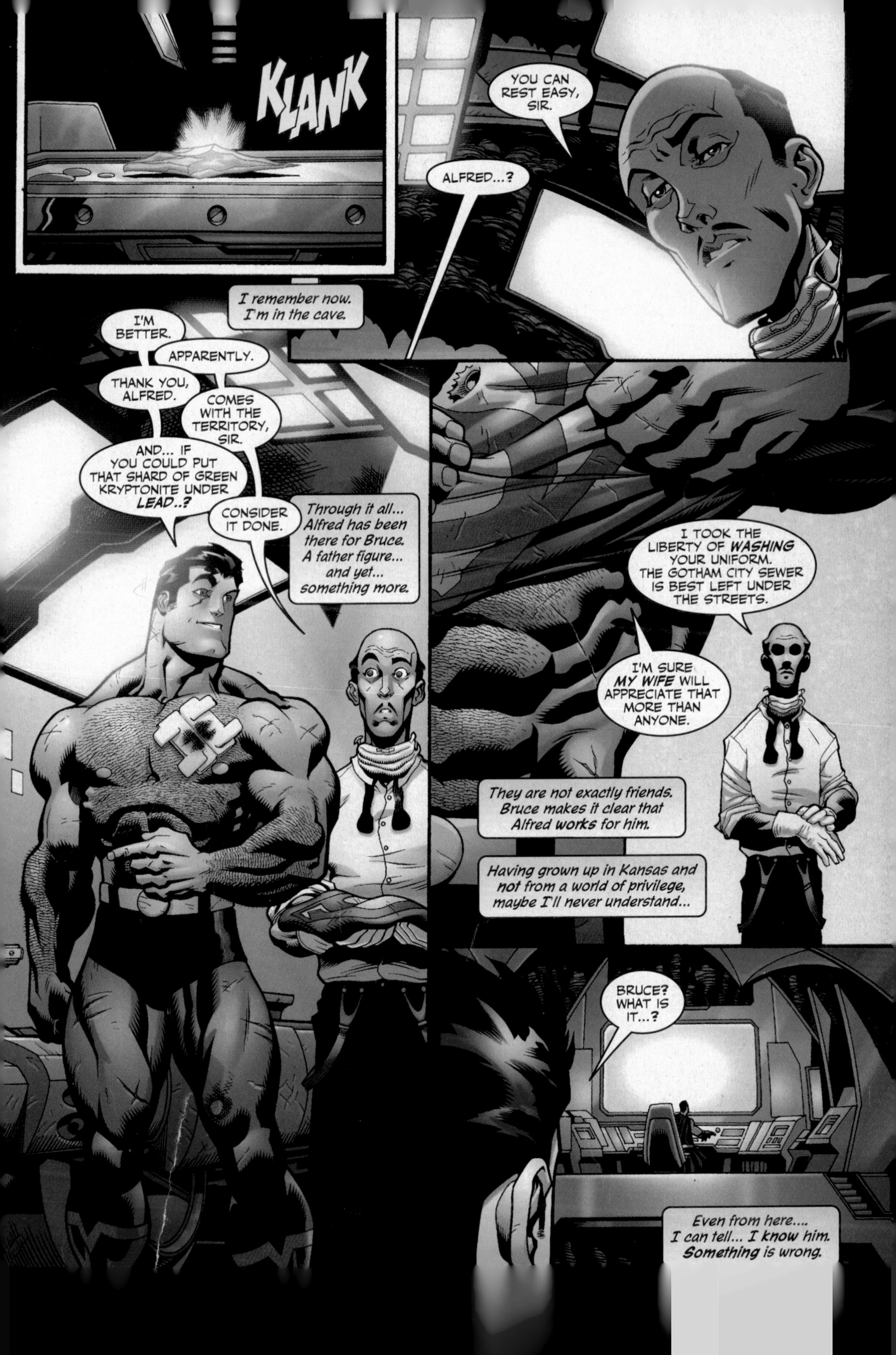
KLANK
YOU CAN REST EASY, SIR.
ALFRED...?
I remember now. I'm in the cave.
I'M BETTER.
APPARENTLY.
THANK YOU, ALFRED.
COMES WITH THE TERRITORY, SIR.
AND... IF YOU COULD PUT THAT SHARD OF GREEN KRYPTONITE UNDER LEAD..?
CONSIDER IT DONE.
Through it all... Alfred has been there for Bruce. A father figure... and yet... something more.
I TOOK THE LIBERTY OF WASHING YOUR UNIFORM. THE GOTHAM CITY SEWER IS BEST LEFT UNDER THE STREETS.
I'M SURE MY WIFE WILL APPRECIATE THAT MORE THAN ANYONE.
They are not exactly friends. Bruce makes it clear that Alfred works for him.
Having grown up in Kansas and not from a world of privilege, maybe I'll never understand...
BRUCE? WHAT IS IT...?
Even from here.... I can tell... I know him. Something is wrong.

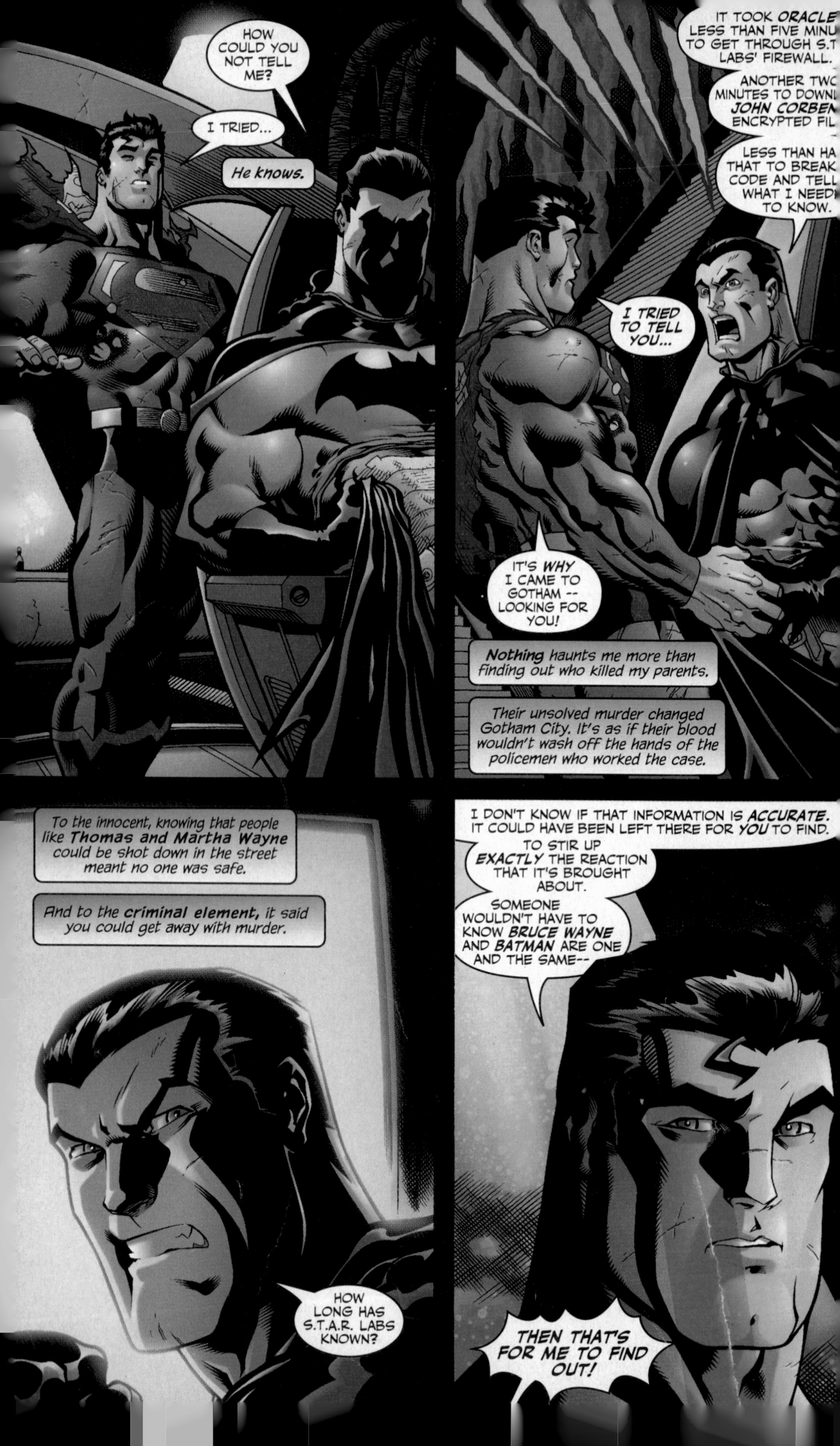

HOW COULD YOU NOT TELL ME?
I TRIED...
He knows.
IT TOOK ORACLE LESS THAN FIVE MINU TO GET THROUGH S.T LABS' FIREWALL.
ANOTHER TWO MINUTES TO DOWNL JOHN CORBEN ENCRYPTED FIL
LESS THAN HA THAT TO BREAK CODE AND TELL WHAT I NEED TO KNOW.
I TRIED TO TELL YOU...
IT'S WHY I CAME TO GOTHAM -- LOOKING FOR YOU!
Nothing haunts me more than finding out who killed my parents.
Their unsolved murder changed Gotham City. It's as if their blood wouldn't wash off the hands of the policemen who worked the case.
To the innocent, knowing that people like Thomas and Martha Wayne could be shot down in the street meant no one was safe.
And to the criminal element, it said you could get away with murder.
HOW LONG HAS S.T.A.R. LABS KNOWN?
I DON'T KNOW IF THAT INFORMATION IS ACCURATE. IT COULD HAVE BEEN LEFT THERE FOR YOU TO FIND.
TO STIR UP EXACTLY THE REACTION THAT IT'S BROUGHT ABOUT.
SOMEONE WOULDN'T HAVE TO KNOW BRUCE WAYNE AND BATMAN ARE ONE AND THE SAME--
THEN THAT'S FOR ME TO FIND OUT!

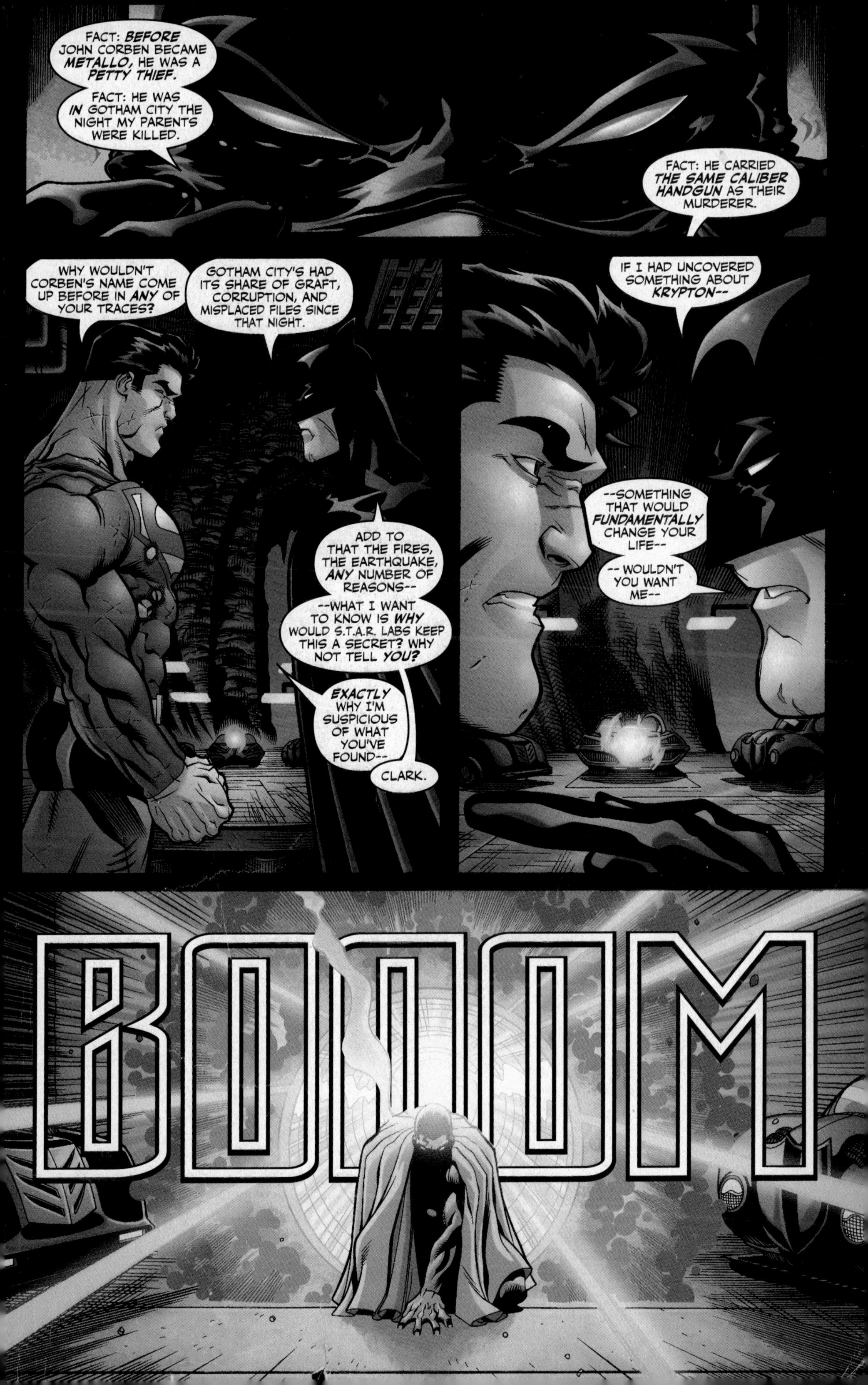
FACT: BEFORE JOHN CORBEN BECAME METALLO, HE WAS A PETTY THIEF.
FACT: HE WAS IN GOTHAM CITY THE NIGHT MY PARENTS WERE KILLED.
FACT: HE CARRIED THE SAME CALIBER HANDGUN AS THEIR MURDERER.
WHY WOULDN'T CORBEN'S NAME COME UP BEFORE IN ANY OF YOUR TRACES?
GOTHAM CITY'S HAD ITS SHARE OF GRAFT, CORRUPTION, AND MISPLACED FILES SINCE THAT NIGHT.
ADD TO THAT THE FIRES, THE EARTHQUAKE, ANY NUMBER OF REASONS--
--WHAT I WANT TO KNOW IS WHY WOULD S.T.A.R. LABS KEEP THIS A SECRET? WHY NOT TELL YOU?
EXACTLY WHY I'M SUSPICIOUS OF WHAT YOU'VE FOUND--
CLARK.
IF I HAD UNCOVERED SOMETHING ABOUT KRYPTON--
--SOMETHING THAT WOULD FUNDAMENTALLY CHANGE YOUR LIFE--
--WOULDN'T YOU WANT ME--
BOOOM

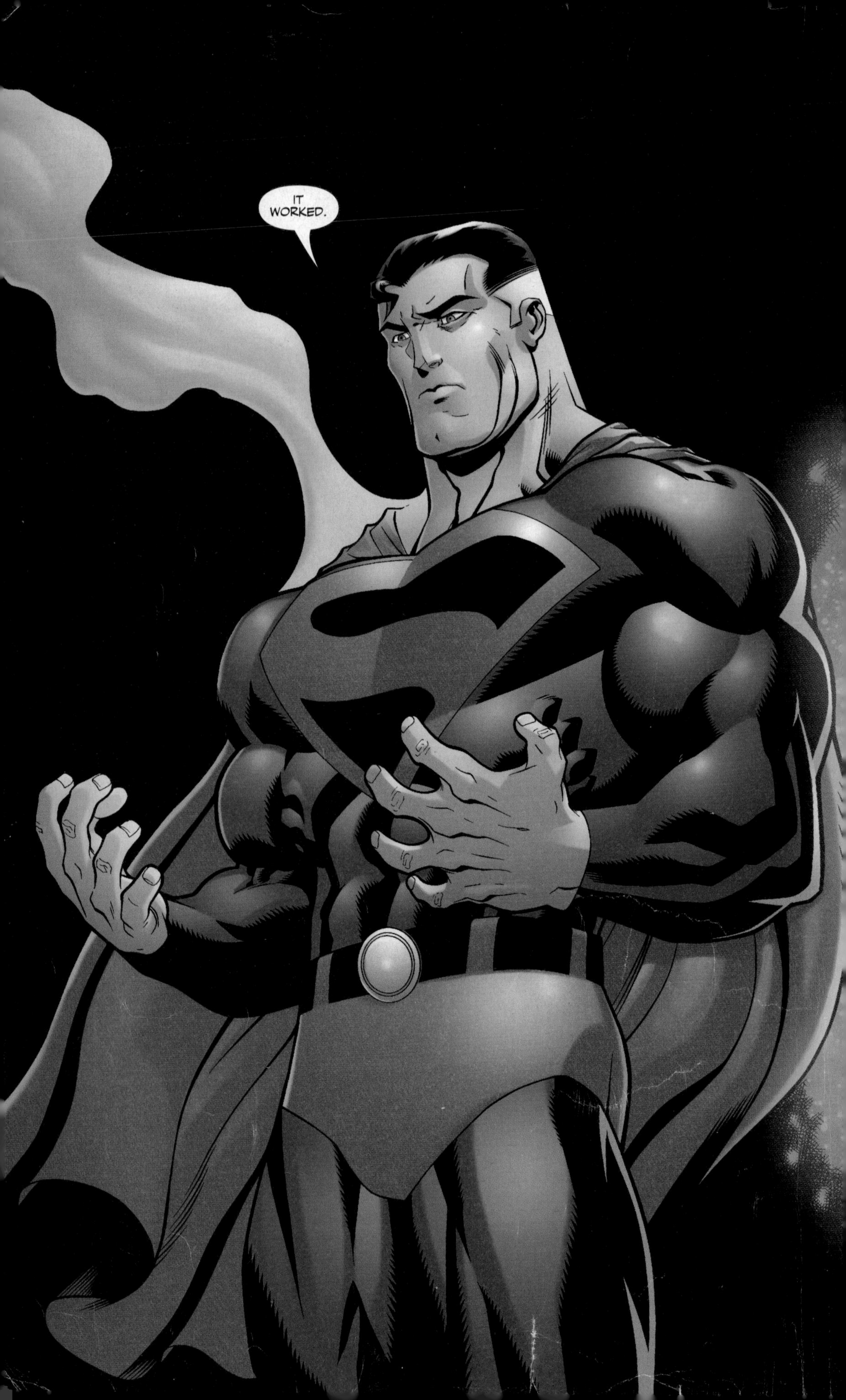
IT WORKED.

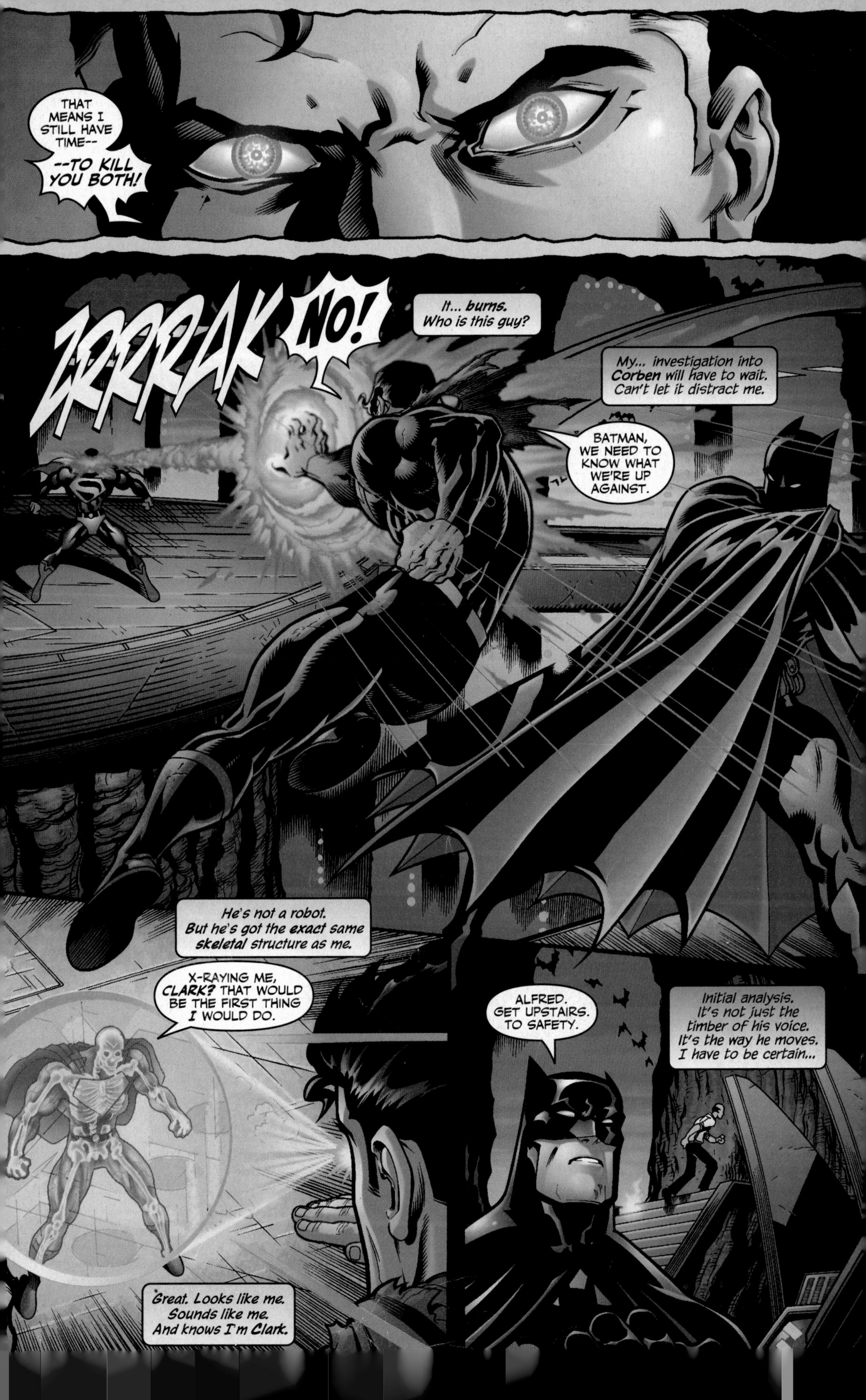
THAT MEANS I STILL HAVE TIME--
--TO KILL YOU BOTH!
ZRRRAK
NO!
It... burns. Who is this guy?
My... investigation into Corben will have to wait. Can't let it distract me.
BATMAN, WE NEED TO KNOW WHAT WE'RE UP AGAINST.
He's not a robot. But he's got the exact same skeletal structure as me.
X-RAYING ME, CLARK? THAT WOULD BE THE FIRST THING I WOULD DO.
Great. Looks like me. Sounds like me. And knows I'm Clark.
ALFRED. GET UPSTAIRS. TO SAFETY.
Initial analysis. It's not just the timber of his voice. It's the way he moves. I have to be certain...

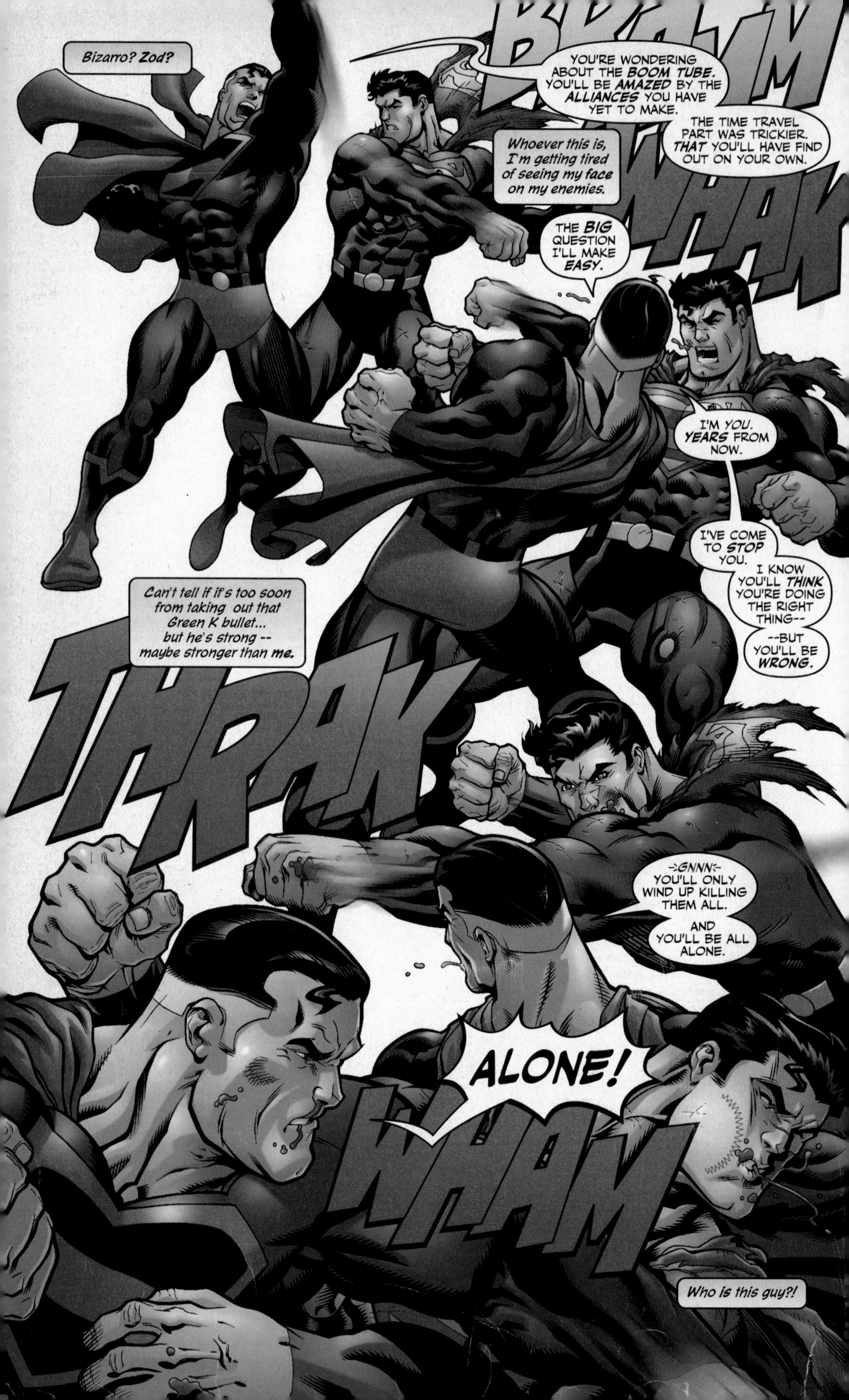

Bizarro? Zod?
YOU'RE WONDERING ABOUT THE BOOM TUBE. YOU'LL BE AMAZED BY THE ALLIANCES YOU HAVE YET TO MAKE.
THE TIME TRAVEL PART WAS TRICKIER. THAT YOU'LL HAVE FIND OUT ON YOUR OWN.
Whoever this is, I'm getting tired of seeing my face on my enemies.
THE BIG QUESTION I'LL MAKE EASY.
I'M YOU. YEARS FROM NOW.
I'VE COME TO STOP YOU.
I KNOW YOU'LL THINK YOU'RE DOING THE RIGHT THING--
--BUT YOU'LL BE WRONG.
Can't tell if it's too soon from taking out that Green K bullet... but he's strong -- maybe stronger than me.
THRAK
-GNNN- YOU'LL ONLY WIND UP KILLING THEM ALL.
AND YOU'LL BE ALL ALONE.
ALONE!
WHAM
Who is this guy?!

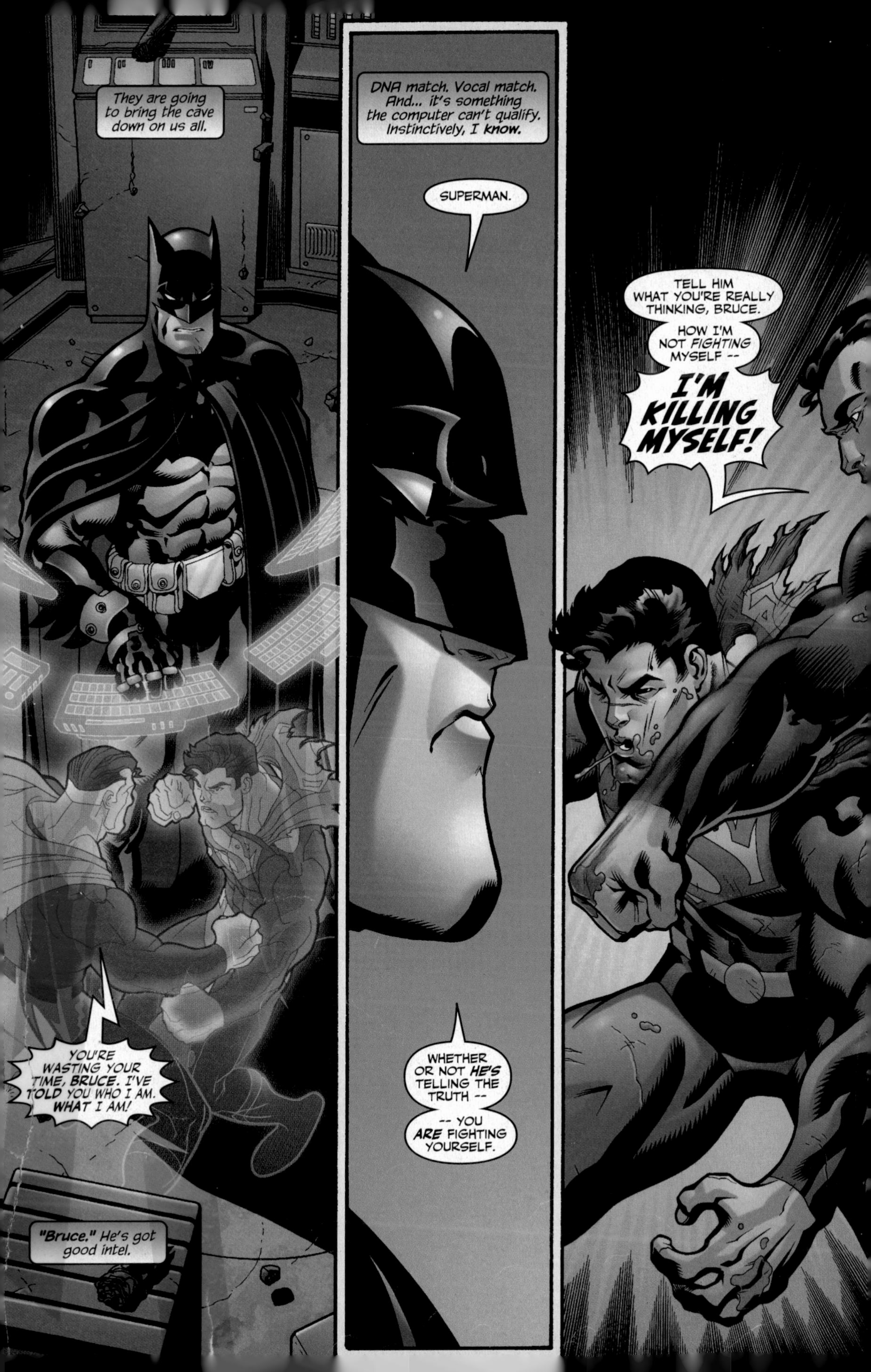
They are going to bring the cave down on us all.
YOU'RE WASTING YOUR TIME, BRUCE. I'VE TOLD YOU WHO I AM. WHAT I AM!
"Bruce." He's got good intel.
DNA match. Vocal match. And... it's something the computer can't qualify. Instinctively, I know.
SUPERMAN.
WHETHER OR NOT HE'S TELLING THE TRUTH --
-- YOU ARE FIGHTING YOURSELF.
TELL HIM WHAT YOU'RE REALLY THINKING, BRUCE.
HOW I'M NOT FIGHTING MYSELF --
I'M KILLING MYSELF!

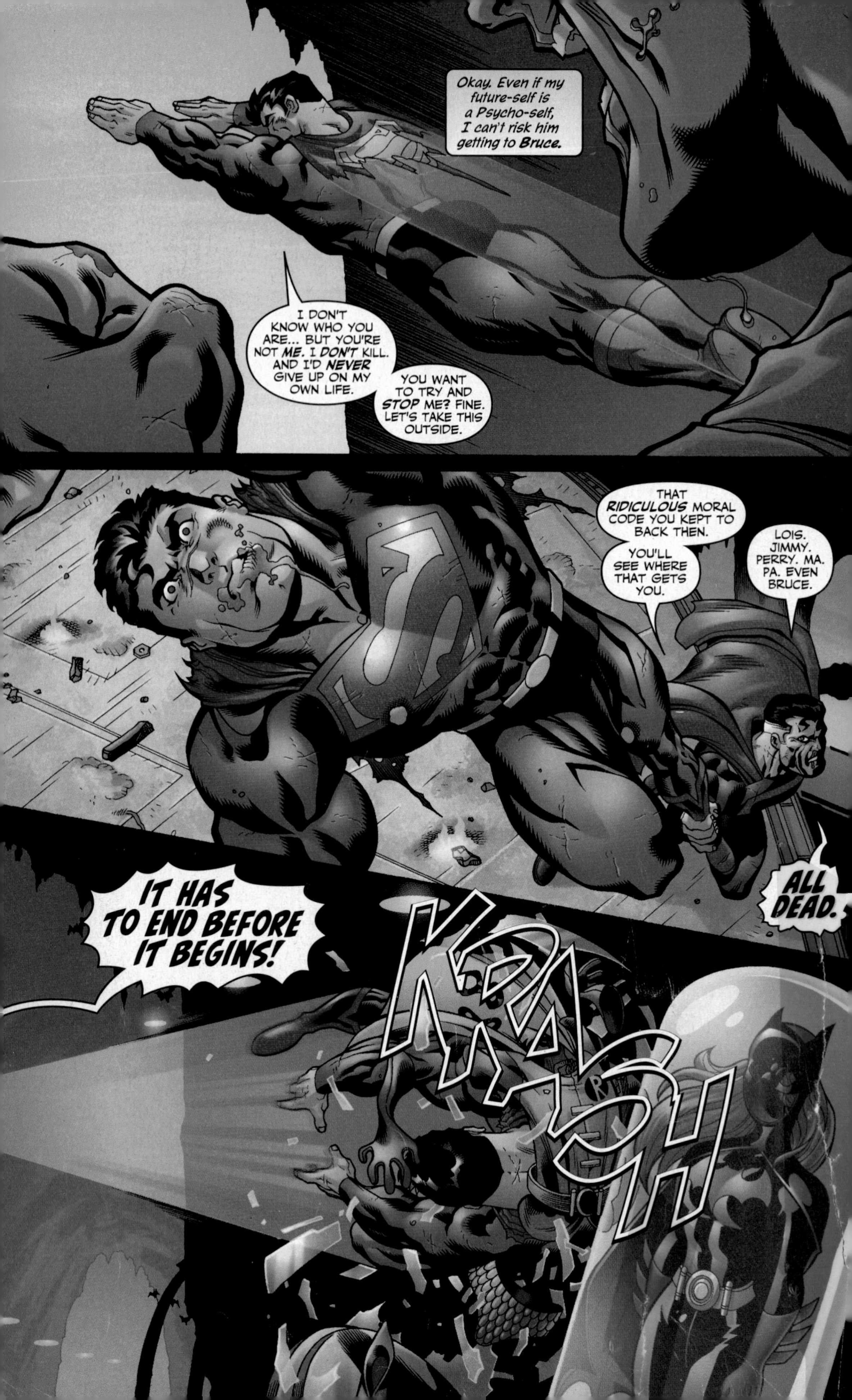
Okay. Even if my future-self is a Psycho-self, I can't risk him getting to Bruce.
I DON'T KNOW WHO YOU ARE... BUT YOU'RE NOT ME. I DON'T KILL. AND I'D NEVER GIVE UP ON MY OWN LIFE.
YOU WANT TO TRY AND STOP ME? FINE. LET'S TAKE THIS OUTSIDE.
THAT RIDICULOUS MORAL CODE YOU KEPT TO BACK THEN.
YOU'LL SEE WHERE THAT GETS YOU.
LOIS. JIMMY. PERRY. MA. PA. EVEN BRUCE.
ALL DEAD.
IT HAS TO END BEFORE IT BEGINS!
KRASH

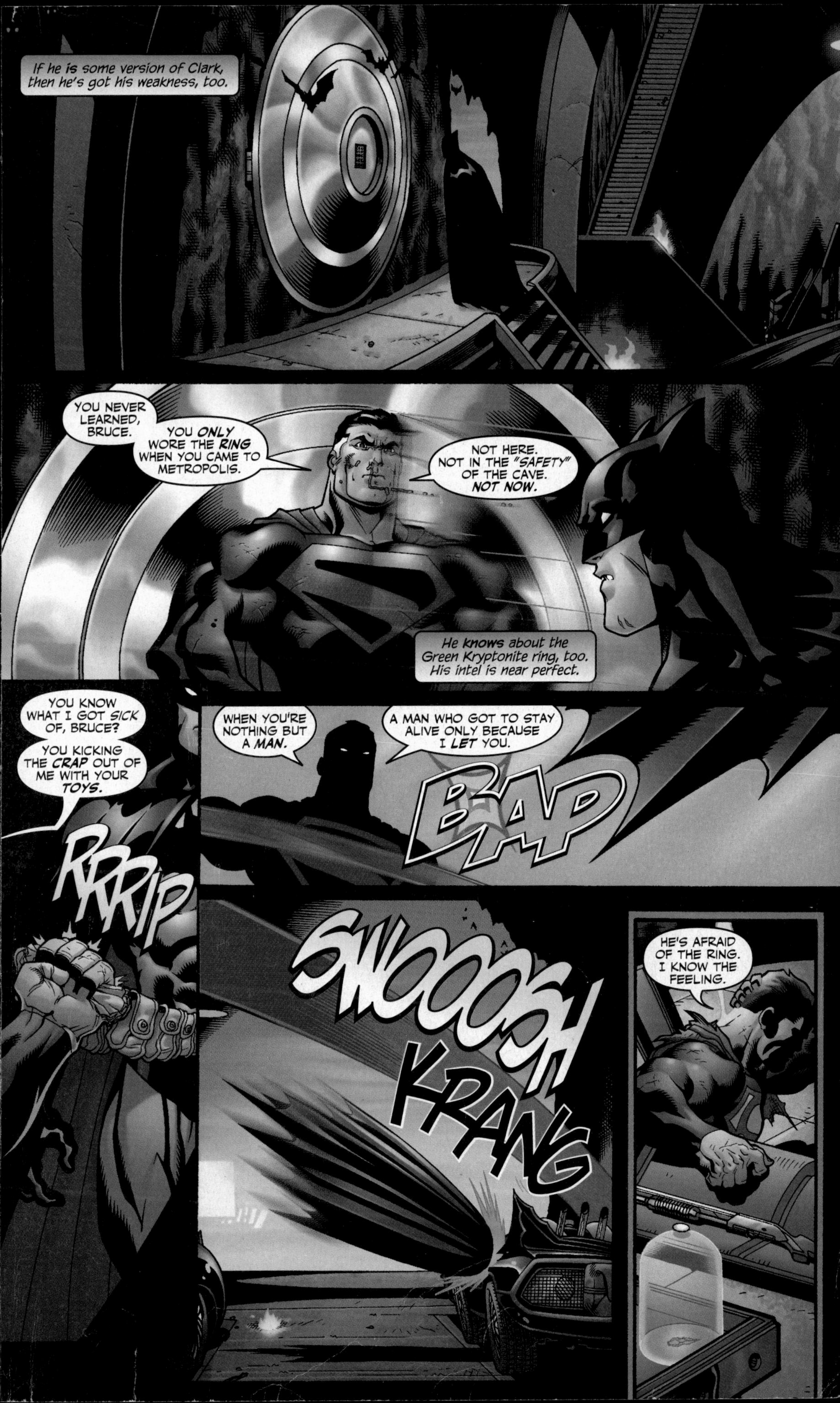
If he is some version of Clark, then he's got his weakness, too.
YOU NEVER LEARNED, BRUCE.
YOU ONLY WORE THE RING WHEN YOU CAME TO METROPOLIS.
NOT HERE. NOT IN THE "SAFETY" OF THE CAVE. NOT NOW.
He knows about the Green Kryptonite ring, too. His intel is near perfect.
YOU KNOW WHAT I GOT SICK OF, BRUCE?
YOU KICKING THE CRAP OUT OF ME WITH YOUR TOYS.
RRRIP
WHEN YOU'RE NOTHING BUT A MAN.
A MAN WHO GOT TO STAY ALIVE ONLY BECAUSE I LET YOU.
BAP
SWOOOSH
KRANG
HE'S AFRAID OF THE RING. I KNOW THE FEELING.

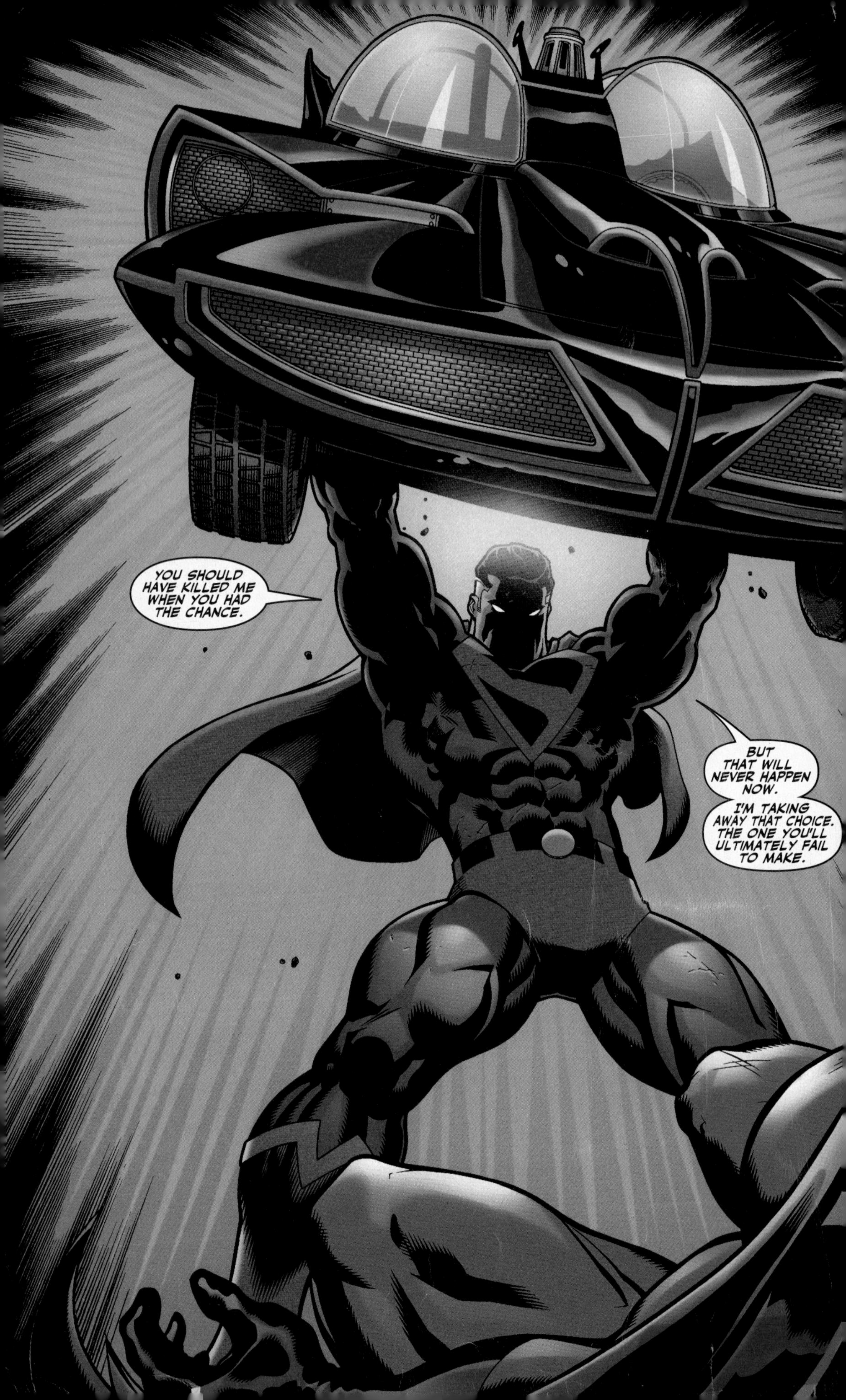
YOU SHOULD HAVE KILLED ME WHEN YOU HAD THE CHANCE.
BUT THAT WILL NEVER HAPPEN NOW.
I'M TAKING AWAY THAT CHOICE. THE ONE YOU'LL ULTIMATELY FAIL TO MAKE.

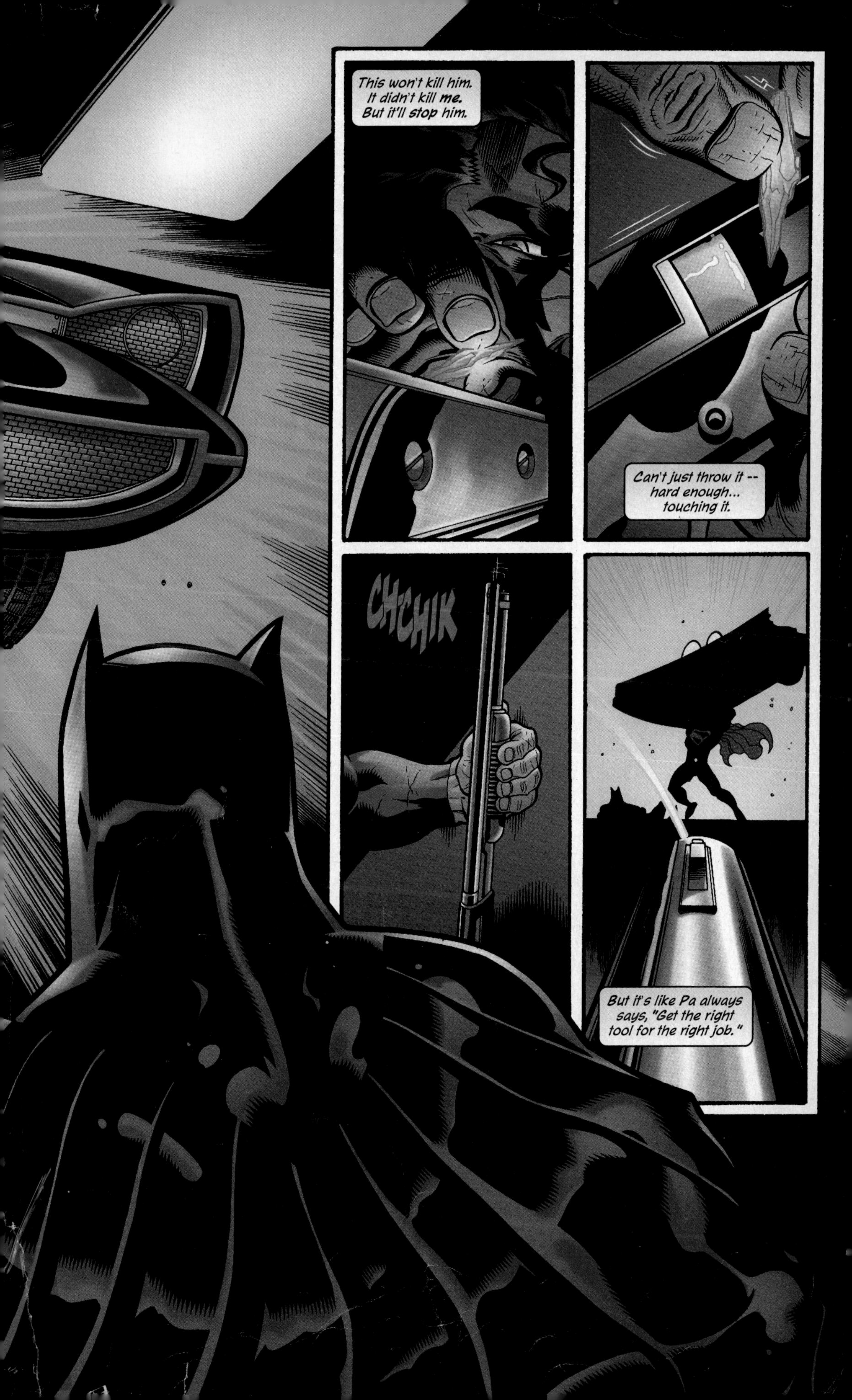
This won't kill him.
It didn't kill me.
But it'll stop him.
Can't just throw it --
hard enough...
touching it.
CHCHIK
But it's like Pa always
says, "Get the right
tool for the right job."

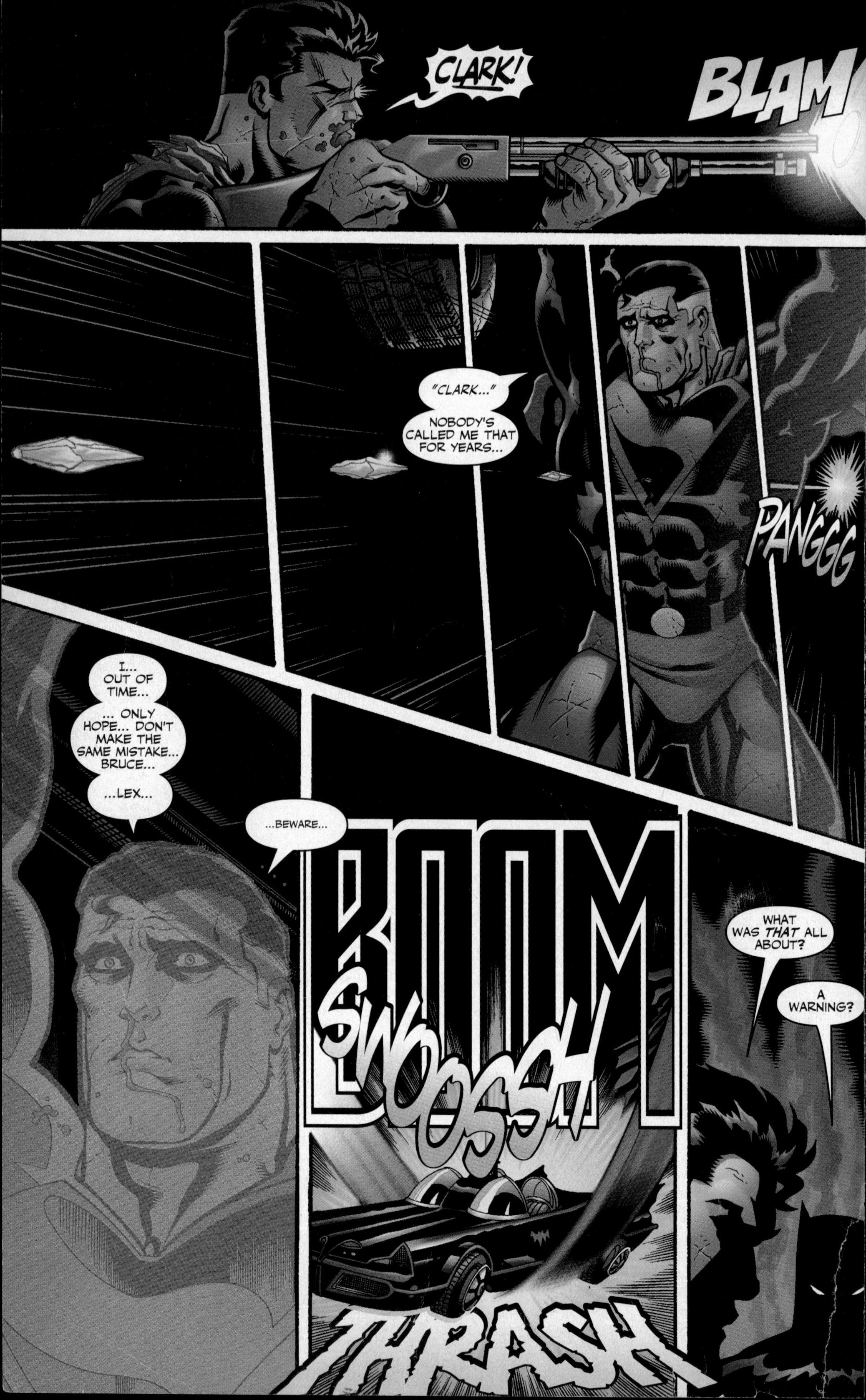
CLARK!
BLAM
"CLARK..."
NOBODY'S CALLED ME THAT FOR YEARS...
PANGGG
I... OUT OF TIME...
... ONLY HOPE... DON'T MAKE THE SAME MISTAKE... BRUCE...
...LEX...
...BEWARE...
BOOM
SWOOSH
THRASH
WHAT WAS THAT ALL ABOUT?
A WARNING?

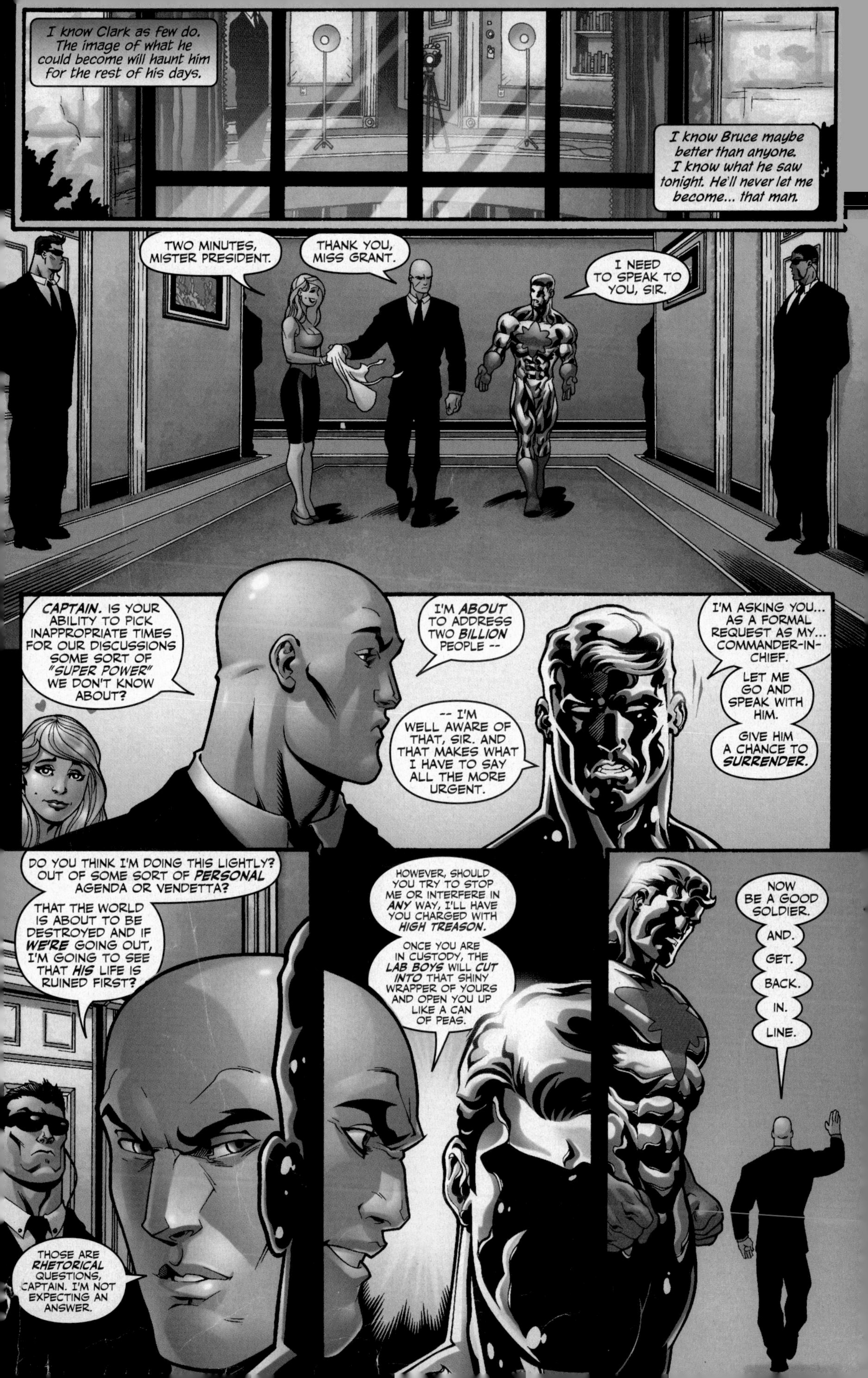

I know Clark as few do. The image of what he could become will haunt him for the rest of his days.
I know Bruce maybe better than anyone. I know what he saw tonight. He'll never let me become... that man.
TWO MINUTES, MISTER PRESIDENT.
THANK YOU, MISS GRANT.
I NEED TO SPEAK TO YOU, SIR.
CAPTAIN. IS YOUR ABILITY TO PICK INAPPROPRIATE TIMES FOR OUR DISCUSSIONS SOME SORT OF "SUPER POWER" WE DON'T KNOW ABOUT?
I'M ABOUT TO ADDRESS TWO BILLION PEOPLE --
-- I'M WELL AWARE OF THAT, SIR. AND THAT MAKES WHAT I HAVE TO SAY ALL THE MORE URGENT.
I'M ASKING YOU... AS A FORMAL REQUEST AS MY... COMMANDER-IN-CHIEF.
LET ME GO AND SPEAK WITH HIM.
GIVE HIM A CHANCE TO SURRENDER.
DO YOU THINK I'M DOING THIS LIGHTLY? OUT OF SOME SORT OF PERSONAL AGENDA OR VENDETTA?
THAT THE WORLD IS ABOUT TO BE DESTROYED AND IF WE'RE GOING OUT, I'M GOING TO SEE THAT HIS LIFE IS RUINED FIRST?
THOSE ARE RHETORICAL QUESTIONS, CAPTAIN. I'M NOT EXPECTING AN ANSWER.
HOWEVER, SHOULD YOU TRY TO STOP ME OR INTERFERE IN ANY WAY, I'LL HAVE YOU CHARGED WITH HIGH TREASON.
ONCE YOU ARE IN CUSTODY, THE LAB BOYS WILL CUT INTO THAT SHINY WRAPPER OF YOURS AND OPEN YOU UP LIKE A CAN OF PEAS.
NOW BE A GOOD SOLDIER.
AND.
GET.
BACK.
IN.
LINE.

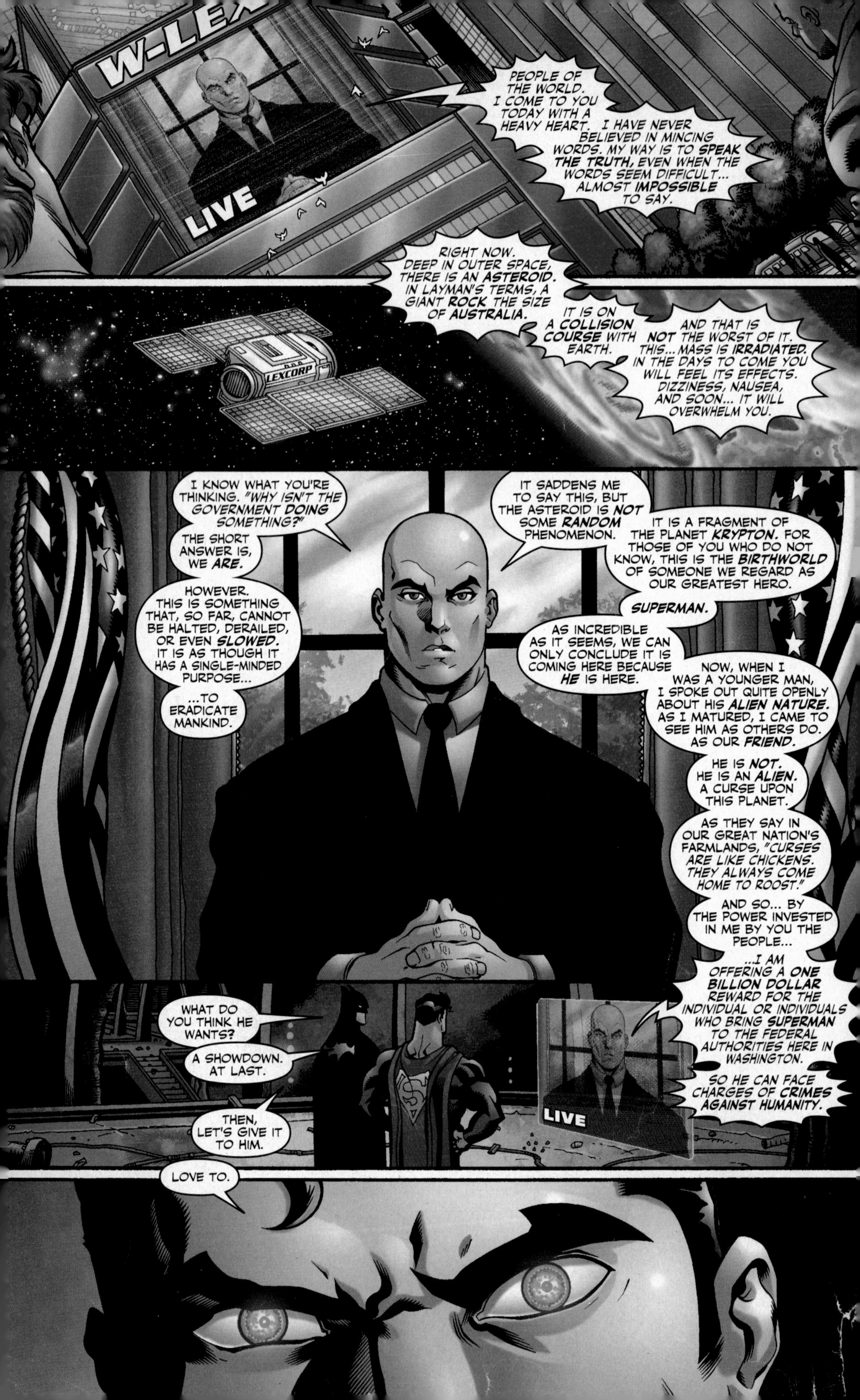
W-LEX
LIVE
PEOPLE OF THE WORLD. I COME TO YOU TODAY WITH A HEAVY HEART. I HAVE NEVER BELIEVED IN MINCING WORDS. MY WAY IS TO SPEAK THE TRUTH, EVEN WHEN THE WORDS SEEM DIFFICULT... ALMOST IMPOSSIBLE TO SAY.
RIGHT NOW. DEEP IN OUTER SPACE, THERE IS AN ASTEROID. IN LAYMAN'S TERMS, A GIANT ROCK THE SIZE OF AUSTRALIA.
IT IS ON A COLLISION COURSE WITH EARTH.
AND THAT IS NOT THE WORST OF IT. THIS... MASS IS IRRADIATED. IN THE DAYS TO COME YOU WILL FEEL ITS EFFECTS. DIZZINESS, NAUSEA, AND SOON... IT WILL OVERWHELM YOU.
LEXCORP
I KNOW WHAT YOU'RE THINKING. "WHY ISN'T THE GOVERNMENT DOING SOMETHING?"
THE SHORT ANSWER IS, WE ARE.
HOWEVER. THIS IS SOMETHING THAT, SO FAR, CANNOT BE HALTED, DERAILED, OR EVEN SLOWED. IT IS AS THOUGH IT HAS A SINGLE-MINDED PURPOSE...
...TO ERADICATE MANKIND.
IT SADDENS ME TO SAY THIS, BUT THE ASTEROID IS NOT SOME RANDOM PHENOMENON.
IT IS A FRAGMENT OF THE PLANET KRYPTON. FOR THOSE OF YOU WHO DO NOT KNOW, THIS IS THE BIRTHWORLD OF SOMEONE WE REGARD AS OUR GREATEST HERO.
SUPERMAN.
AS INCREDIBLE AS IT SEEMS, WE CAN ONLY CONCLUDE IT IS COMING HERE BECAUSE HE IS HERE.
NOW, WHEN I WAS A YOUNGER MAN, I SPOKE OUT QUITE OPENLY ABOUT HIS ALIEN NATURE. AS I MATURED, I CAME TO SEE HIM AS OTHERS DO. AS OUR FRIEND.
HE IS NOT. HE IS AN ALIEN. A CURSE UPON THIS PLANET.
AS THEY SAY IN OUR GREAT NATION'S FARMLANDS, "CURSES ARE LIKE CHICKENS. THEY ALWAYS COME HOME TO ROOST."
AND SO... BY THE POWER INVESTED IN ME BY YOU THE PEOPLE...
...I AM OFFERING A ONE BILLION DOLLAR REWARD FOR THE INDIVIDUAL OR INDIVIDUALS WHO BRING SUPERMAN TO THE FEDERAL AUTHORITIES HERE IN WASHINGTON.
SO HE CAN FACE CHARGES OF CRIMES AGAINST HUMANITY.
WHAT DO YOU THINK HE WANTS?
A SHOWDOWN. AT LAST.
THEN, LET'S GIVE IT TO HIM.
LIVE
LOVE TO.

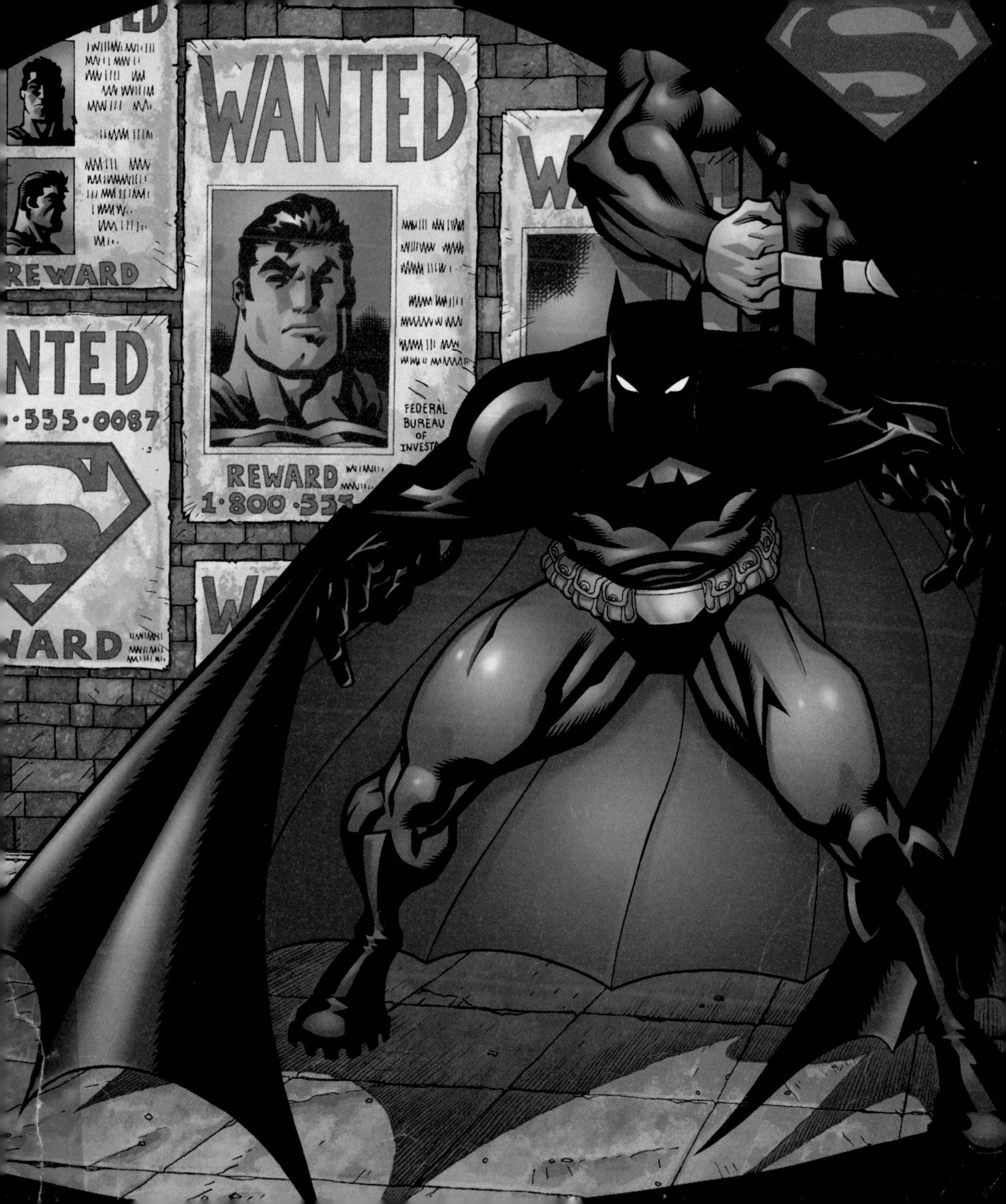

WANTED
REWARD
NTED
·555·0087
ARD
WANTED
FEDERAL
BUREAU
OF
INVESTA
REWARD
1·800·555

"I told you Luthor wouldn't go quietly..."

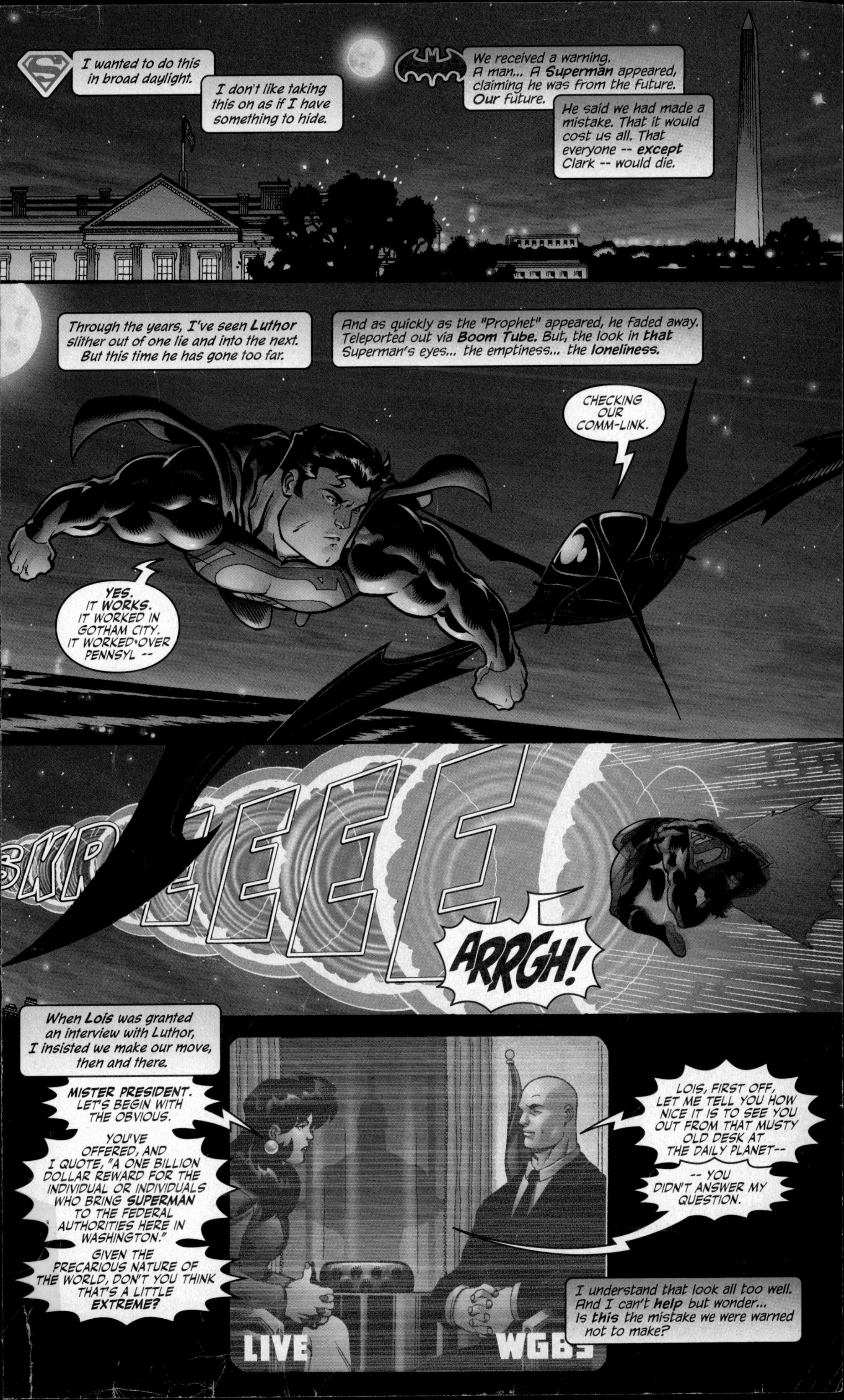

I wanted to do this in broad daylight.
I don't like taking this on as if I have something to hide.
We received a warning. A man... A Superman appeared, claiming he was from the future. Our future.
He said we had made a mistake. That it would cost us all. That everyone -- except Clark -- would die.
Through the years, I've seen Luthor slither out of one lie and into the next. But this time he has gone too far.
And as quickly as the "Prophet" appeared, he faded away. Teleported out via Boom Tube. But, the look in that Superman's eyes... the emptiness... the loneliness.
CHECKING OUR COMM-LINK.
YES. IT WORKS. IT WORKED IN GOTHAM CITY. IT WORKED OVER PENNSYL --
SKREEEEE
ARRGH!
When Lois was granted an interview with Luthor, I insisted we make our move, then and there.
MISTER PRESIDENT. LET'S BEGIN WITH THE OBVIOUS.
YOU'VE OFFERED, AND I QUOTE, "A ONE BILLION DOLLAR REWARD FOR THE INDIVIDUAL OR INDIVIDUALS WHO BRING SUPERMAN TO THE FEDERAL AUTHORITIES HERE IN WASHINGTON."
GIVEN THE PRECARIOUS NATURE OF THE WORLD, DON'T YOU THINK THAT'S A LITTLE EXTREME?
LOIS, FIRST OFF, LET ME TELL YOU HOW NICE IT IS TO SEE YOU OUT FROM THAT MUSTY OLD DESK AT THE DAILY PLANET--
-- YOU DIDN'T ANSWER MY QUESTION.
I understand that look all too well. And I can't help but wonder... Is this the mistake we were warned not to make?
LIVE
WGBS

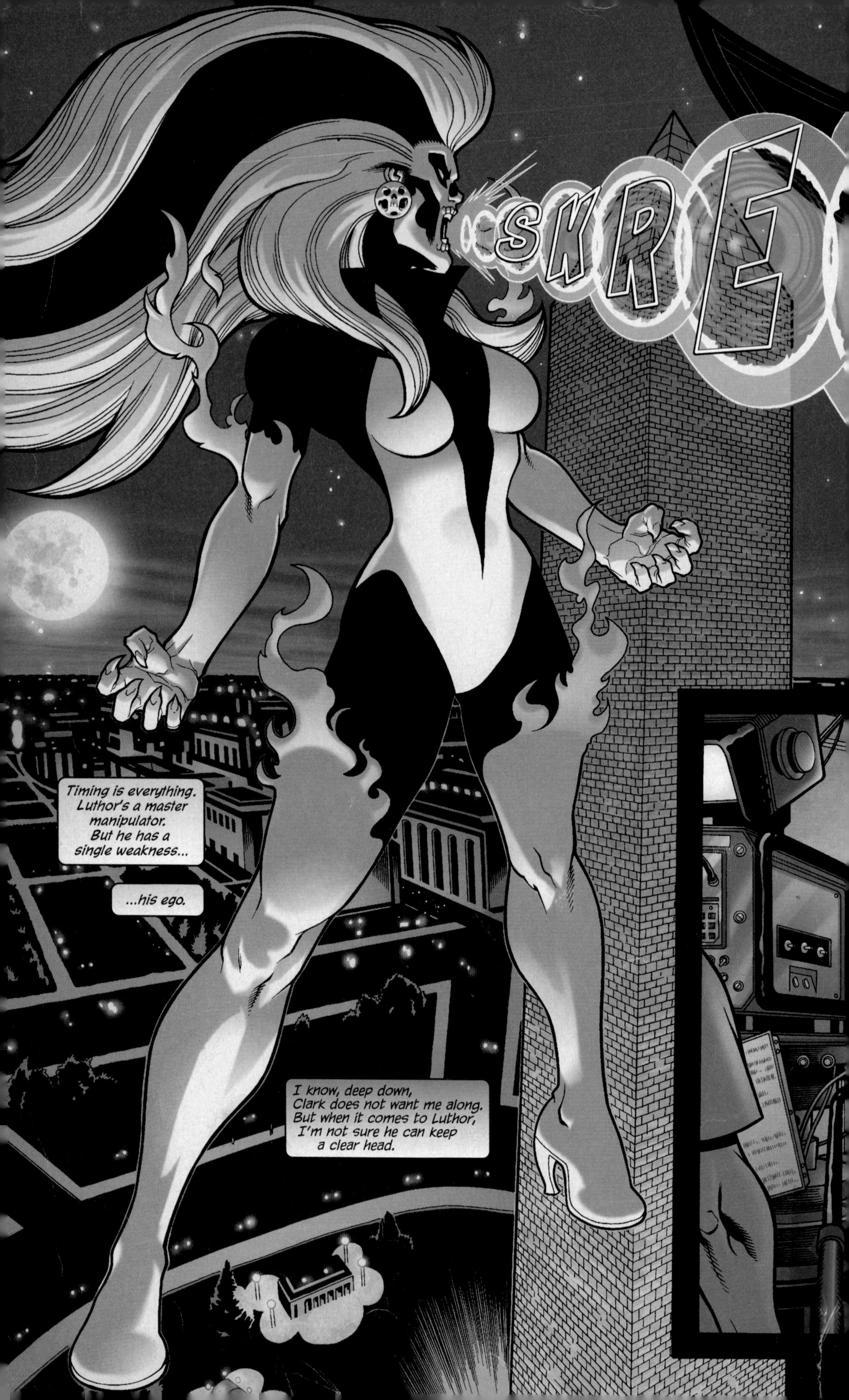
SKRE
Timing is everything. Luthor's a master manipulator. But he has a single weakness...
...his ego.
I know, deep down, Clark does not want me along. But when it comes to Luthor, I'm not sure he can keep a clear head.

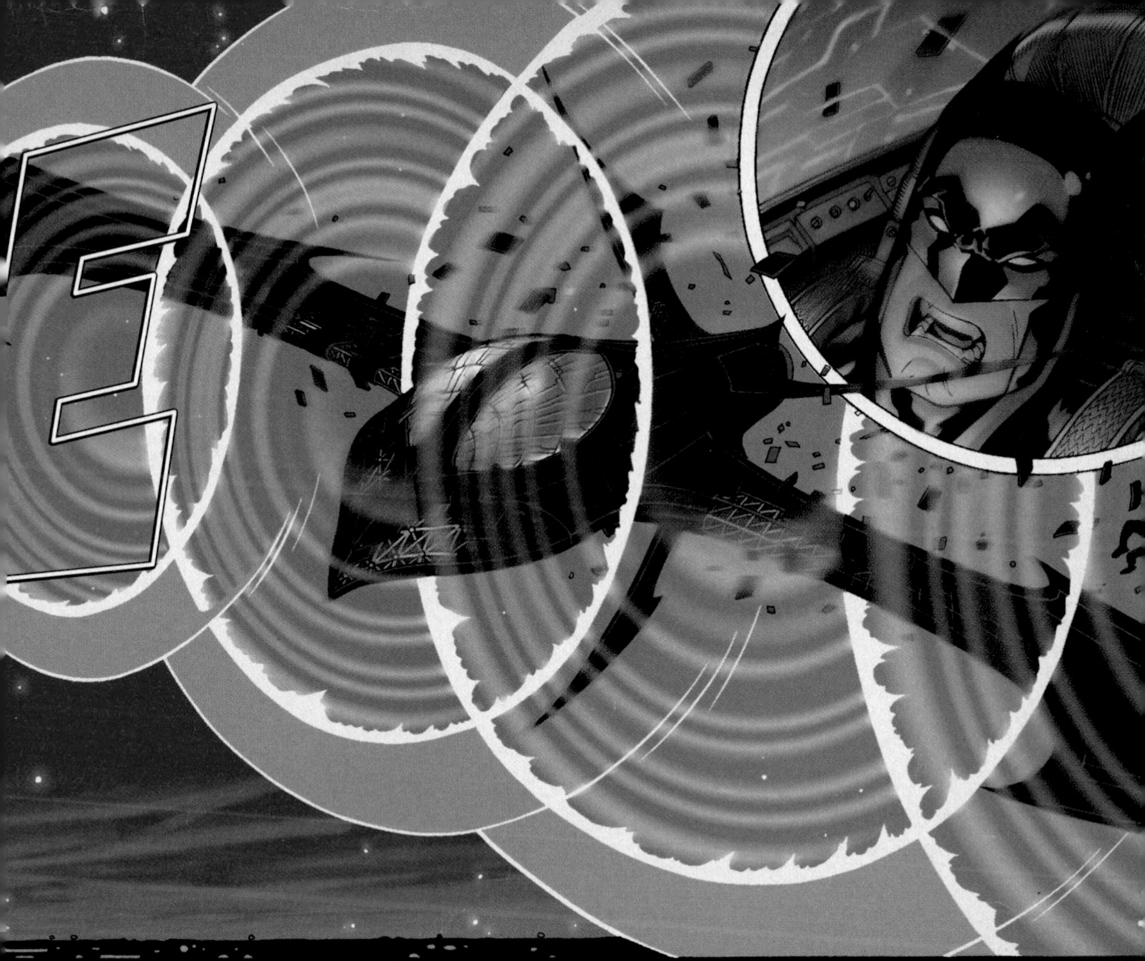

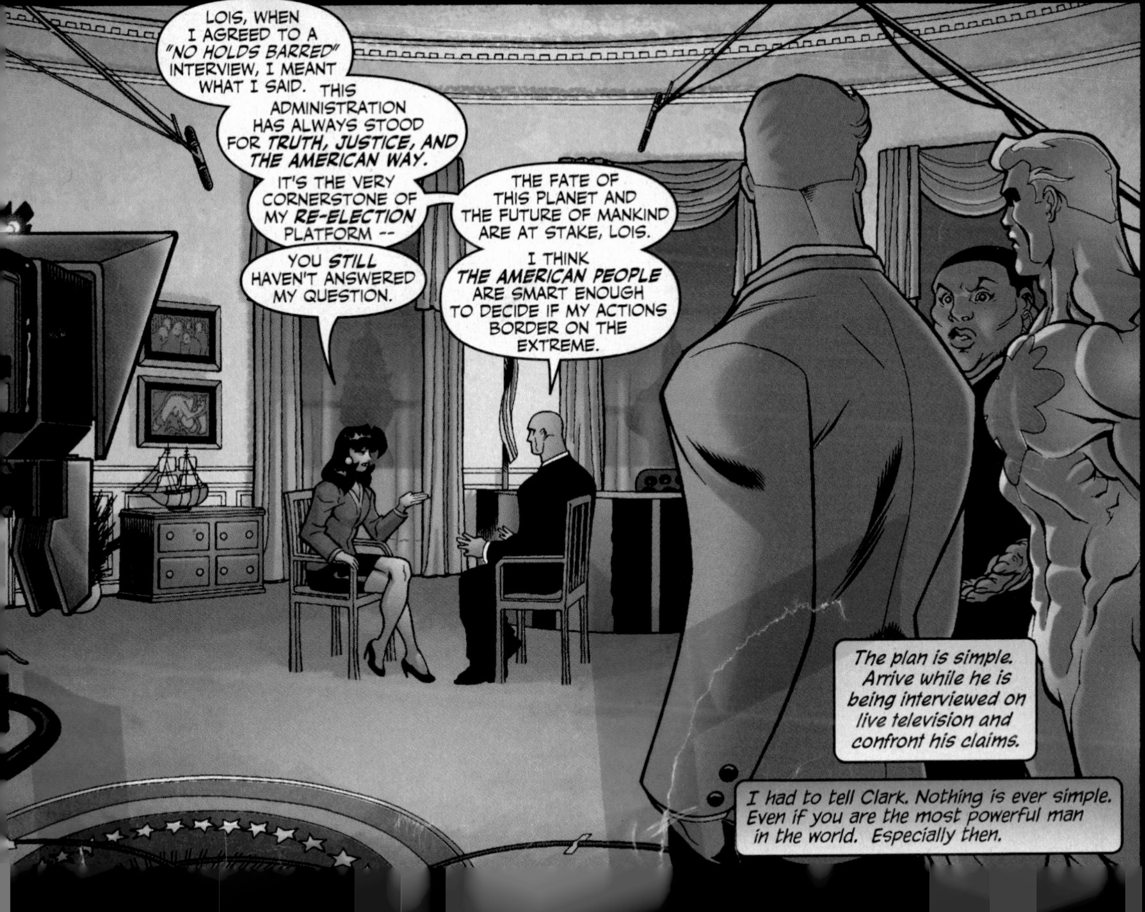

LOIS, WHEN I AGREED TO A "NO HOLDS BARRED" INTERVIEW, I MEANT WHAT I SAID.
THIS ADMINISTRATION HAS ALWAYS STOOD FOR TRUTH, JUSTICE, AND THE AMERICAN WAY.
IT'S THE VERY CORNERSTONE OF MY RE-ELECTION PLATFORM --
YOU STILL HAVEN'T ANSWERED MY QUESTION.
THE FATE OF THIS PLANET AND THE FUTURE OF MANKIND ARE AT STAKE, LOIS.
I THINK THE AMERICAN PEOPLE ARE SMART ENOUGH TO DECIDE IF MY ACTIONS BORDER ON THE EXTREME.
The plan is simple. Arrive while he is being interviewed on live television and confront his claims.
I had to tell Clark. Nothing is ever simple. Even if you are the most powerful man in the world. Especially then.

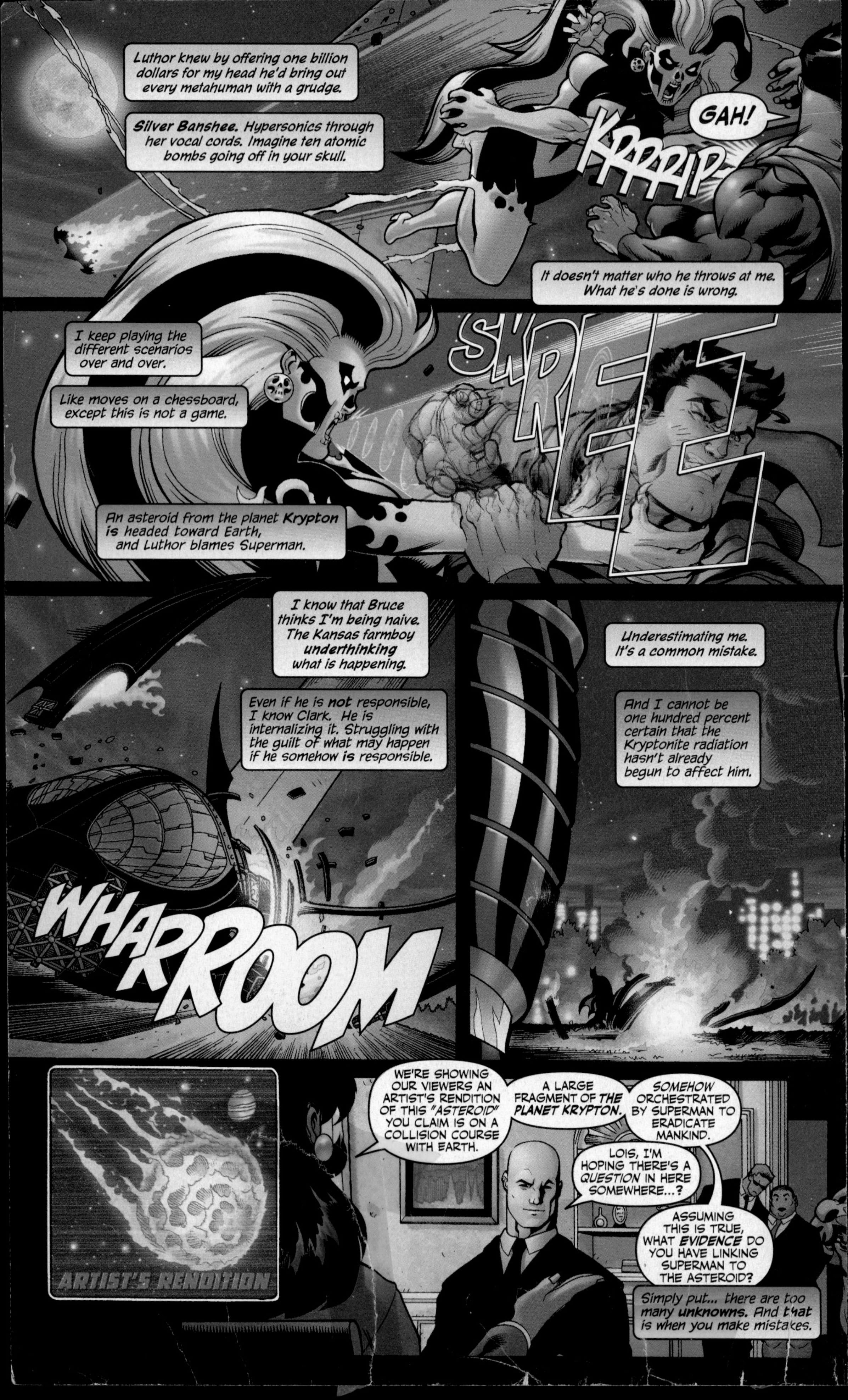

Luthor knew by offering one billion dollars for my head he'd bring out every metahuman with a grudge.
Silver Banshee. Hypersonics through her vocal cords. Imagine ten atomic bombs going off in your skull.
GAH!
KRRRRIP
It doesn't matter who he throws at me. What he's done is wrong.
I keep playing the different scenarios over and over.
Like moves on a chessboard, except this is not a game.
SKREEE
An asteroid from the planet Krypton is headed toward Earth, and Luthor blames Superman.
I know that Bruce thinks I'm being naive. The Kansas farmboy underthinking what is happening.
Even if he is not responsible, I know Clark. He is internalizing it. Struggling with the guilt of what may happen if he somehow is responsible.
WHARROOM
Underestimating me. It's a common mistake.
And I cannot be one hundred percent certain that the Kryptonite radiation hasn't already begun to affect him.
ARTIST'S RENDITION
WE'RE SHOWING OUR VIEWERS AN ARTIST'S RENDITION OF THIS "ASTEROID" YOU CLAIM IS ON A COLLISION COURSE WITH EARTH.
A LARGE FRAGMENT OF THE PLANET KRYPTON.
SOMEHOW ORCHESTRATED BY SUPERMAN TO ERADICATE MANKIND.
LOIS, I'M HOPING THERE'S A QUESTION IN HERE SOMEWHERE...?
ASSUMING THIS IS TRUE, WHAT EVIDENCE DO YOU HAVE LINKING SUPERMAN TO THE ASTEROID?
Simply put... there are too many unknowns. And that is when you make mistakes.

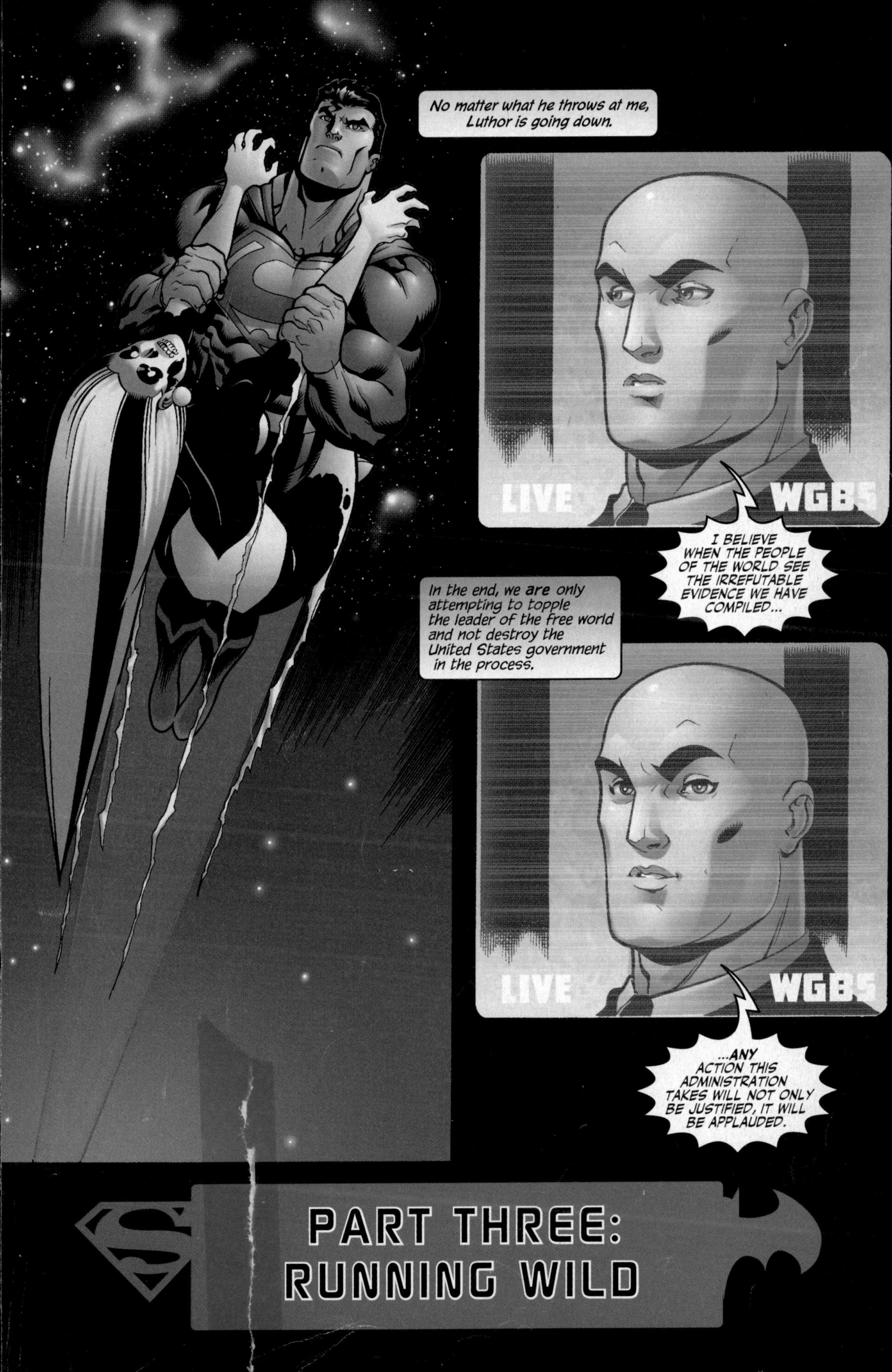
No matter what he throws at me, Luthor is going down.
LIVE
WGBS
I BELIEVE WHEN THE PEOPLE OF THE WORLD SEE THE IRREFUTABLE EVIDENCE WE HAVE COMPILED...
In the end, we **are** only attempting to topple the leader of the free world and not destroy the United States government in the process.
LIVE
WGBS
...**ANY** ACTION THIS ADMINISTRATION TAKES WILL NOT ONLY BE JUSTIFIED, IT WILL BE APPLAUDED.
PART THREE: RUNNING WILD

Mister Freeze. Captain Cold. Icicle. Killer Frost.

LITTLE BUSY AT THE MOMENT, B.

Criminals who have essentially the *same* modus operandi. Subzero thermals as a weapon.

WHEN YOU CAN. BRING THE HEAT.

"S"...

FRZZZZZZZZZ

PFFFT

DKUSH

UNDERSTOOD. IF YOU COULD MOVE ABOUT THREE FEET TO YOUR LEFT...

They may have never worked *together* before but money often overcomes such boundaries.

SO, YOUR ENTIRE BASIS FOR CHARGE OF "CRIMES AGAINST HUMANITY" THAT YOU'VE LEVELED ON SUPERMAN --

-- IS THIS EVIDENCE. CARE TO SHARE ANY OF THAT WITH YOUR *VOTERS*, I MEAN, FELLOW CITIZENS?

NOT AT THIS TIME. IT SIMPLY WOULDN'T BE PRUDENT.

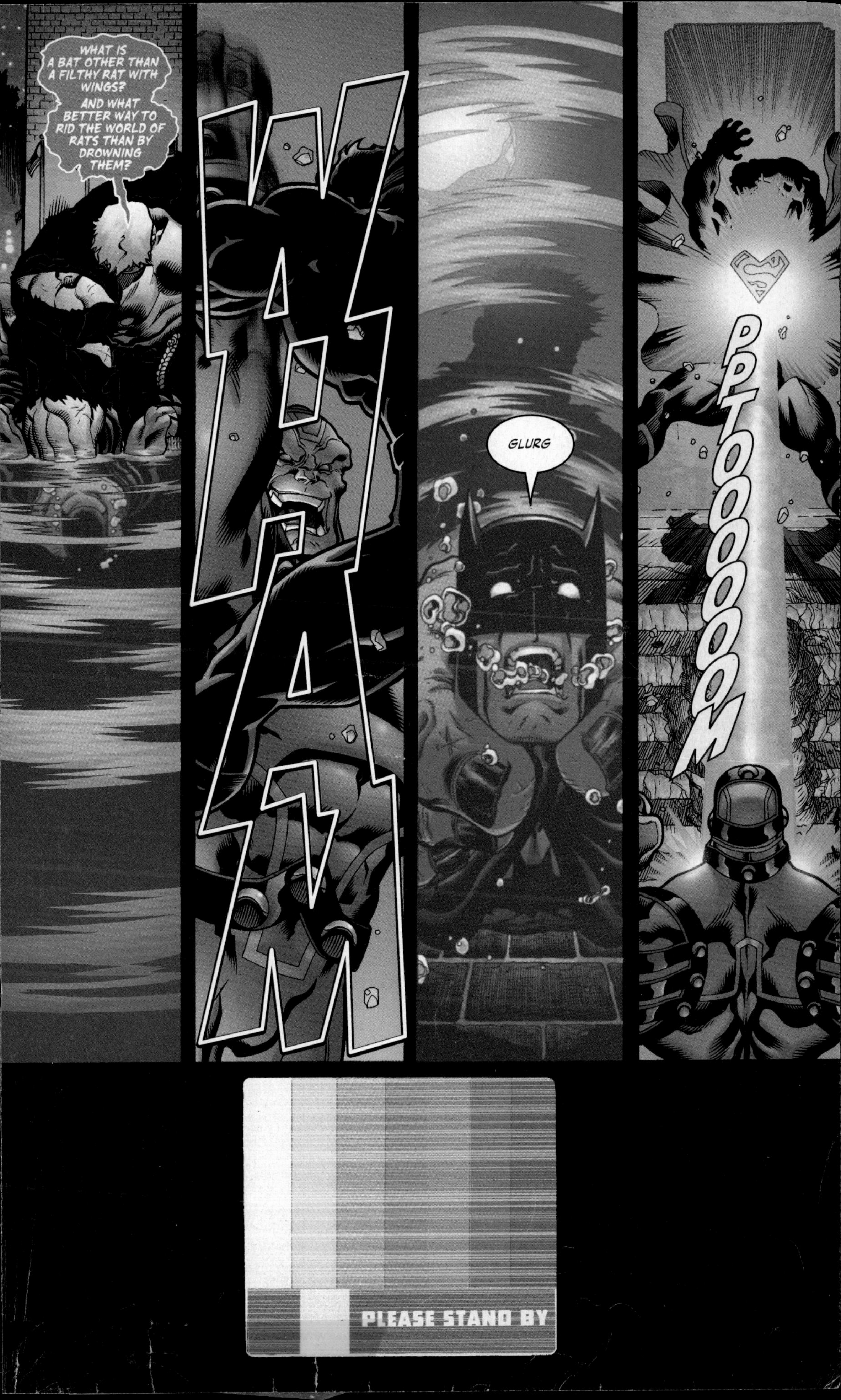

WHAT IS A BAT OTHER THAN A FILTHY RAT WITH WINGS? AND WHAT BETTER WAY TO RID THE WORLD OF RATS THAN BY DROWNING THEM?
WHAM
GLURG
PPTOOOOOOM
PLEASE STAND BY

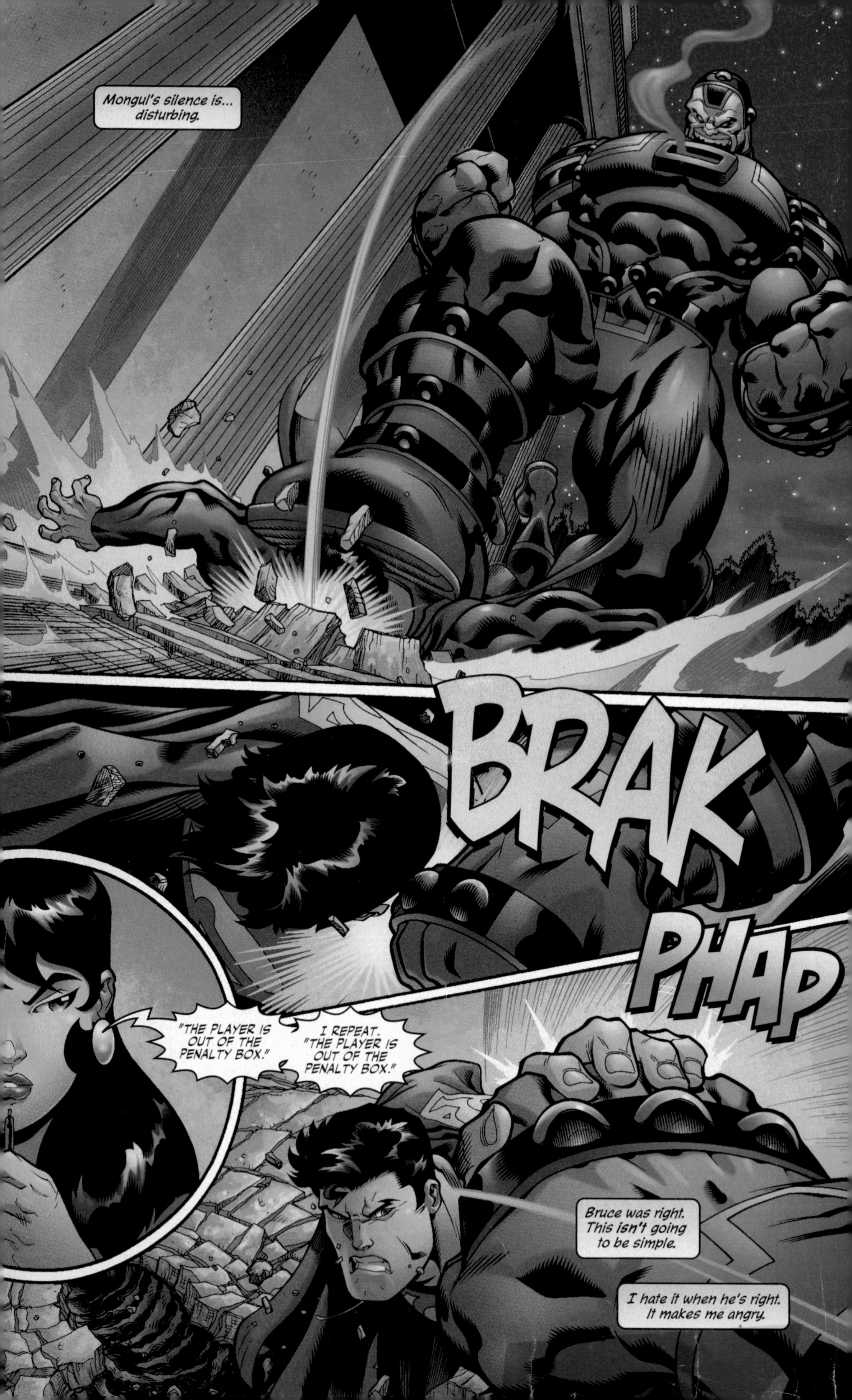

Mongul's silence is... disturbing.
BRAK
PHAP
"THE PLAYER IS OUT OF THE PENALTY BOX."
I REPEAT. "THE PLAYER IS OUT OF THE PENALTY BOX."
Bruce was right. This isn't going to be simple.
I hate it when he's right. It makes me angry.

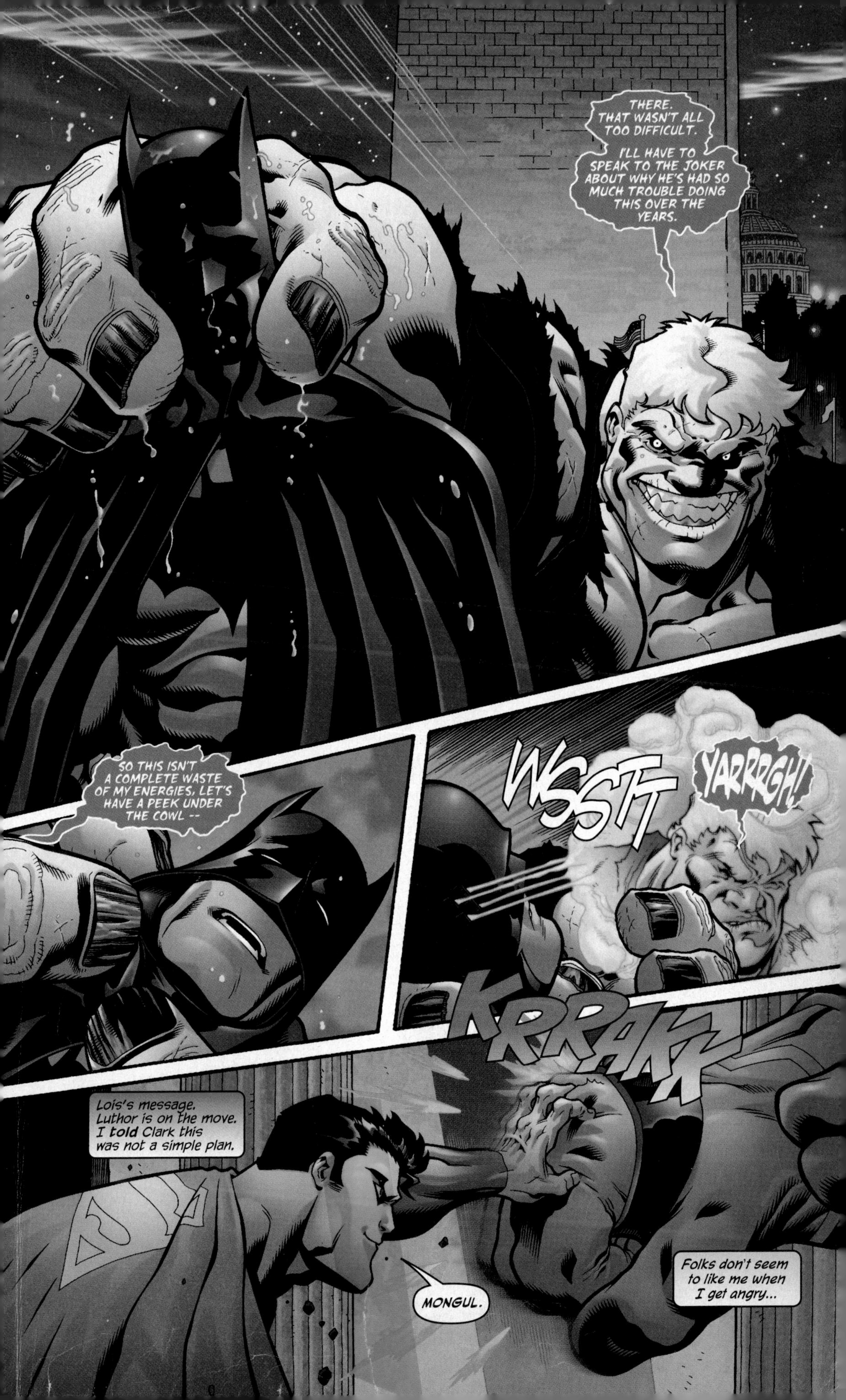
THERE. THAT WASN'T ALL TOO DIFFICULT.
I'LL HAVE TO SPEAK TO THE JOKER ABOUT WHY HE'S HAD SO MUCH TROUBLE DOING THIS OVER THE YEARS.
SO THIS ISN'T A COMPLETE WASTE OF MY ENERGIES, LET'S HAVE A PEEK UNDER THE COWL --
WSSFT
YARRRGH!
KRRAKK
Lois's message. Luthor is on the move. I told Clark this was not a simple plan.
MONGUL.
Folks don't seem to like me when I get angry...

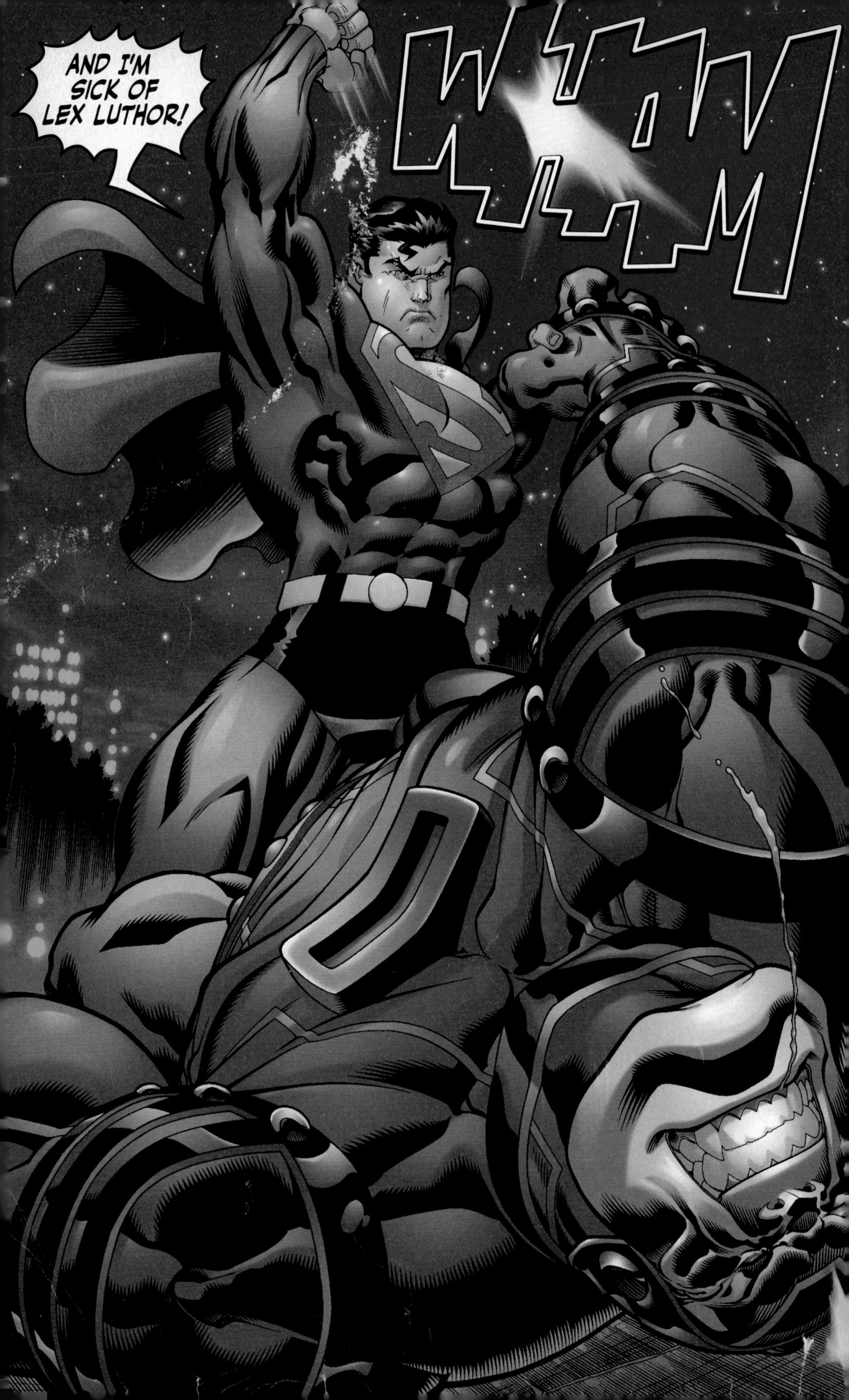
AND I'M SICK OF LEX LUTHOR!
WHAM

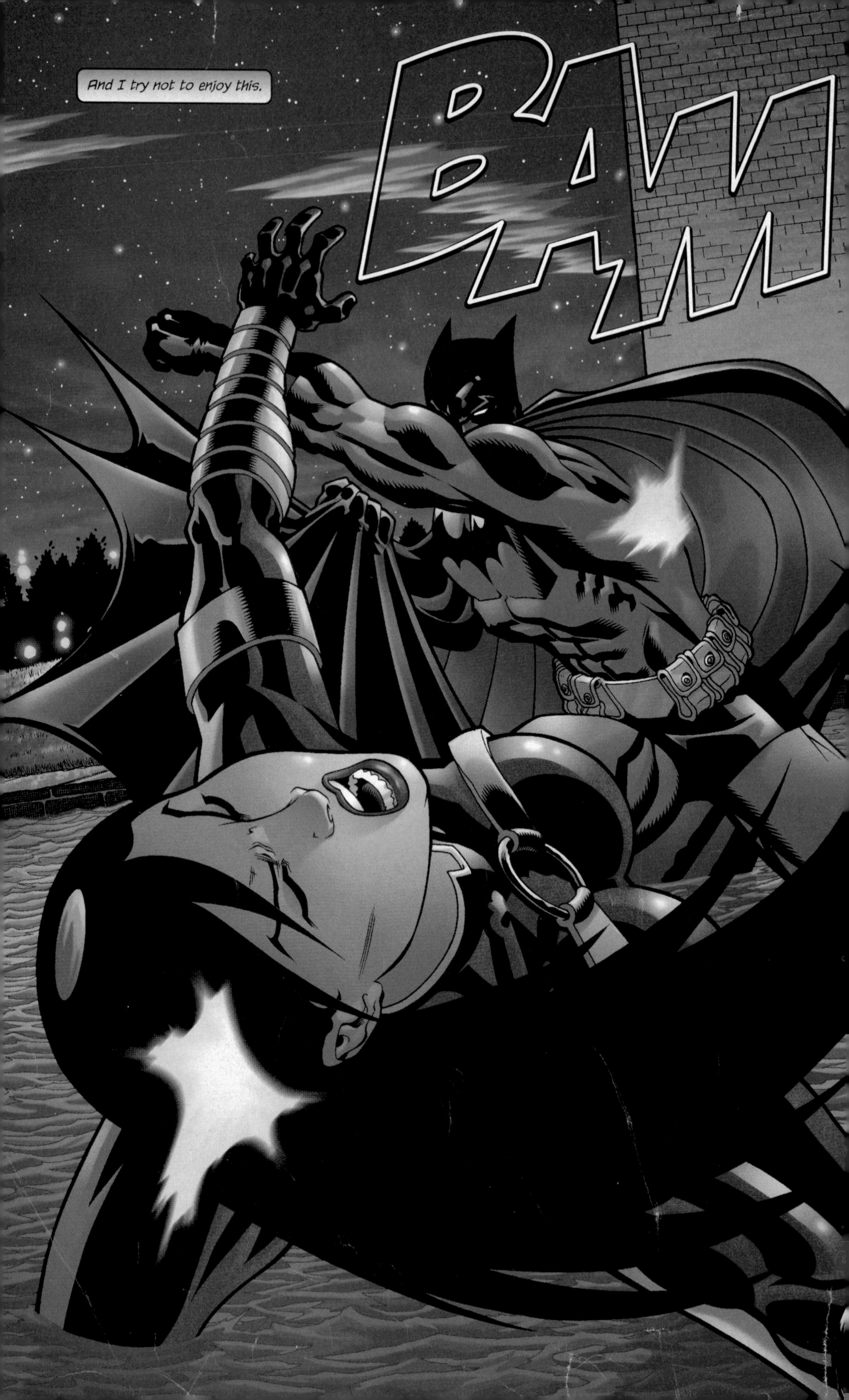
And I try not to enjoy this.
BAM

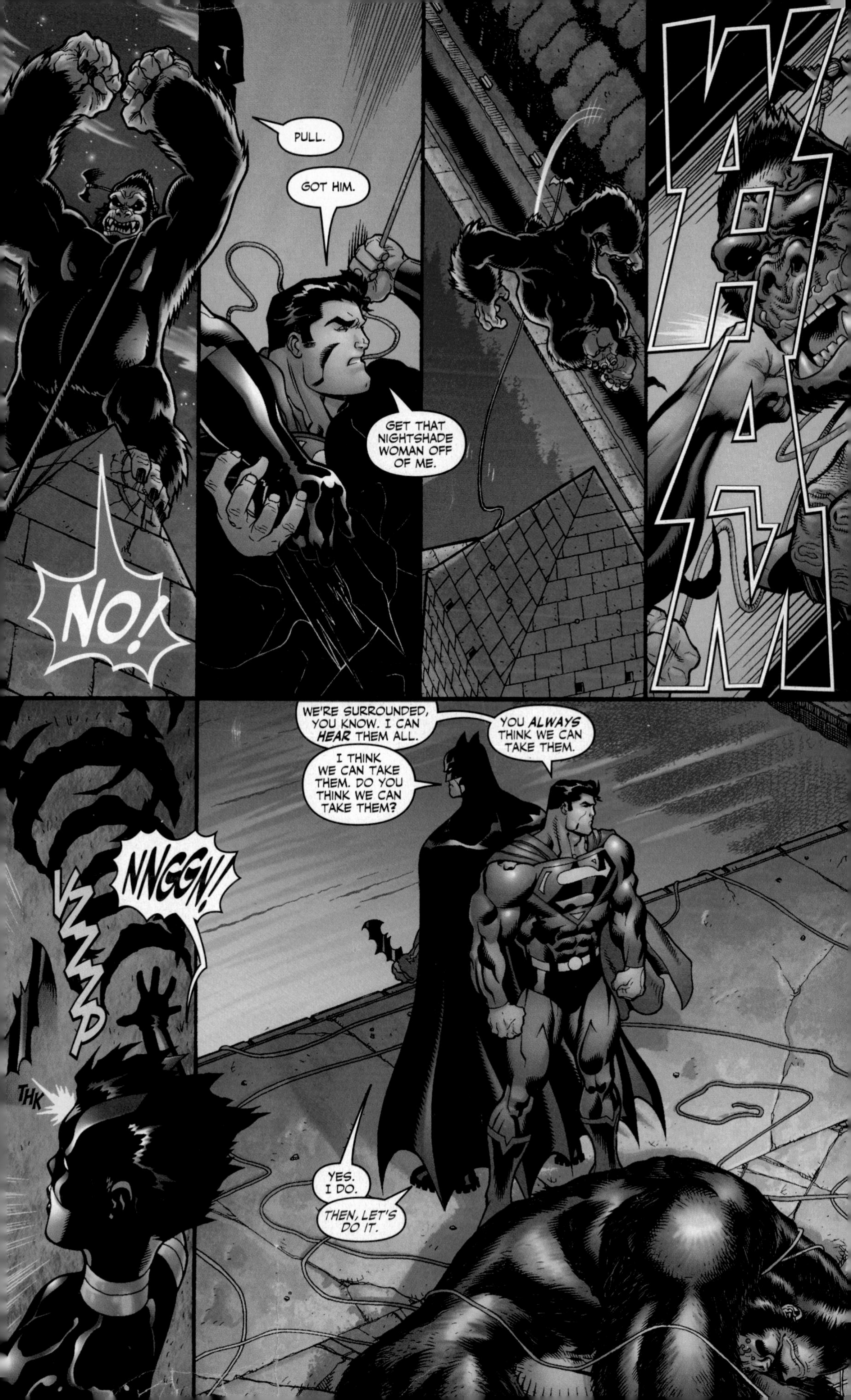

NO!
PULL.
GOT HIM.
GET THAT NIGHTSHADE WOMAN OFF OF ME.
WHAM
NNGGN!
VZZZAP
THK
WE'RE SURROUNDED, YOU KNOW. I CAN HEAR THEM ALL.
YOU ALWAYS THINK WE CAN TAKE THEM.
I THINK WE CAN TAKE THEM. DO YOU THINK WE CAN TAKE THEM?
YES. I DO.
THEN, LET'S DO IT.

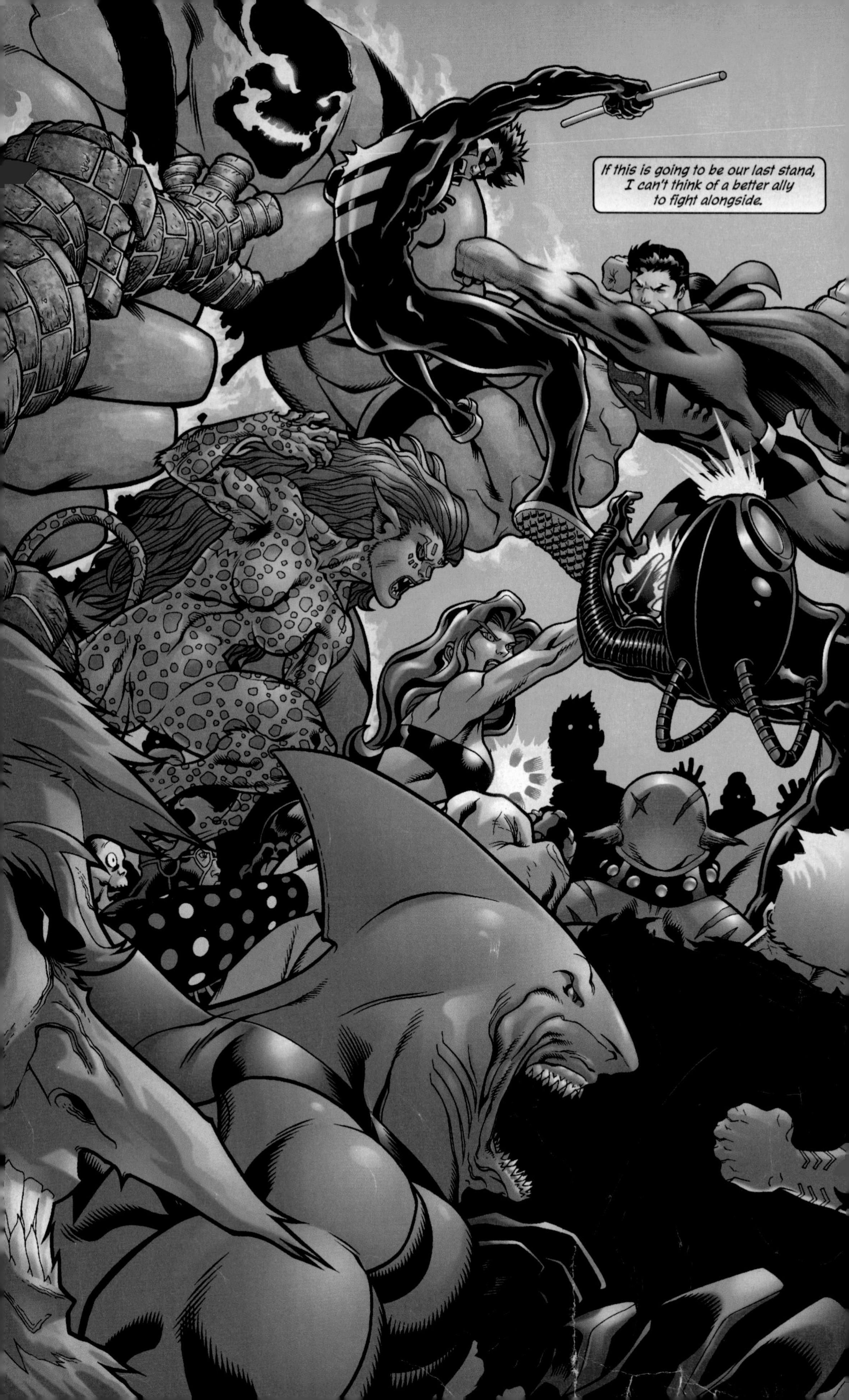
If this is going to be our last stand, I can't think of a better ally to fight alongside.

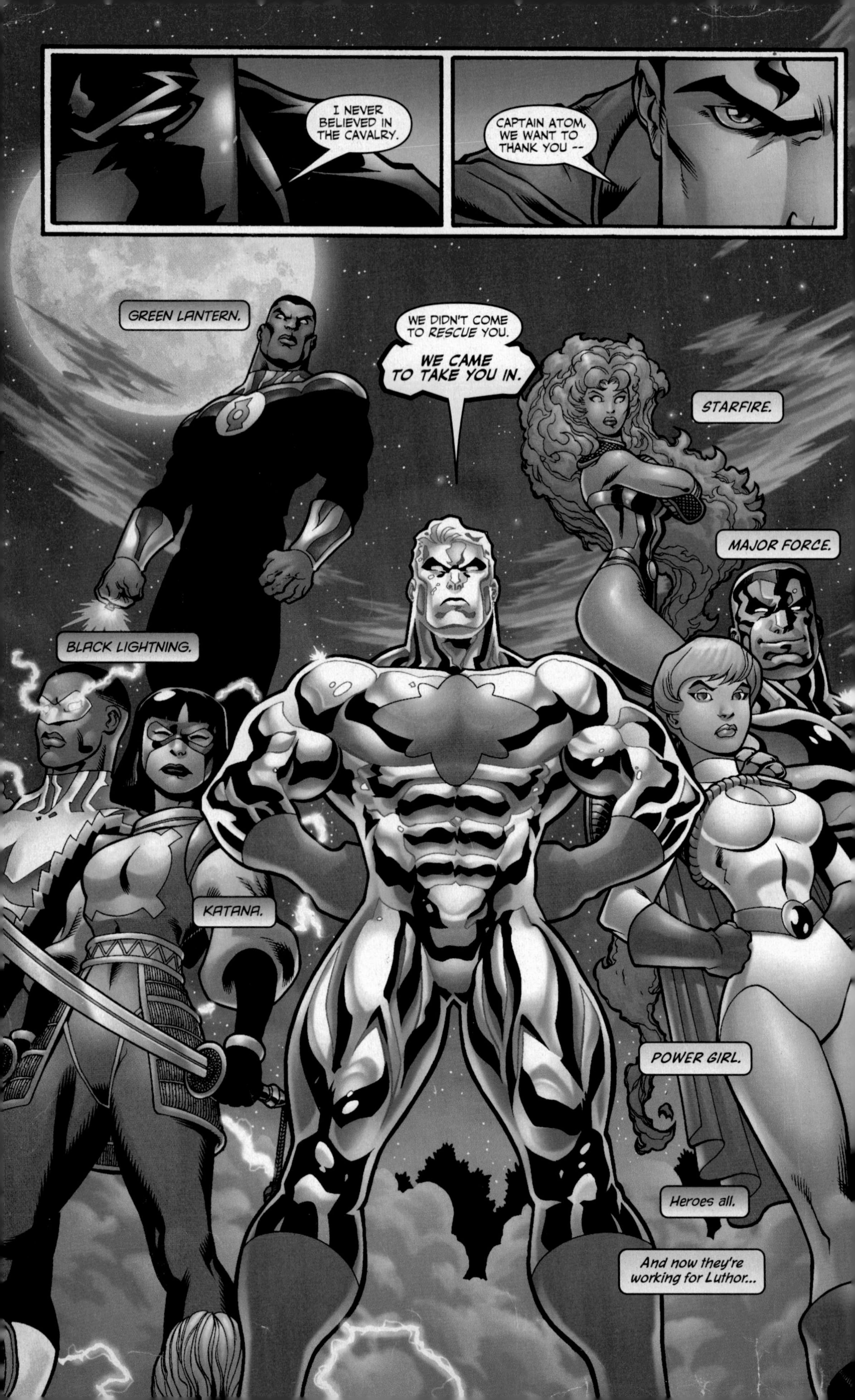
I NEVER BELIEVED IN THE CAVALRY.
CAPTAIN ATOM, WE WANT TO THANK YOU --
GREEN LANTERN.
WE DIDN'T COME TO RESCUE YOU.
WE CAME TO TAKE YOU IN.
STARFIRE.
MAJOR FORCE.
BLACK LIGHTNING.
KATANA.
POWER GIRL.
Heroes all.
And now they're working for Luthor...

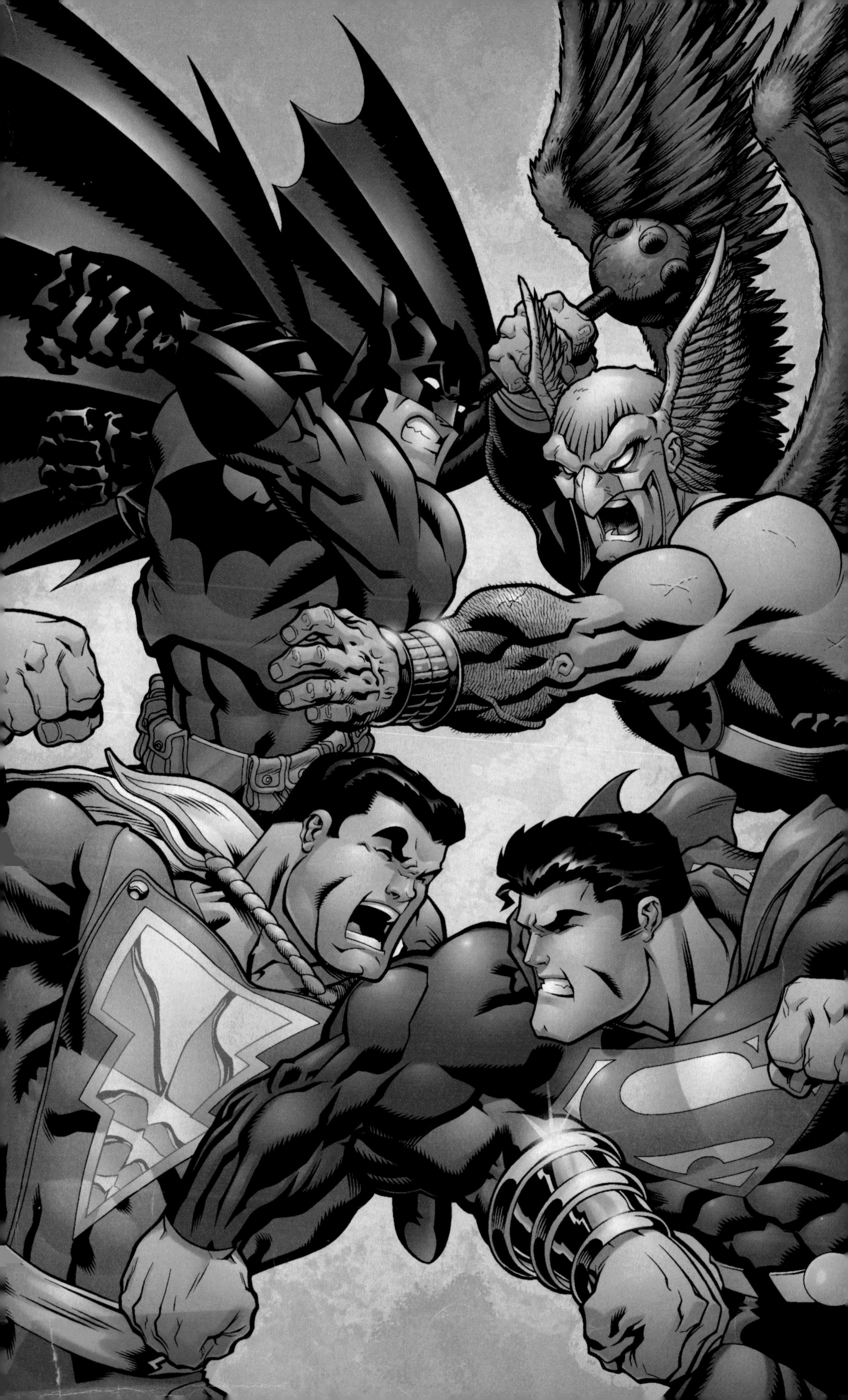

"In times of war, circumstances dictate action."

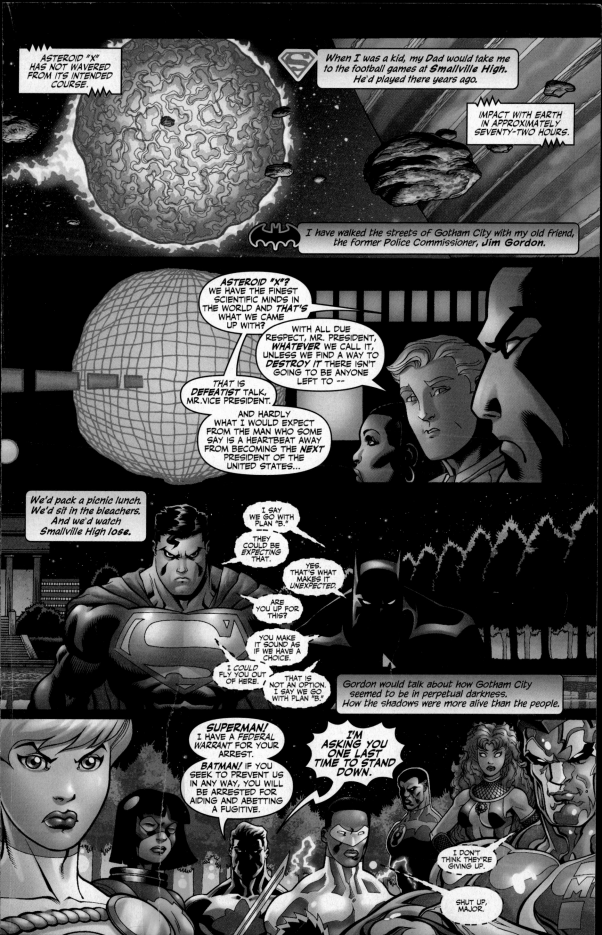

ASTEROID "X" HAS NOT WAVERED FROM ITS INTENDED COURSE.

When I was a kid, my Dad would take me to the football games at *Smallville High.* He'd played there years ago.

IMPACT WITH EARTH IN APPROXIMATELY SEVENTY-TWO HOURS.

I have walked the streets of Gotham City with my old friend, the former Police Commissioner, *Jim Gordon.*

ASTEROID "X"? WE HAVE THE FINEST SCIENTIFIC MINDS IN THE WORLD AND *THAT'S* WHAT WE CAME UP WITH?

WITH ALL DUE RESPECT, MR. PRESIDENT, *WHATEVER* WE CALL IT, UNLESS WE FIND A WAY TO *DESTROY IT* THERE ISN'T GOING TO BE ANYONE LEFT TO --

THAT IS *DEFEATIST* TALK, MR. VICE PRESIDENT.

AND HARDLY WHAT I WOULD EXPECT FROM THE MAN WHO SOME SAY IS A HEARTBEAT AWAY FROM BECOMING THE *NEXT* PRESIDENT OF THE UNITED STATES...

We'd pack a picnic lunch. We'd sit in the bleachers. And we'd watch Smallville High *lose.*

I SAY WE GO WITH PLAN "B."

THEY COULD BE EXPECTING THAT.

YES. THAT'S WHAT MAKES IT *UNEXPECTED.*

ARE YOU UP FOR THIS?

YOU MAKE IT SOUND AS IF WE HAVE A CHOICE.

I COULD FLY YOU OUT OF HERE.

THAT IS NOT AN OPTION. I SAY WE GO WITH PLAN "B."

Gordon would talk about how Gotham City seemed to be in perpetual darkness. How the shadows were more alive than the people.

SUPERMAN! I HAVE A *FEDERAL* WARRANT FOR YOUR ARREST.

BATMAN! IF YOU SEEK TO PREVENT US IN ANY WAY, YOU WILL BE ARRESTED FOR AIDING AND ABETTING A FUGITIVE.

I'M ASKING YOU ONE LAST TIME TO STAND DOWN.

I DON'T THINK THEY'RE GIVING UP.

SHUT UP, MAJOR.

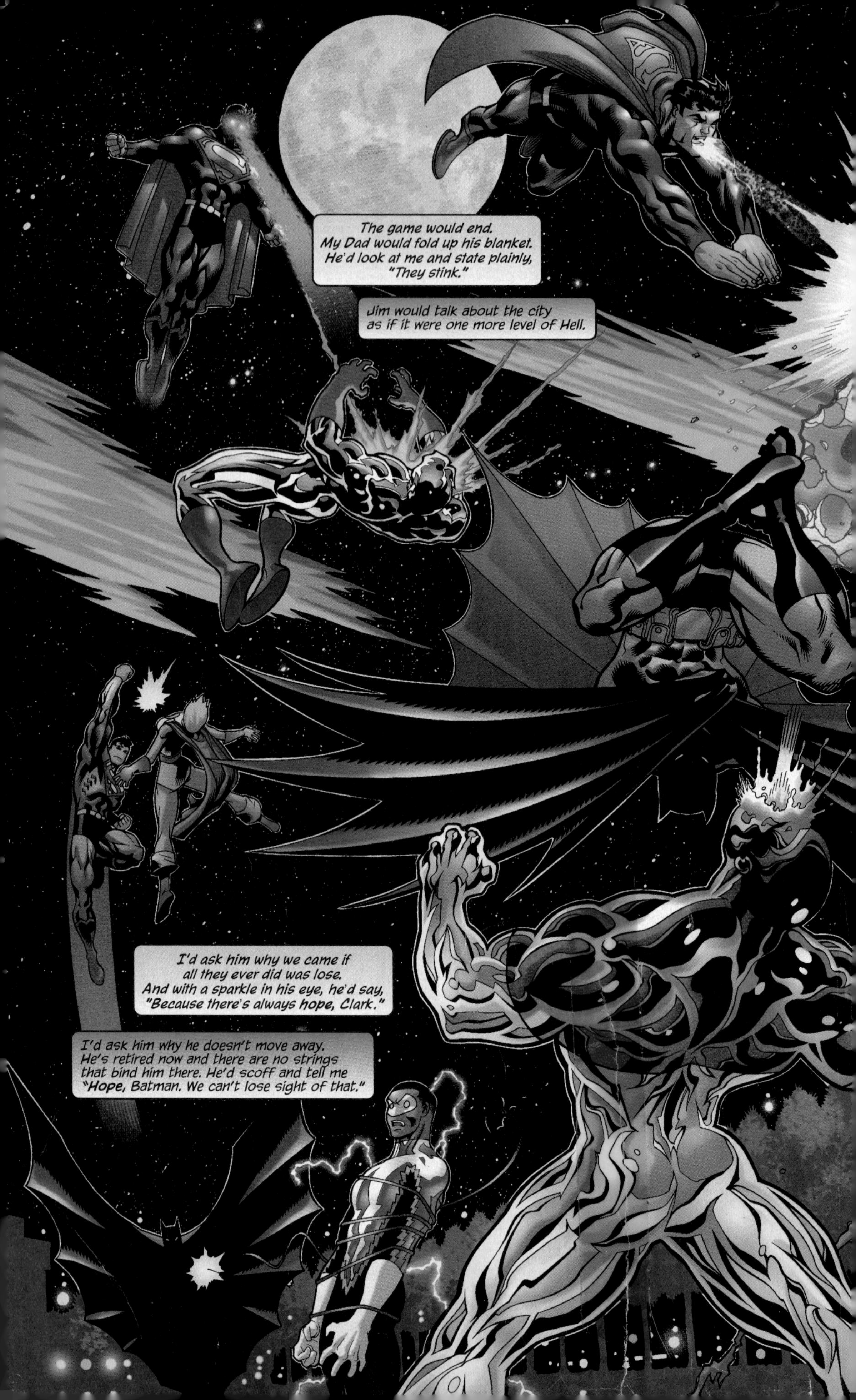
The game would end. My Dad would fold up his blanket. He'd look at me and state plainly, "They stink."
Jim would talk about the city as if it were one more level of Hell.
I'd ask him why we came if all they ever did was lose. And with a sparkle in his eye, he'd say, "Because there's always **hope**, Clark."
I'd ask him why he doesn't move away. He's retired now and there are no strings that bind him there. He'd scoff and tell me "**Hope**, Batman. We can't lose sight of that."

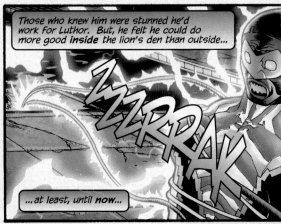

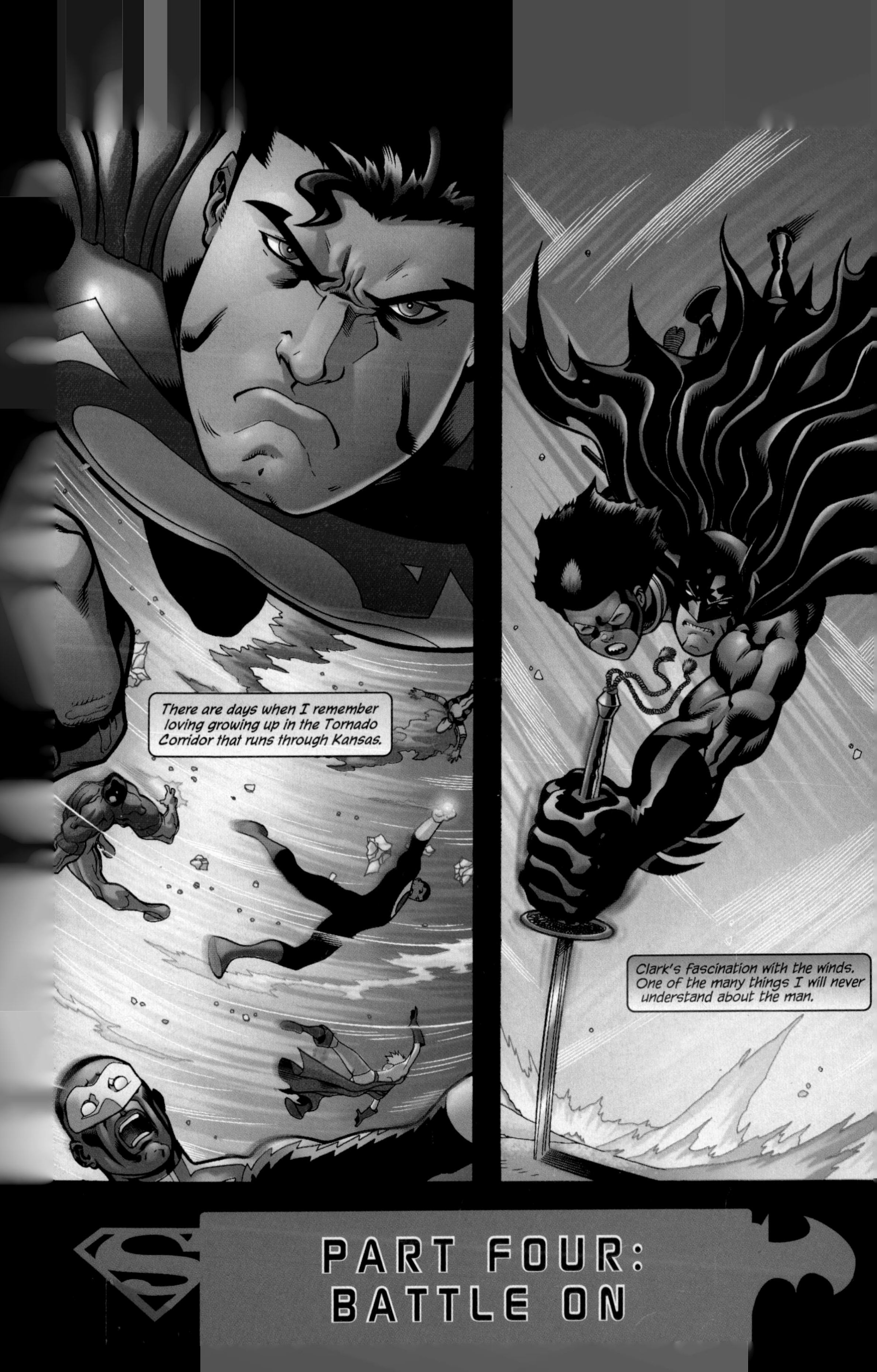
There are days when I remember loving growing up in the Tornado Corridor that runs through Kansas.
Clark's fascination with the winds. One of the many things I will never understand about the man.
PART FOUR: BATTLE ON

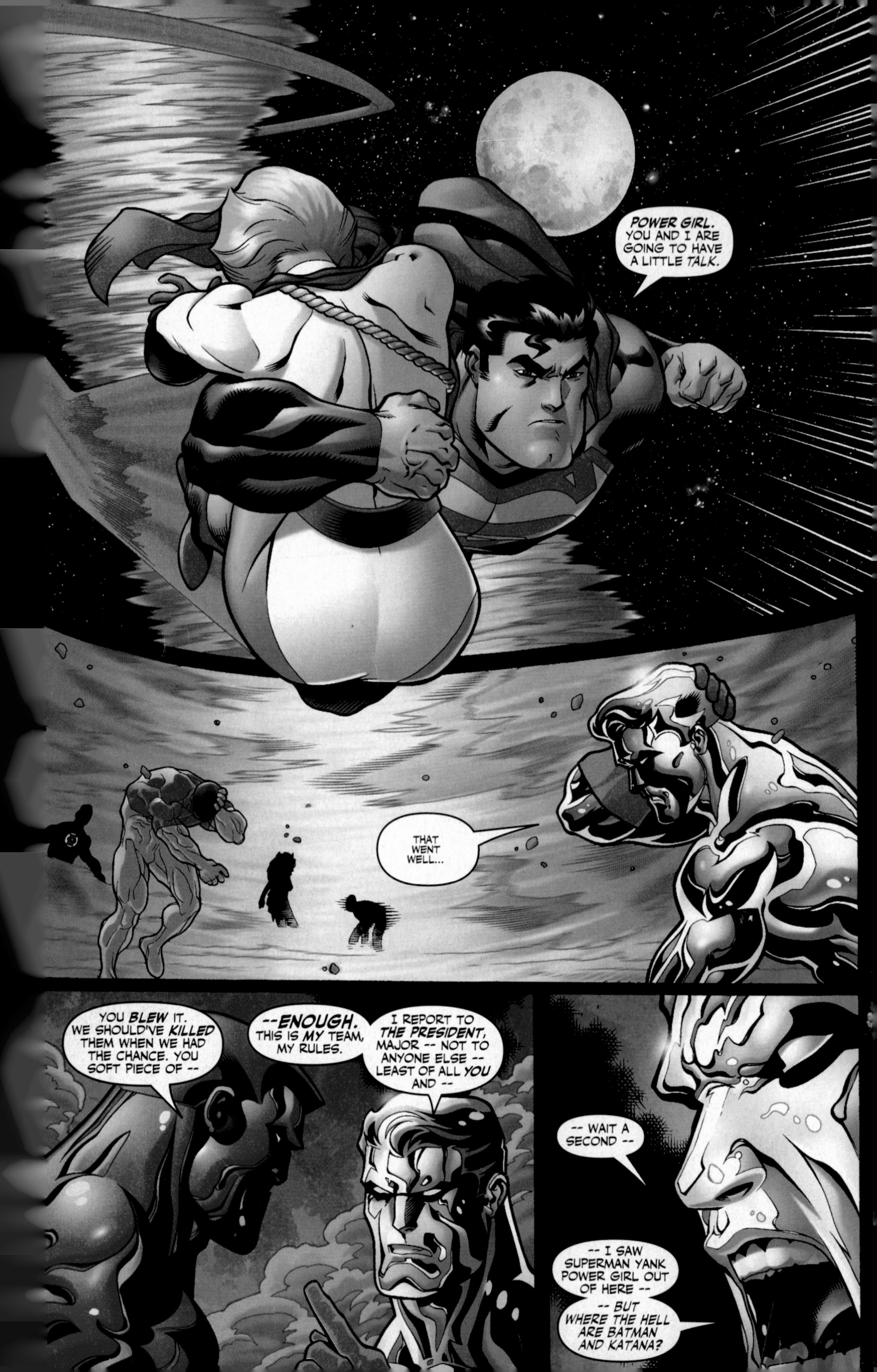
POWER GIRL. YOU AND I ARE GOING TO HAVE A LITTLE TALK.
THAT WENT WELL...
YOU BLEW IT. WE SHOULD'VE KILLED THEM WHEN WE HAD THE CHANCE. YOU SOFT PIECE OF --
--ENOUGH. THIS IS MY TEAM, MY RULES.
I REPORT TO THE PRESIDENT, MAJOR -- NOT TO ANYONE ELSE -- LEAST OF ALL YOU AND --
-- WAIT A SECOND --
-- I SAW SUPERMAN YANK POWER GIRL OUT OF HERE --
-- BUT WHERE THE HELL ARE BATMAN AND KATANA?

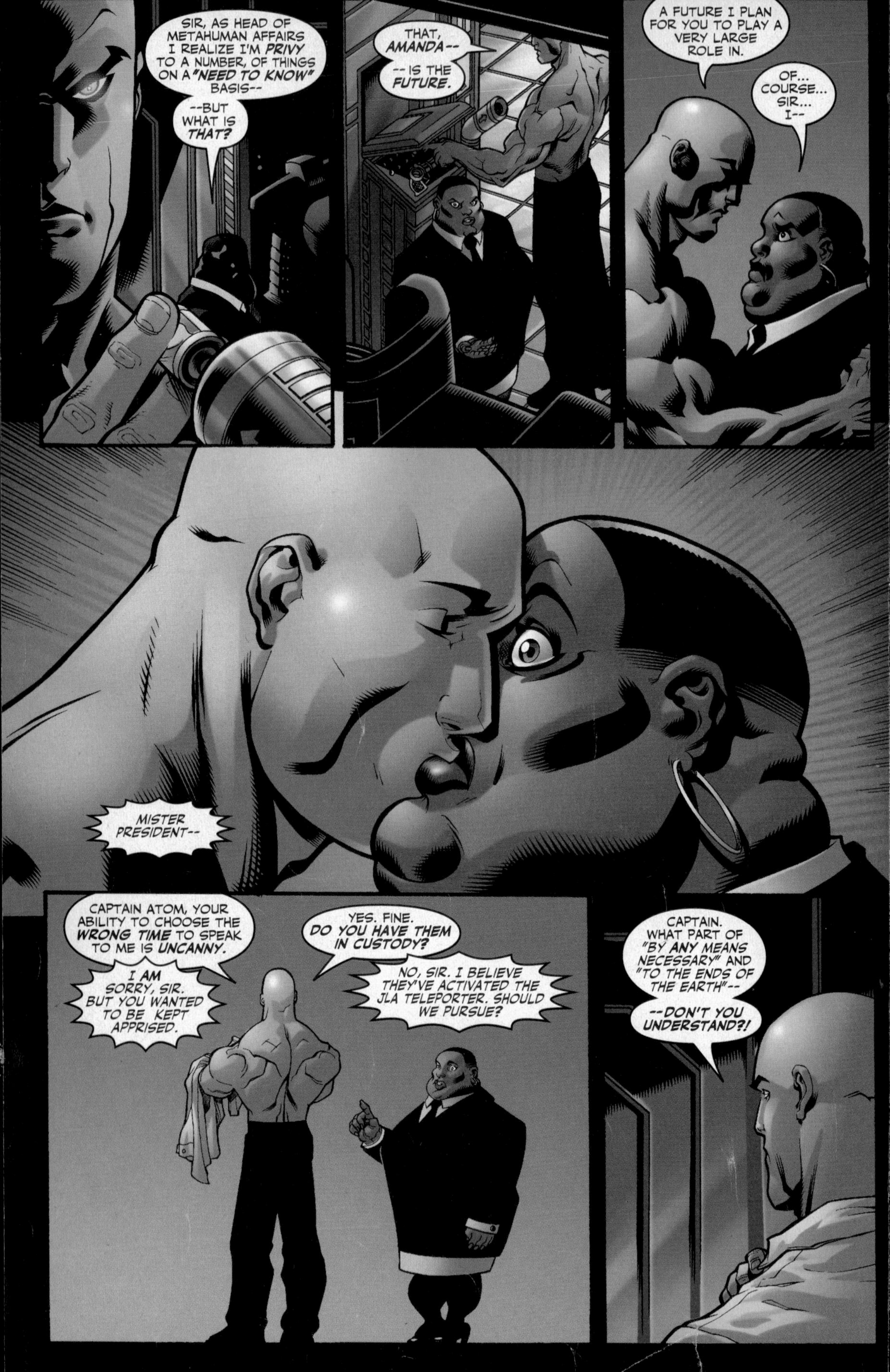
SIR, AS HEAD OF METAHUMAN AFFAIRS I REALIZE I'M PRIVY TO A NUMBER, OF THINGS ON A "NEED TO KNOW" BASIS--
--BUT WHAT IS THAT?
THAT, AMANDA--
--IS THE FUTURE.
A FUTURE I PLAN FOR YOU TO PLAY A VERY LARGE ROLE IN.
OF... COURSE... SIR... I--
MISTER PRESIDENT--
CAPTAIN ATOM, YOUR ABILITY TO CHOOSE THE WRONG TIME TO SPEAK TO ME IS UNCANNY.
I AM SORRY, SIR. BUT YOU WANTED TO BE KEPT APPRISED.
YES. FINE. DO YOU HAVE THEM IN CUSTODY?
NO, SIR. I BELIEVE THEY'VE ACTIVATED THE JLA TELEPORTER. SHOULD WE PURSUE?
CAPTAIN. WHAT PART OF "BY ANY MEANS NECESSARY" AND "TO THE ENDS OF THE EARTH"--
--DON'T YOU UNDERSTAND?!

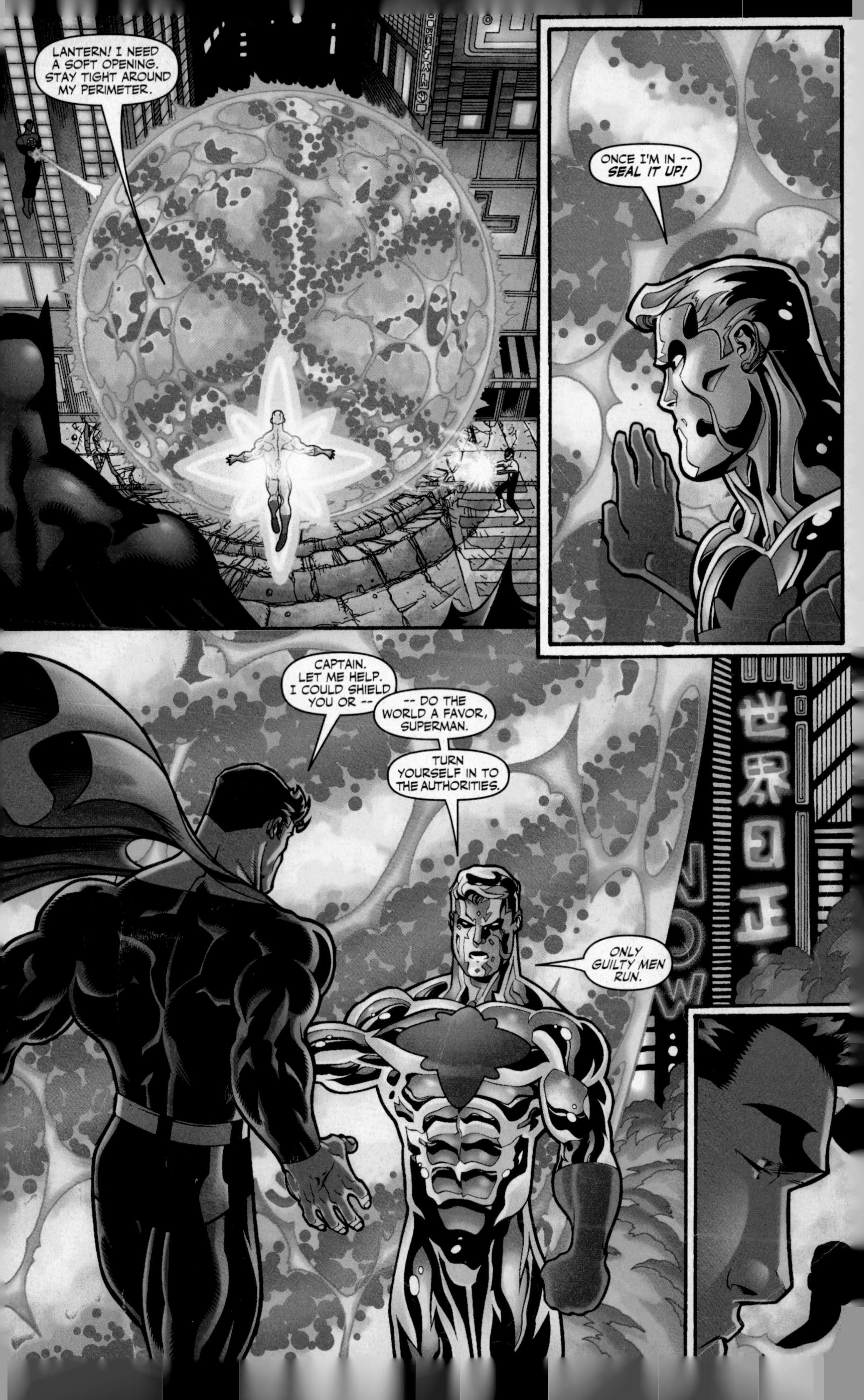
LANTERN! I NEED A SOFT OPENING. STAY TIGHT AROUND MY PERIMETER.
ONCE I'M IN -- SEAL IT UP!
CAPTAIN. LET ME HELP. I COULD SHIELD YOU OR --
-- DO THE WORLD A FAVOR, SUPERMAN.
TURN YOURSELF IN TO THE AUTHORITIES.
ONLY GUILTY MEN RUN.
世界日正
NOW

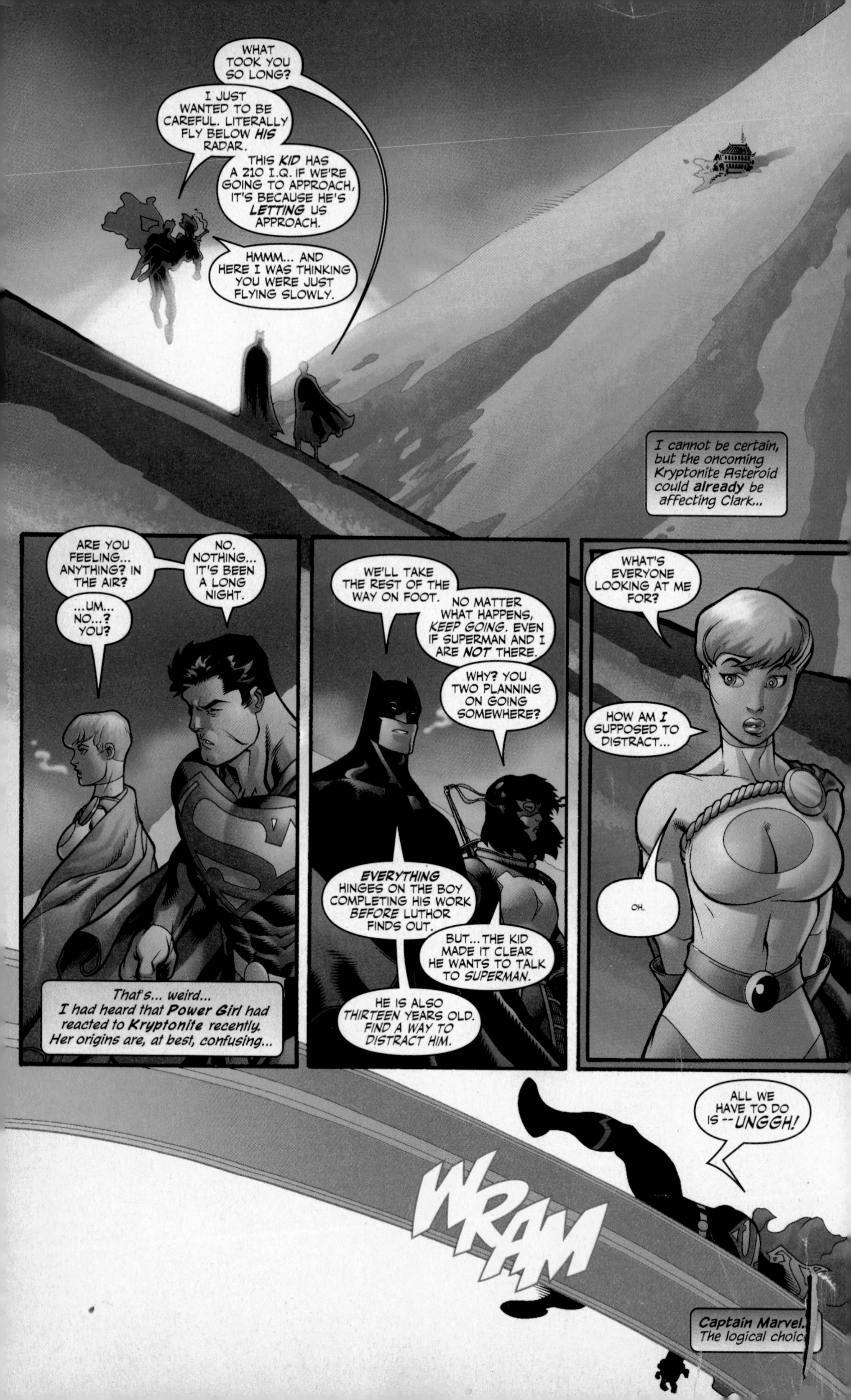
WHAT TOOK YOU SO LONG?
I JUST WANTED TO BE CAREFUL. LITERALLY FLY BELOW *HIS* RADAR.
THIS *KID* HAS A 210 I.Q. IF WE'RE GOING TO APPROACH, IT'S BECAUSE HE'S *LETTING* US APPROACH.
HMMM... AND HERE I WAS THINKING YOU WERE JUST FLYING SLOWLY.
I cannot be certain, but the oncoming Kryptonite Asteroid could **already** be affecting Clark...
ARE YOU FEELING... ANYTHING? IN THE AIR?
NO. NOTHING... IT'S BEEN A LONG NIGHT.
...UM... NO...? YOU?
That's... weird... I had heard that **Power Girl** had reacted to **Kryptonite** recently. Her origins are, at best, confusing...
WE'LL TAKE THE REST OF THE WAY ON FOOT.
NO MATTER WHAT HAPPENS, *KEEP GOING*. EVEN IF SUPERMAN AND I ARE *NOT* THERE.
WHY? YOU TWO PLANNING ON GOING SOMEWHERE?
EVERYTHING HINGES ON THE BOY COMPLETING HIS WORK *BEFORE* LUTHOR FINDS OUT.
BUT... THE KID MADE IT CLEAR HE WANTS TO TALK TO *SUPERMAN*.
HE IS ALSO *THIRTEEN YEARS OLD. FIND A WAY TO DISTRACT HIM.*
WHAT'S EVERYONE LOOKING AT ME FOR?
HOW AM *I* SUPPOSED TO DISTRACT...
OH.
ALL WE HAVE TO DO IS -- *UNGGH!*
WRAM
Captain Marvel. The logical choic

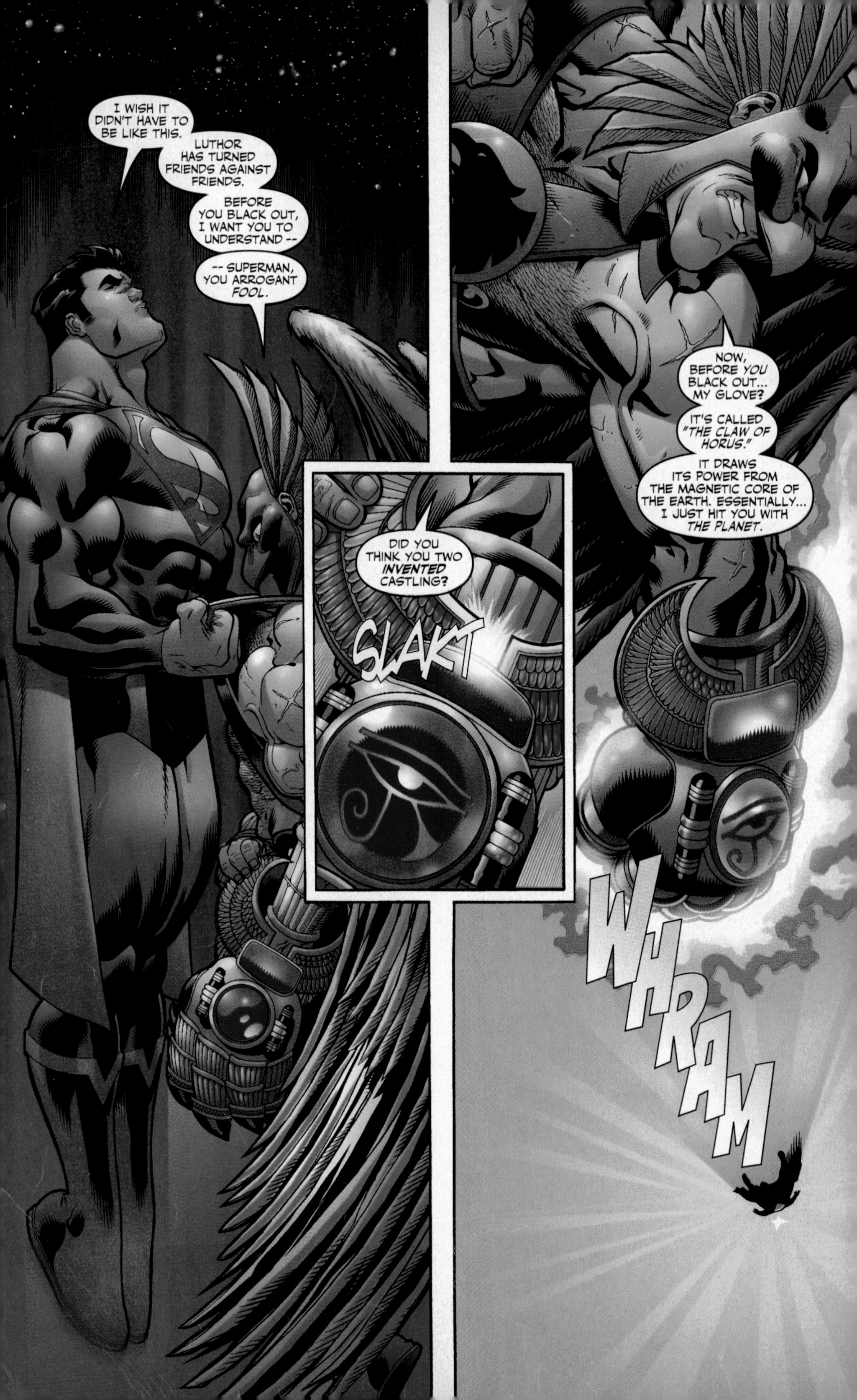
I WISH IT DIDN'T HAVE TO BE LIKE THIS.
LUTHOR HAS TURNED FRIENDS AGAINST FRIENDS.
BEFORE YOU BLACK OUT, I WANT YOU TO UNDERSTAND --
-- SUPERMAN, YOU ARROGANT *FOOL*.
DID YOU THINK YOU TWO *INVENTED* CASTLING?
SLAKT
NOW, BEFORE *YOU* BLACK OUT... MY GLOVE?
IT'S CALLED *"THE CLAW OF HORUS."*
IT DRAWS ITS POWER FROM THE MAGNETIC CORE OF THE EARTH. ESSENTIALLY... I JUST HIT YOU WITH *THE PLANET*.
WHRAM

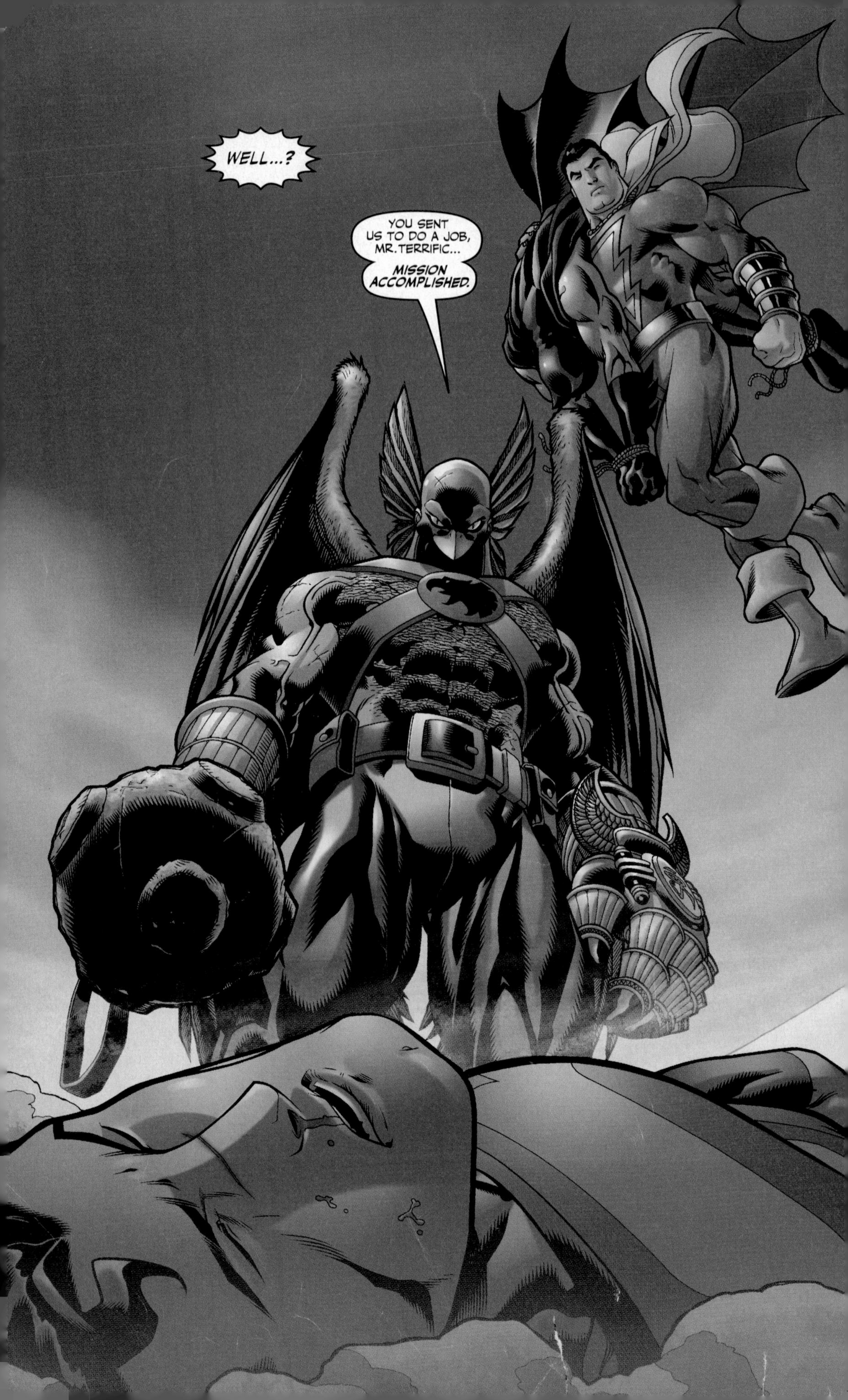
WELL...?
YOU SENT US TO DO A JOB, MR.TERRIFIC... MISSION ACCOMPLISHED.

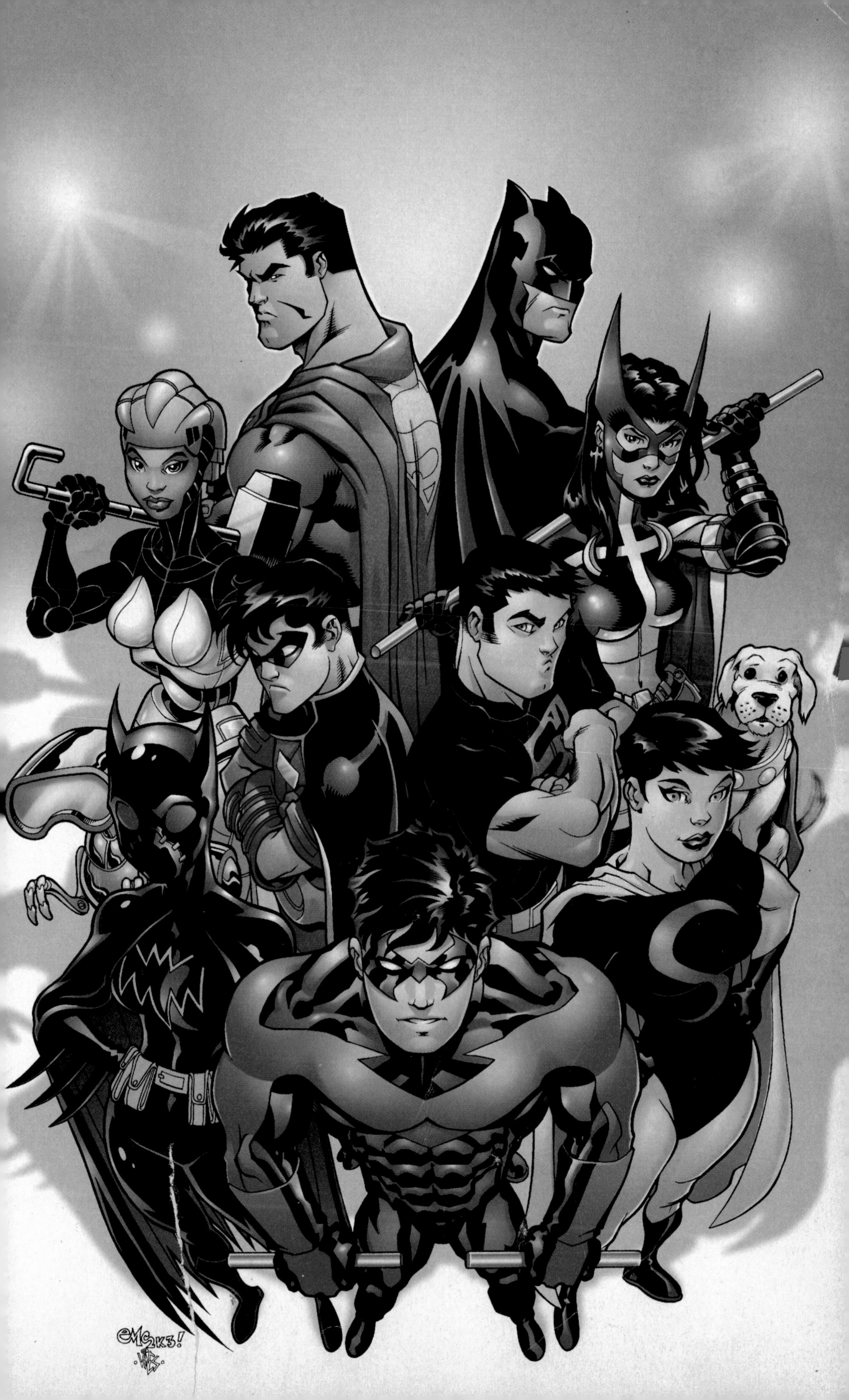

"Give me what I've always wanted — the end of you."

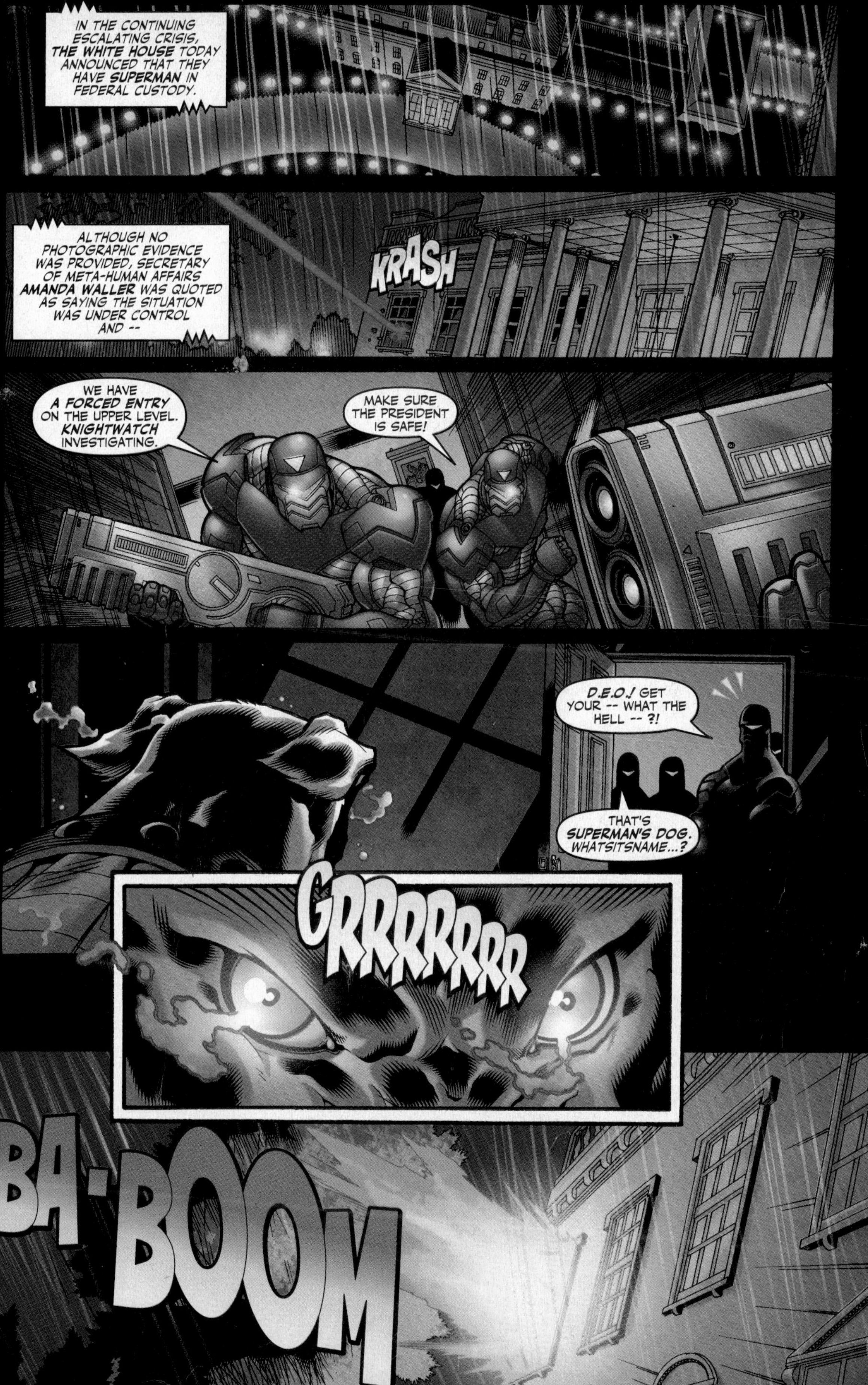
IN THE CONTINUING ESCALATING CRISIS, THE WHITE HOUSE TODAY ANNOUNCED THAT THEY HAVE SUPERMAN IN FEDERAL CUSTODY.
ALTHOUGH NO PHOTOGRAPHIC EVIDENCE WAS PROVIDED, SECRETARY OF META-HUMAN AFFAIRS AMANDA WALLER WAS QUOTED AS SAYING THE SITUATION WAS UNDER CONTROL AND --
KRASH
WE HAVE A FORCED ENTRY ON THE UPPER LEVEL. KNIGHTWATCH INVESTIGATING.
MAKE SURE THE PRESIDENT IS SAFE!
D.E.O.! GET YOUR -- WHAT THE HELL -- ?!
THAT'S SUPERMAN'S DOG. WHATSITSNAME...?
GRRRRRRR
BA-BOOM

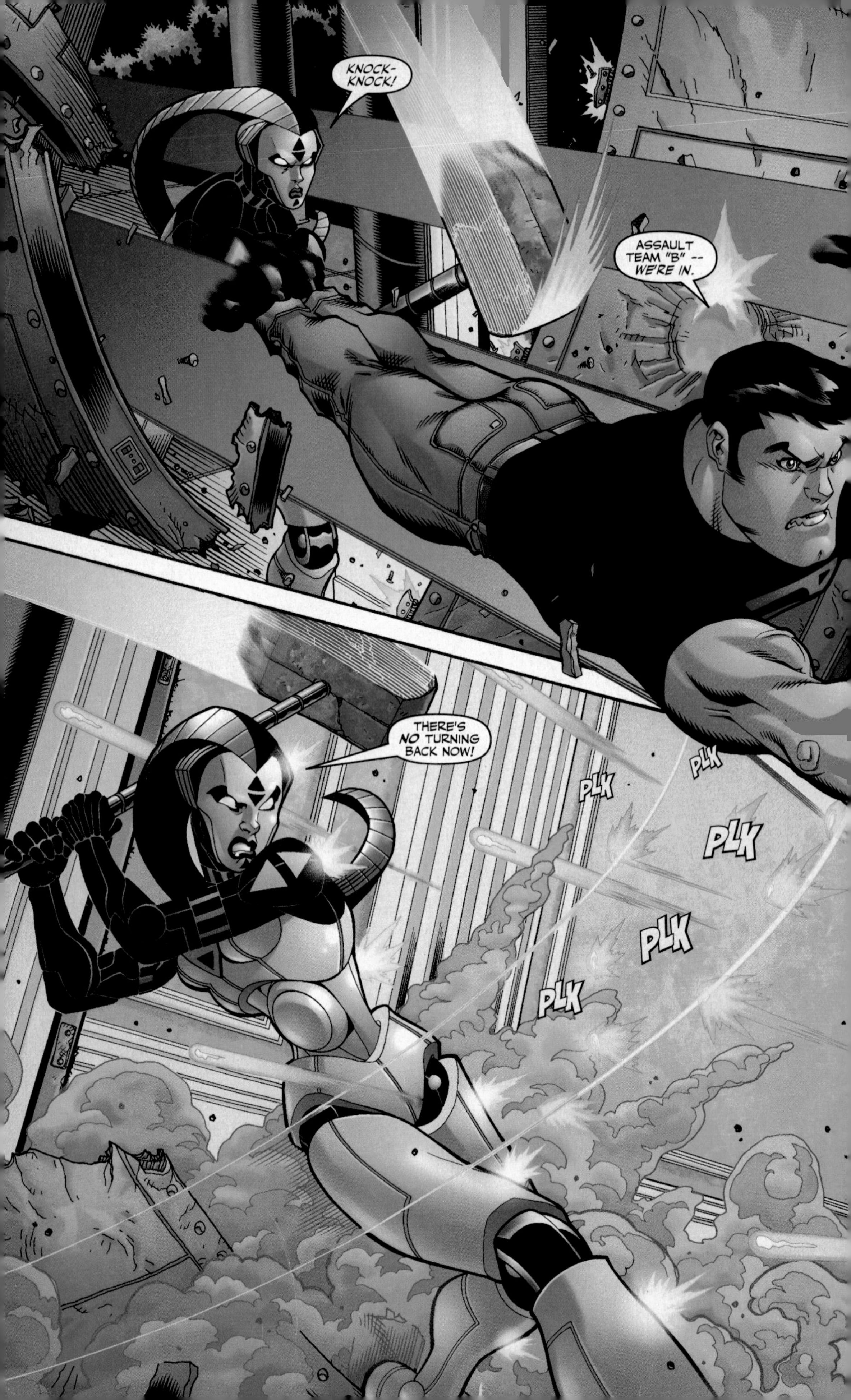
KNOCK-KNOCK!
ASSAULT TEAM "B" -- WE'RE IN.
THERE'S NO TURNING BACK NOW!
PLK
PLK
PLK
PLK
PLK

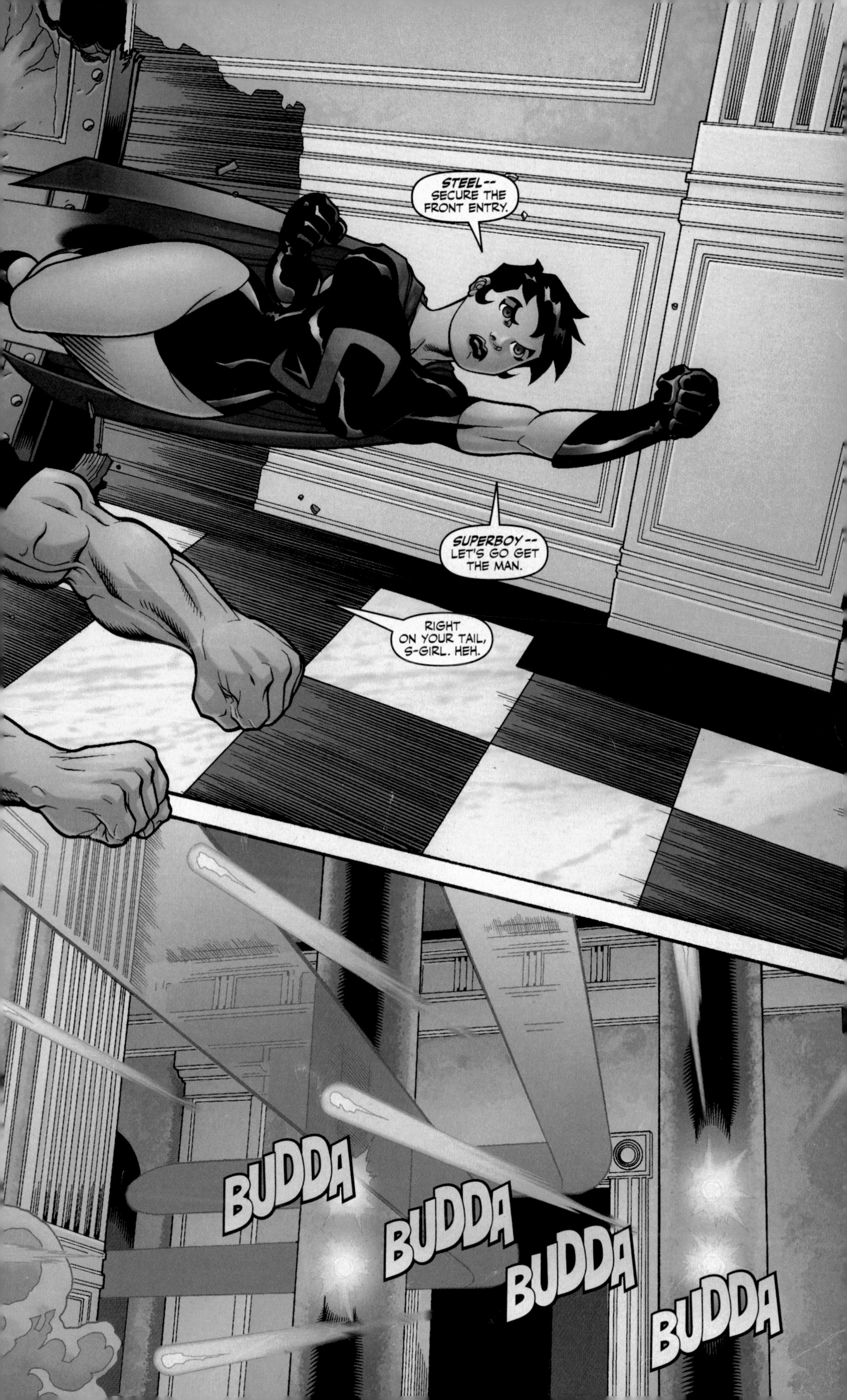
STEEL-- SECURE THE FRONT ENTRY.
SUPERBOY-- LET'S GO GET THE MAN.
RIGHT ON YOUR TAIL, S-GIRL. HEH.
BUDDA
BUDDA
BUDDA
BUDDA

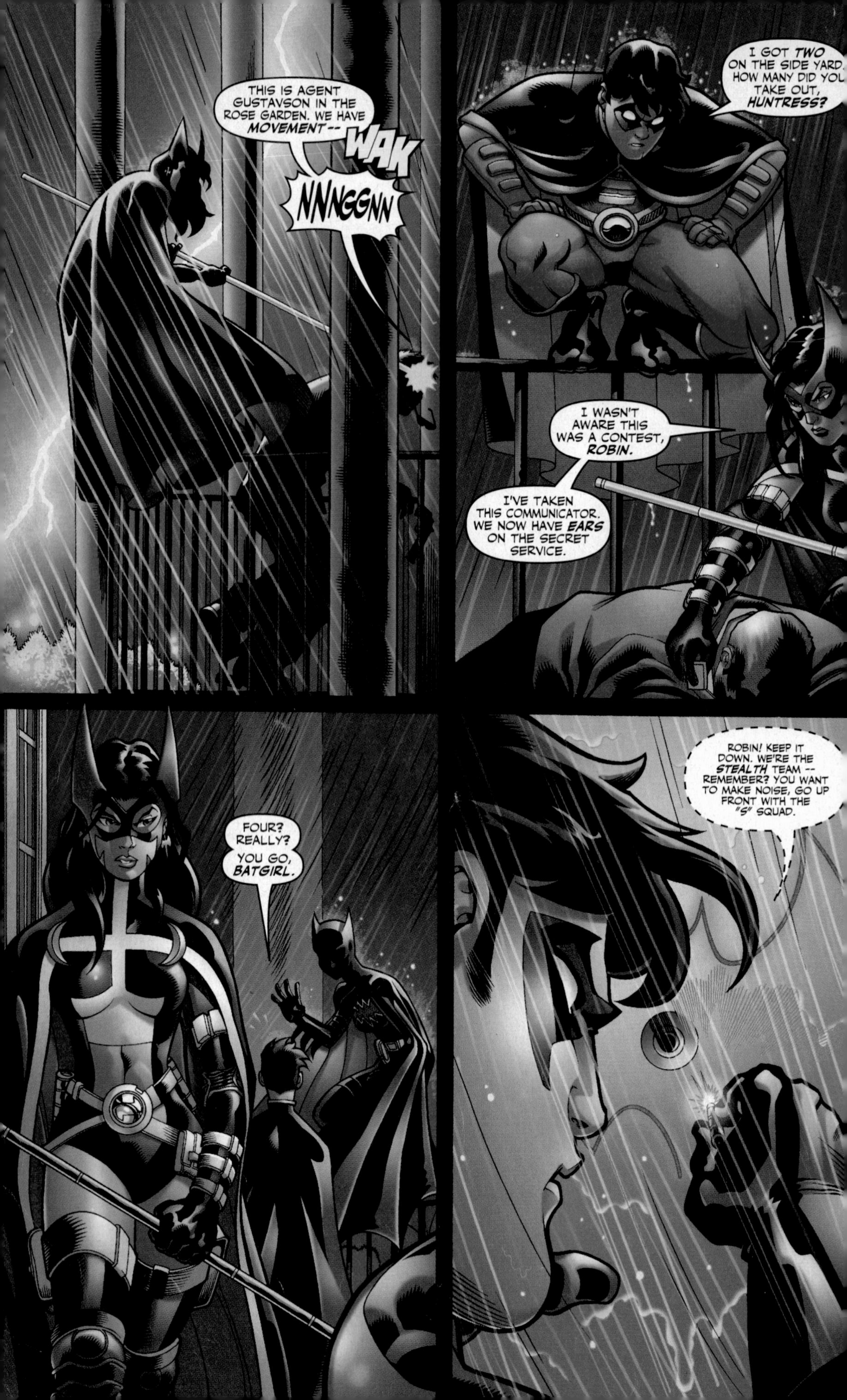
THIS IS AGENT GUSTAVSON IN THE ROSE GARDEN. WE HAVE MOVEMENT--
WAK
NNNGGNN
I GOT TWO ON THE SIDE YARD. HOW MANY DID YOU TAKE OUT, HUNTRESS?
I WASN'T AWARE THIS WAS A CONTEST, ROBIN.
I'VE TAKEN THIS COMMUNICATOR. WE NOW HAVE EARS ON THE SECRET SERVICE.
FOUR? REALLY? YOU GO, BATGIRL.
ROBIN! KEEP IT DOWN. WE'RE THE STEALTH TEAM -- REMEMBER? YOU WANT TO MAKE NOISE, GO UP FRONT WITH THE "S" SQUAD.

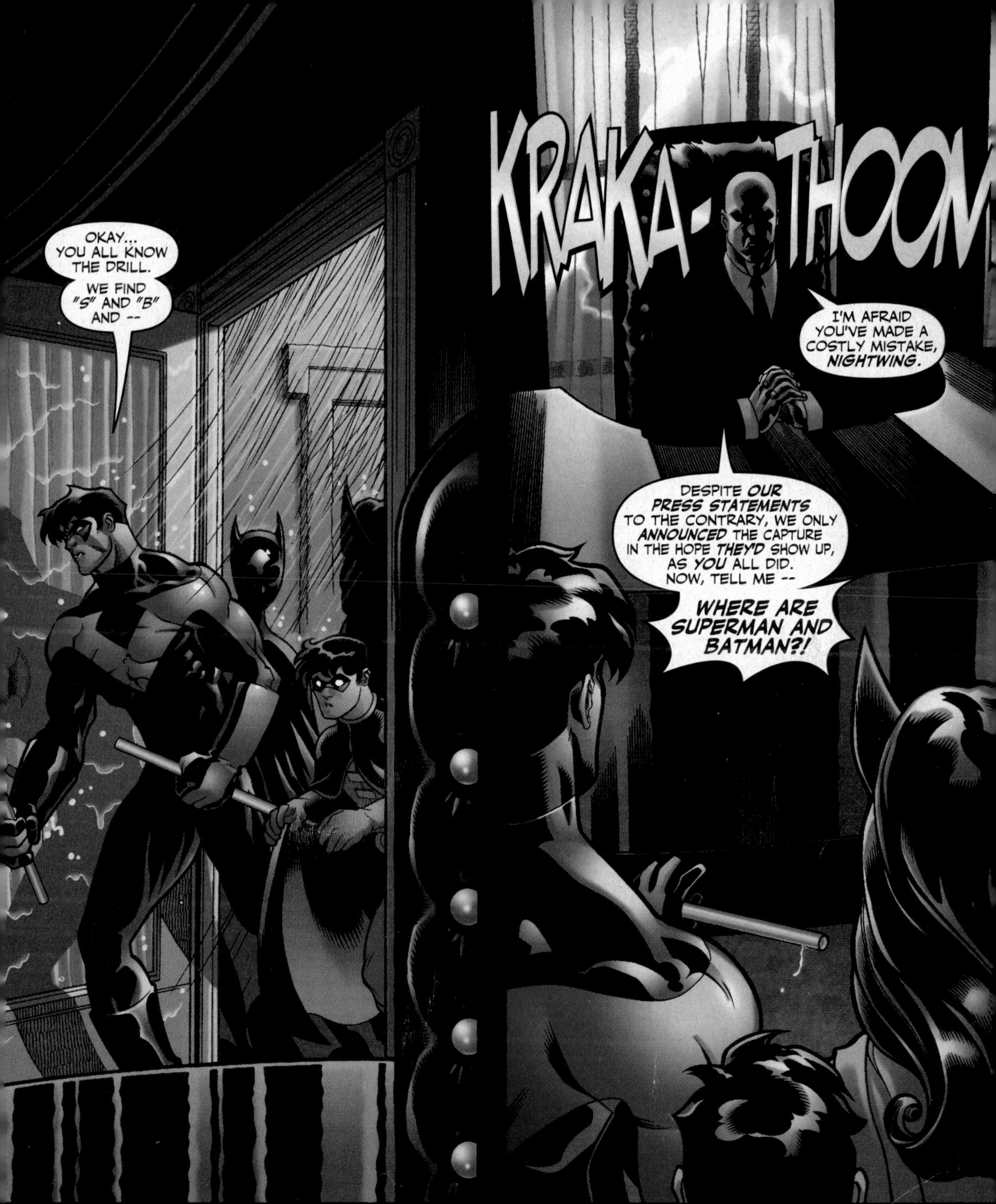
KRAKA-THOOM
OKAY... YOU ALL KNOW THE DRILL.
WE FIND "S" AND "B" AND --
I'M AFRAID YOU'VE MADE A COSTLY MISTAKE, NIGHTWING.
DESPITE OUR PRESS STATEMENTS TO THE CONTRARY, WE ONLY ANNOUNCED THE CAPTURE IN THE HOPE THEY'D SHOW UP, AS YOU ALL DID. NOW, TELL ME --
WHERE ARE SUPERMAN AND BATMAN?!

PART FIVE: STATE OF SIEGE

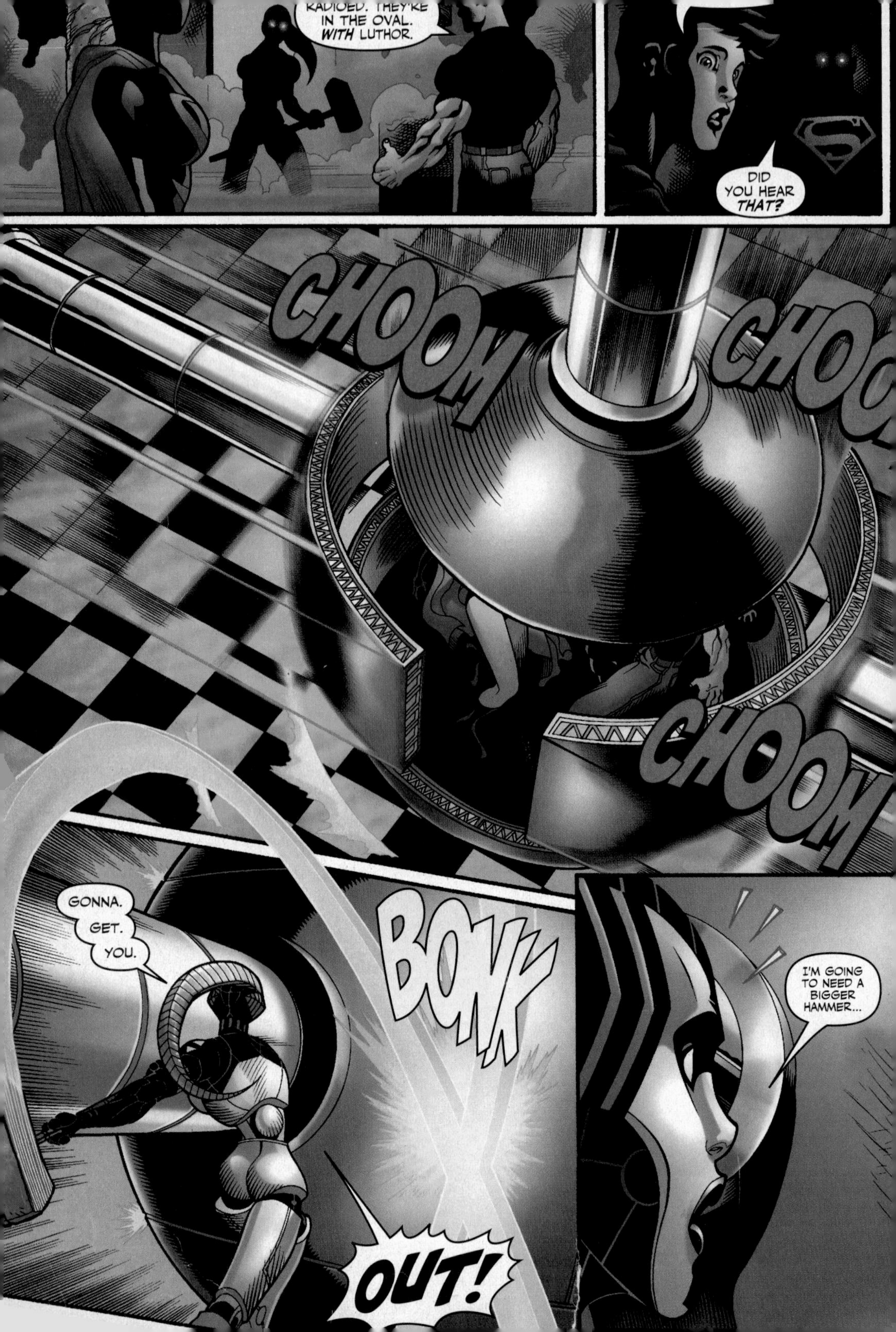
RADIOED. THEY'RE IN THE OVAL. *WITH* LUTHOR.
DID YOU HEAR *THAT?*
CHOOM
CHOO
CHOOM
GONNA. GET. YOU.
BONK
OUT!
I'M GOING TO NEED A BIGGER HAMMER...

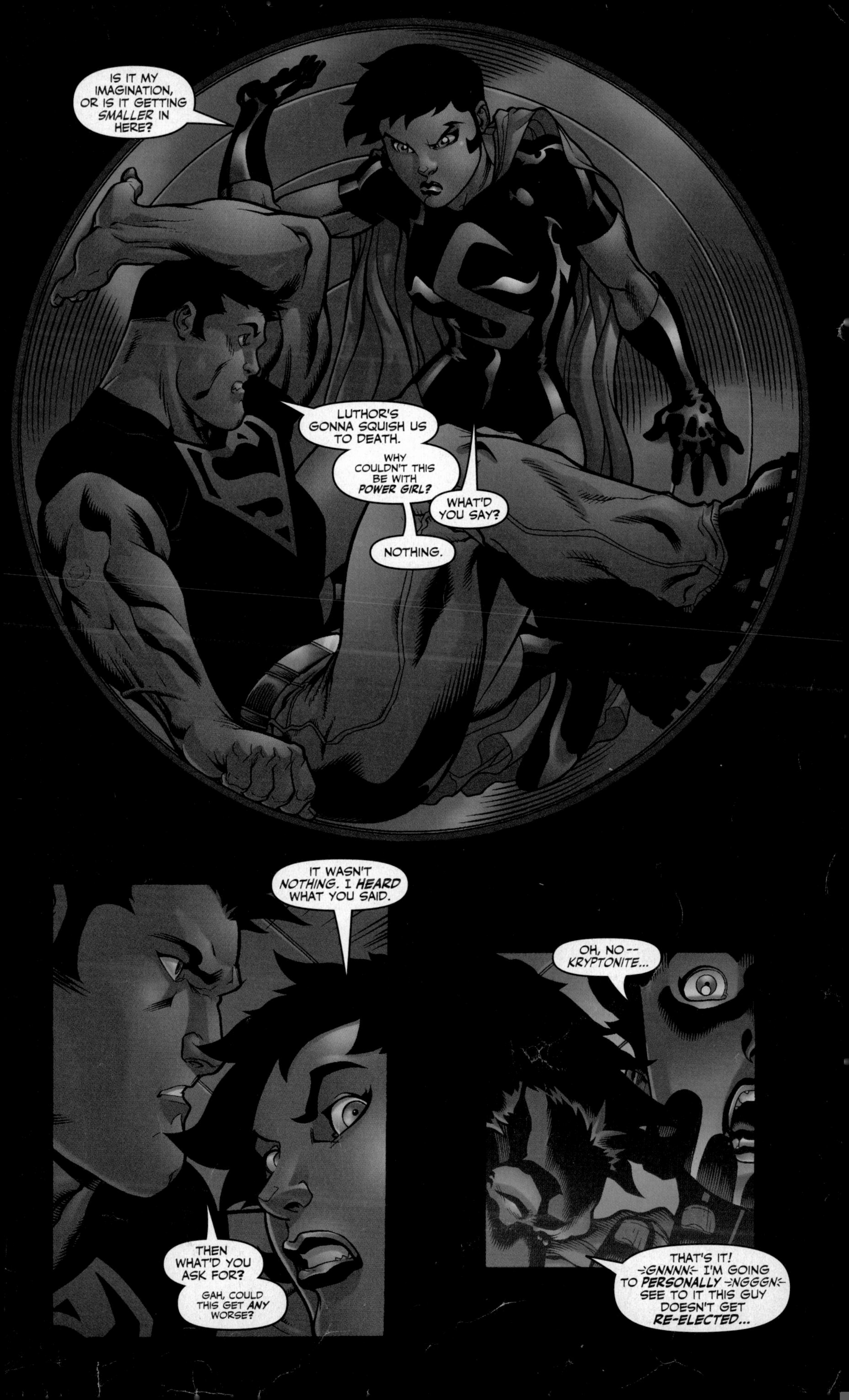

IS IT MY IMAGINATION, OR IS IT GETTING SMALLER IN HERE?
LUTHOR'S GONNA SQUISH US TO DEATH.
WHY COULDN'T THIS BE WITH POWER GIRL?
WHAT'D YOU SAY?
NOTHING.
IT WASN'T NOTHING. I HEARD WHAT YOU SAID.
THEN WHAT'D YOU ASK FOR?
GAH, COULD THIS GET ANY WORSE?
OH, NO-- KRYPTONITE...
THAT'S IT! =GNNNN= I'M GOING TO PERSONALLY =NGGGN= SEE TO IT THIS GUY DOESN'T GET RE-ELECTED...

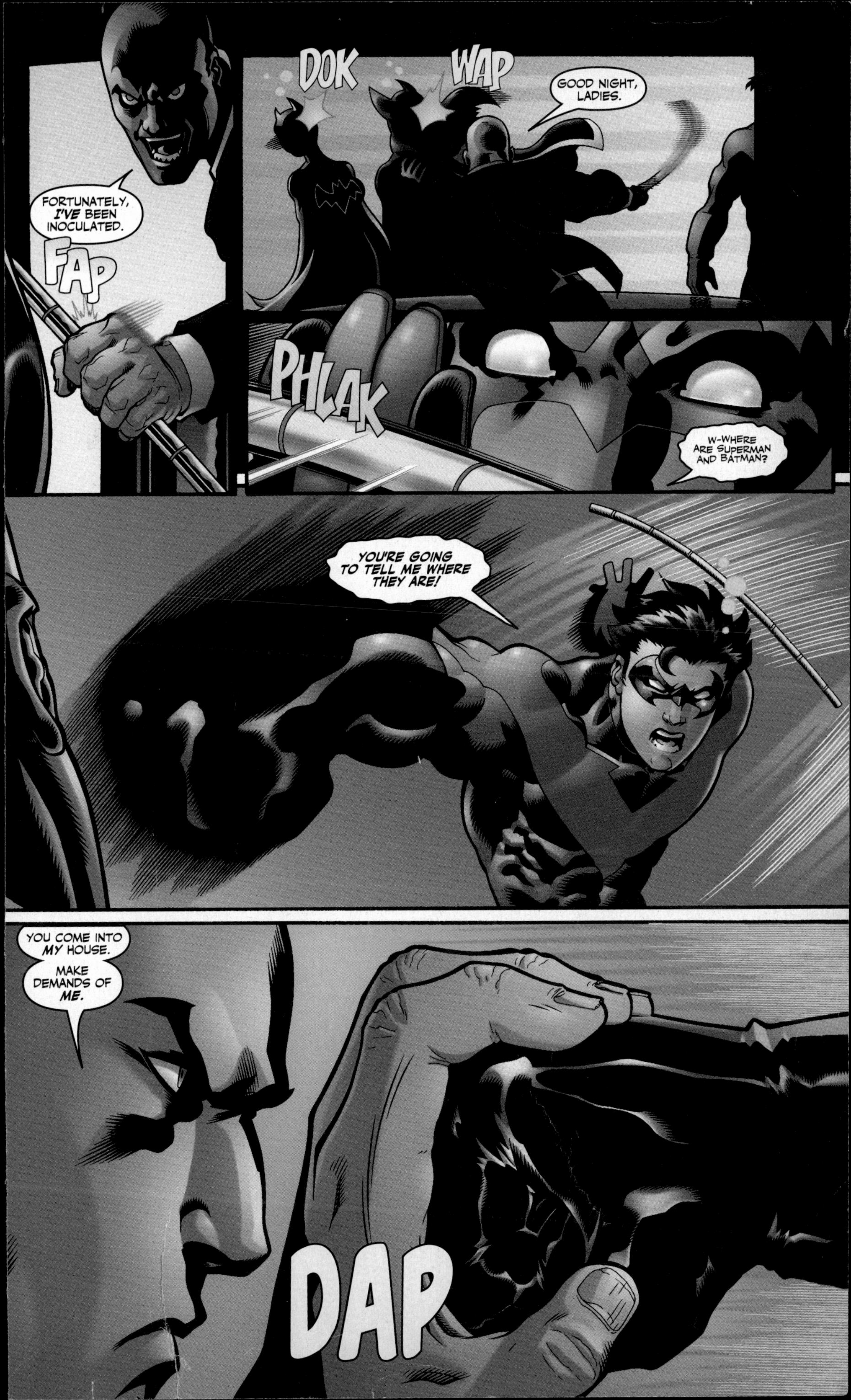
FORTUNATELY, *I'VE* BEEN INOCULATED.
FAP
DOK
WAP
GOOD NIGHT, LADIES.
PHLAK
W-WHERE ARE SUPERMAN AND BATMAN?
YOU'RE GOING TO TELL ME WHERE THEY ARE!
YOU COME INTO *MY* HOUSE.
MAKE DEMANDS OF *ME*.
DAP

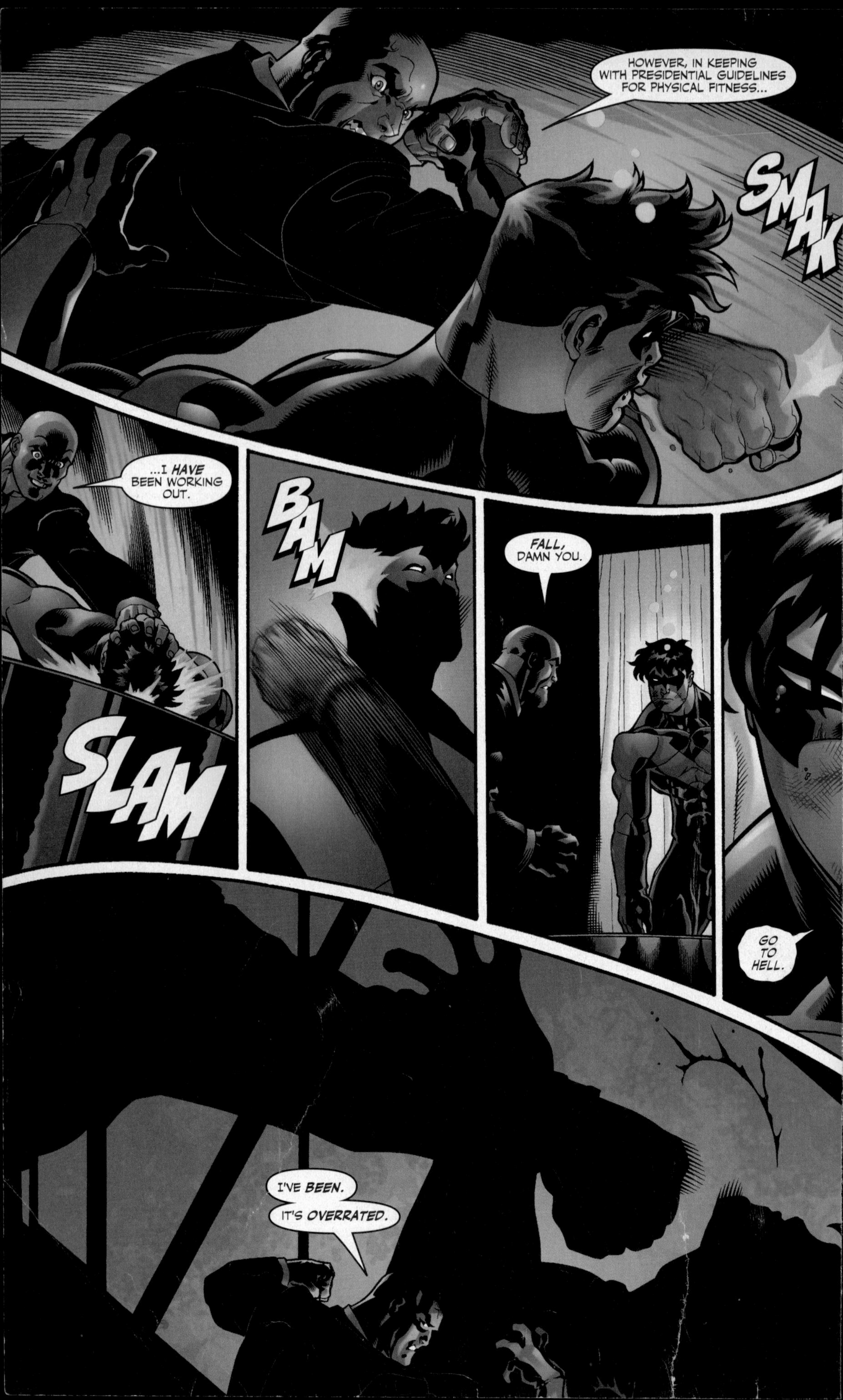
HOWEVER, IN KEEPING WITH PRESIDENTIAL GUIDELINES FOR PHYSICAL FITNESS...
SMAK
...I HAVE BEEN WORKING OUT.
SLAM
BAM
FALL, DAMN YOU.
GO TO HELL.
I'VE BEEN.
IT'S OVERRATED.

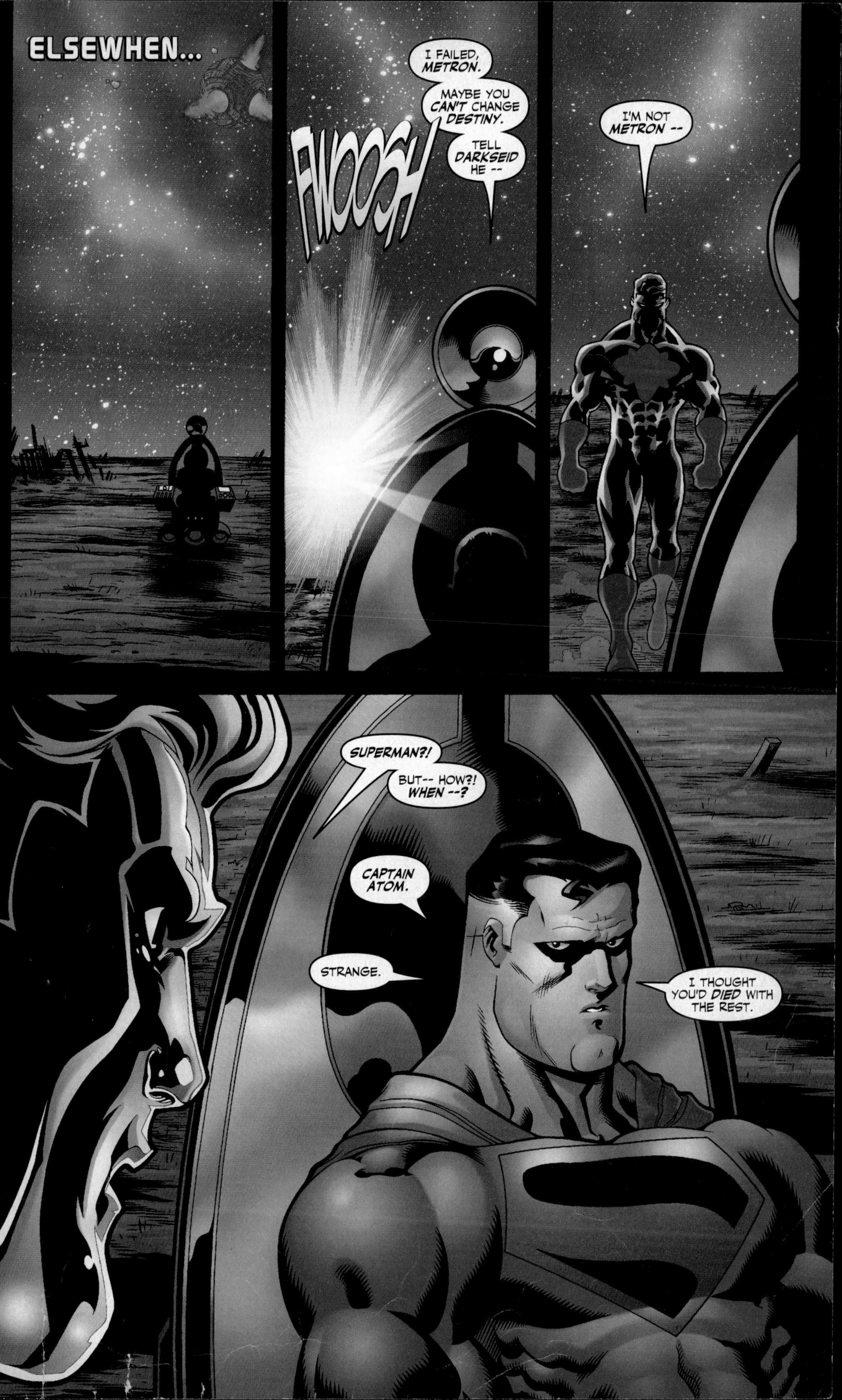

ELSEWHEN...
I FAILED, METRON.
MAYBE YOU CAN'T CHANGE DESTINY.
TELL DARKSEID HE --
FWOOSH
I'M NOT METRON --
SUPERMAN?!
BUT-- HOW?! WHEN --?
CAPTAIN ATOM.
STRANGE.
I THOUGHT YOU'D DIED WITH THE REST.

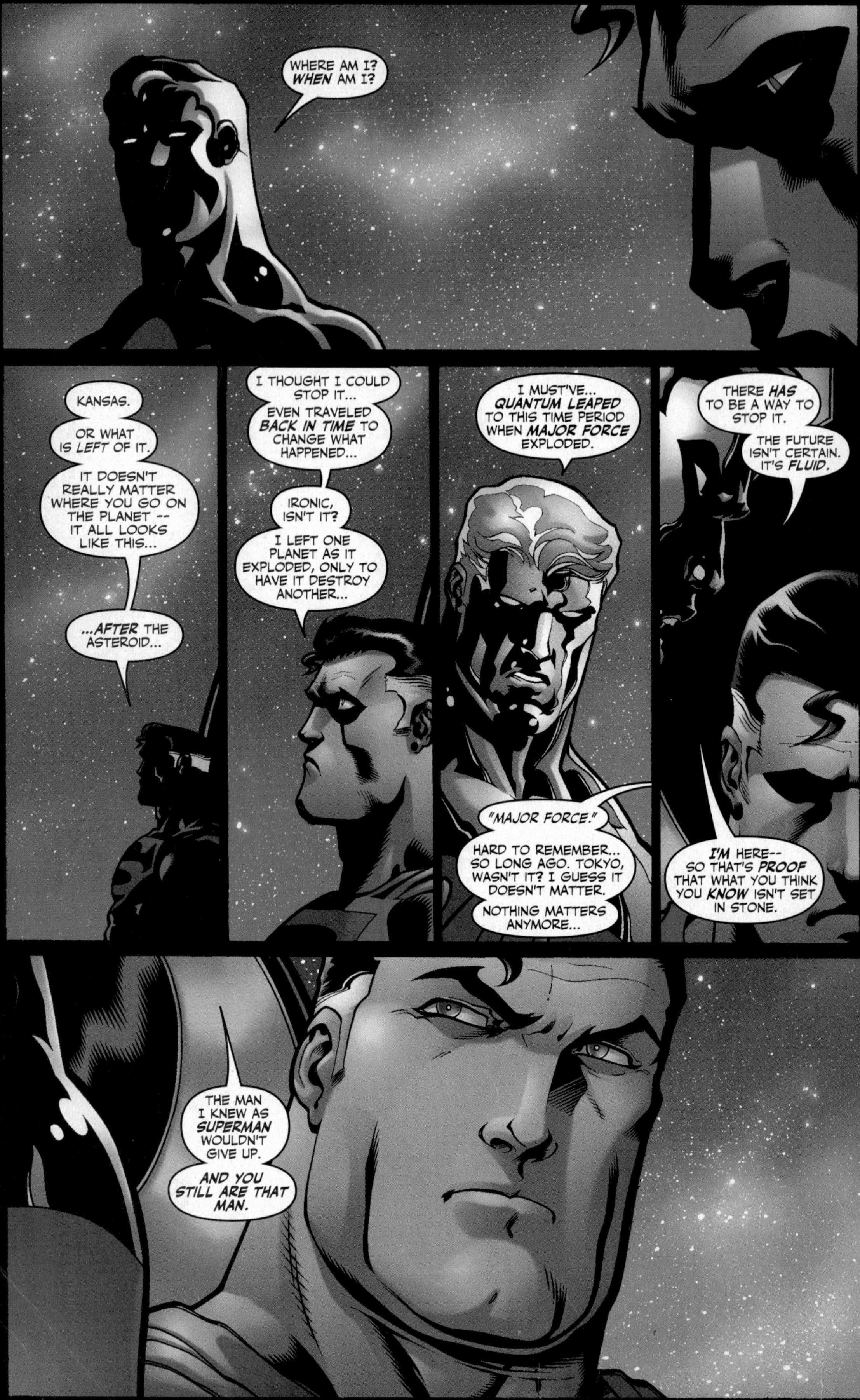
WHERE AM I? WHEN AM I?
KANSAS.
OR WHAT IS LEFT OF IT.
IT DOESN'T REALLY MATTER WHERE YOU GO ON THE PLANET -- IT ALL LOOKS LIKE THIS...
...AFTER THE ASTEROID...
I THOUGHT I COULD STOP IT... EVEN TRAVELED BACK IN TIME TO CHANGE WHAT HAPPENED...
IRONIC, ISN'T IT?
I LEFT ONE PLANET AS IT EXPLODED, ONLY TO HAVE IT DESTROY ANOTHER...
I MUST'VE... QUANTUM LEAPED TO THIS TIME PERIOD WHEN MAJOR FORCE EXPLODED.
"MAJOR FORCE."
HARD TO REMEMBER... SO LONG AGO. TOKYO, WASN'T IT? I GUESS IT DOESN'T MATTER.
NOTHING MATTERS ANYMORE...
THERE HAS TO BE A WAY TO STOP IT.
THE FUTURE ISN'T CERTAIN. IT'S FLUID.
I'M HERE-- SO THAT'S PROOF THAT WHAT YOU THINK YOU KNOW ISN'T SET IN STONE.
THE MAN I KNEW AS SUPERMAN WOULDN'T GIVE UP.
AND YOU STILL ARE THAT MAN.

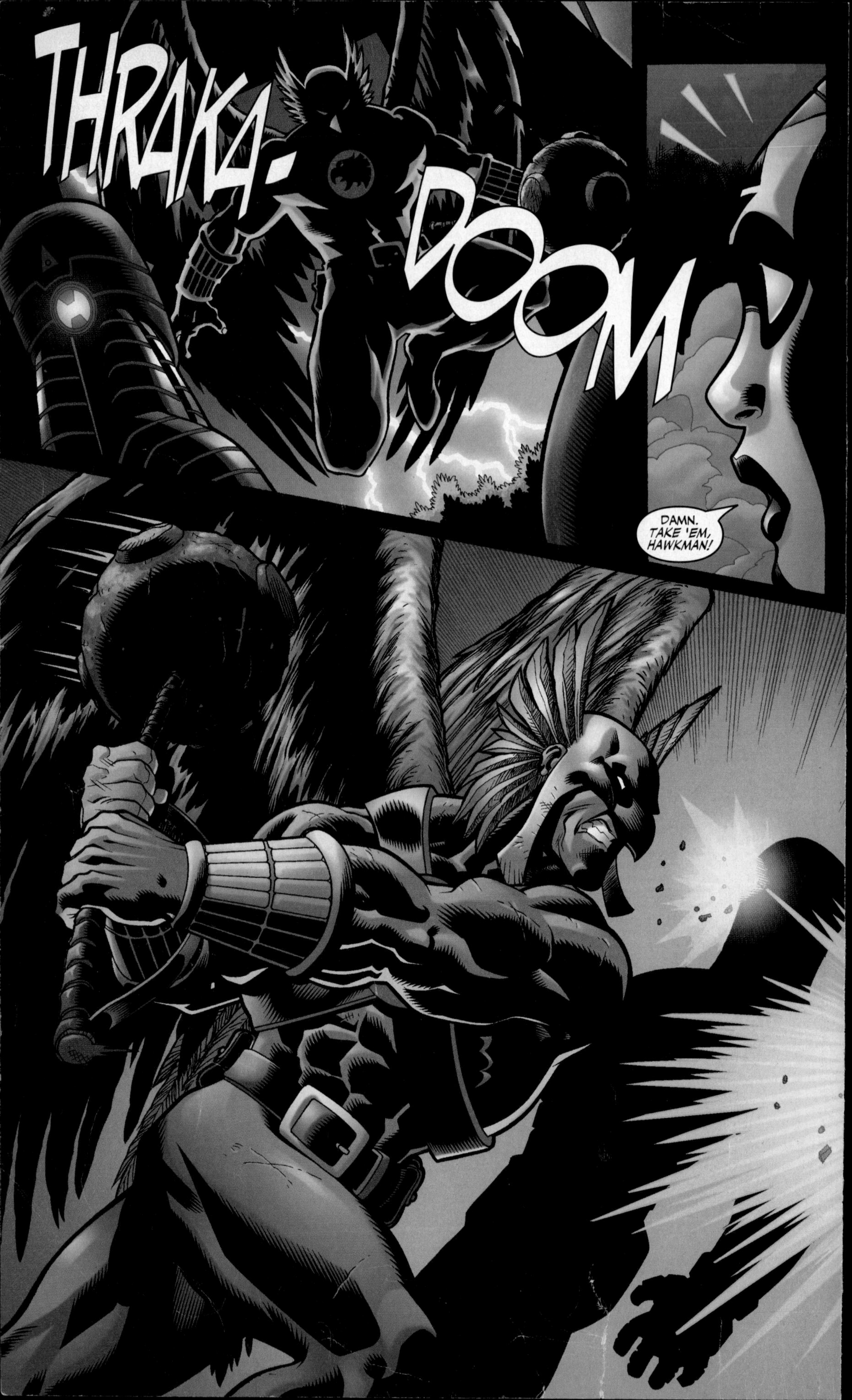
THRAKA-DOOM
DAMN. TAKE 'EM, HAWKMAN!

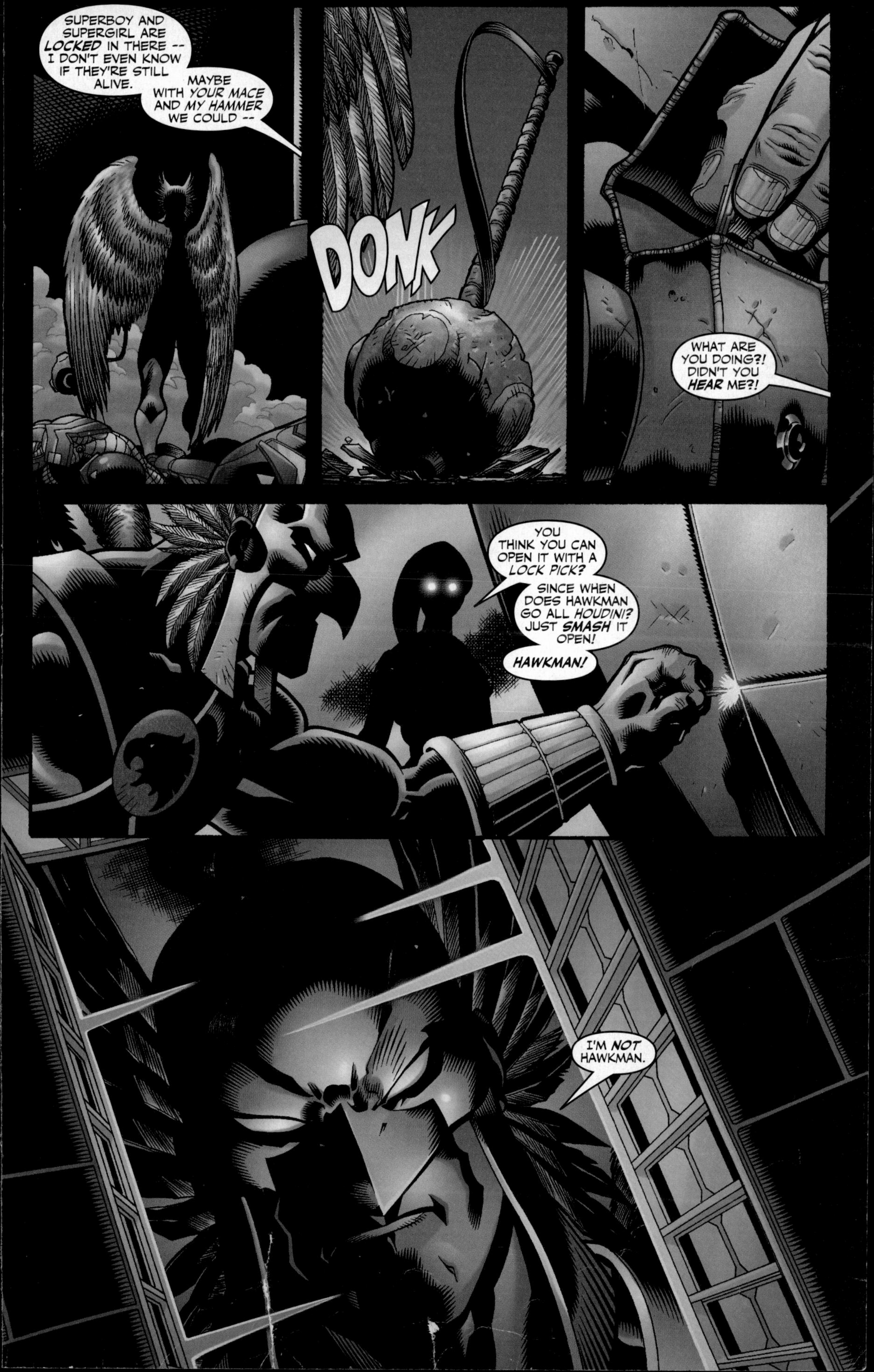
SUPERBOY AND SUPERGIRL ARE LOCKED IN THERE -- I DON'T EVEN KNOW IF THEY'RE STILL ALIVE.
MAYBE WITH YOUR MACE AND MY HAMMER WE COULD --
DONK
WHAT ARE YOU DOING?! DIDN'T YOU HEAR ME?!
YOU THINK YOU CAN OPEN IT WITH A LOCK PICK?
SINCE WHEN DOES HAWKMAN GO ALL HOUDINI? JUST SMASH IT OPEN!
HAWKMAN!
I'M NOT HAWKMAN.

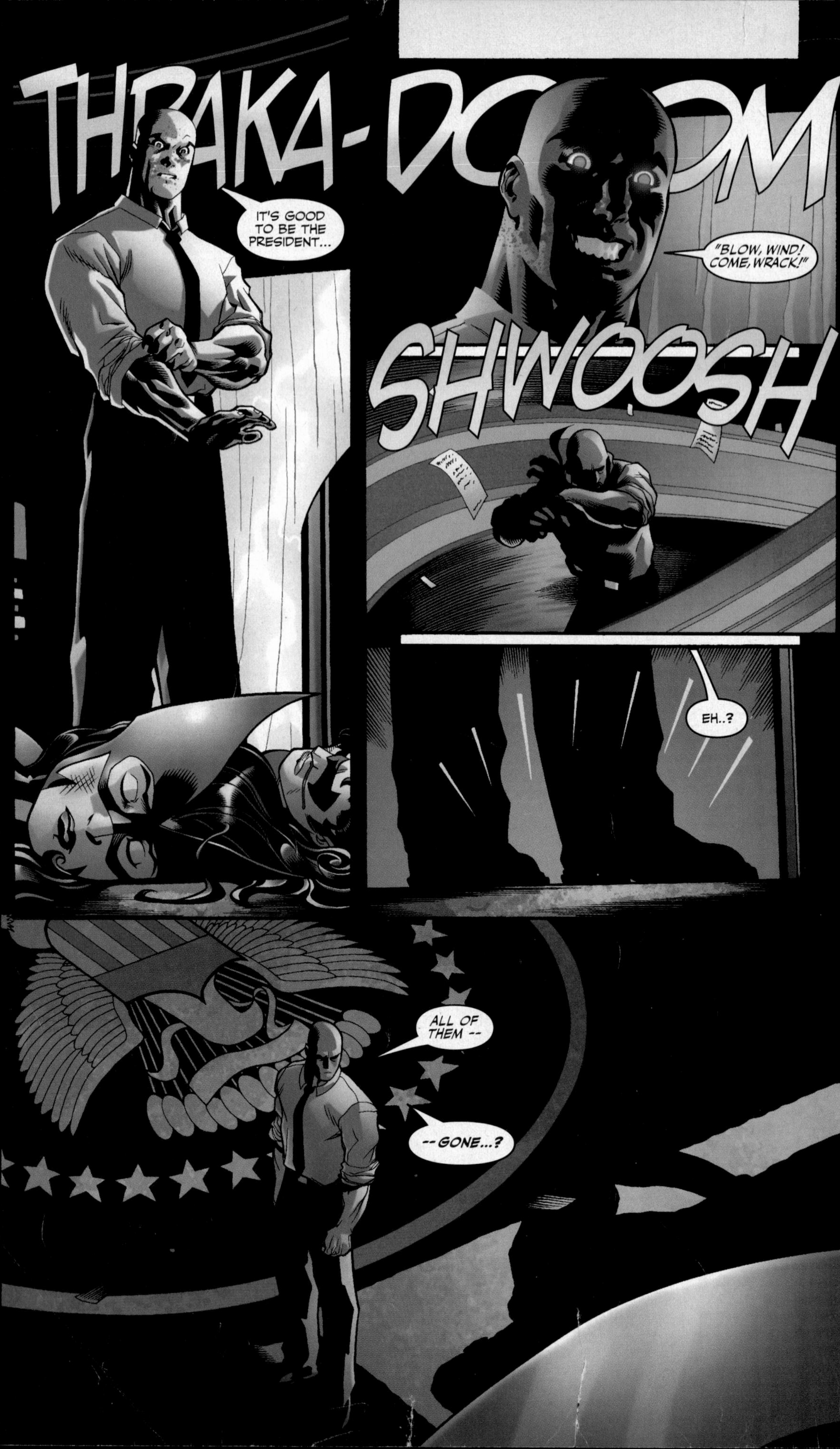
THRAKA-DOOOM
IT'S GOOD TO BE THE PRESIDENT...
"BLOW, WIND! COME, WRACK!"
SHWOOSH
EH..?
ALL OF THEM --
-- GONE...?

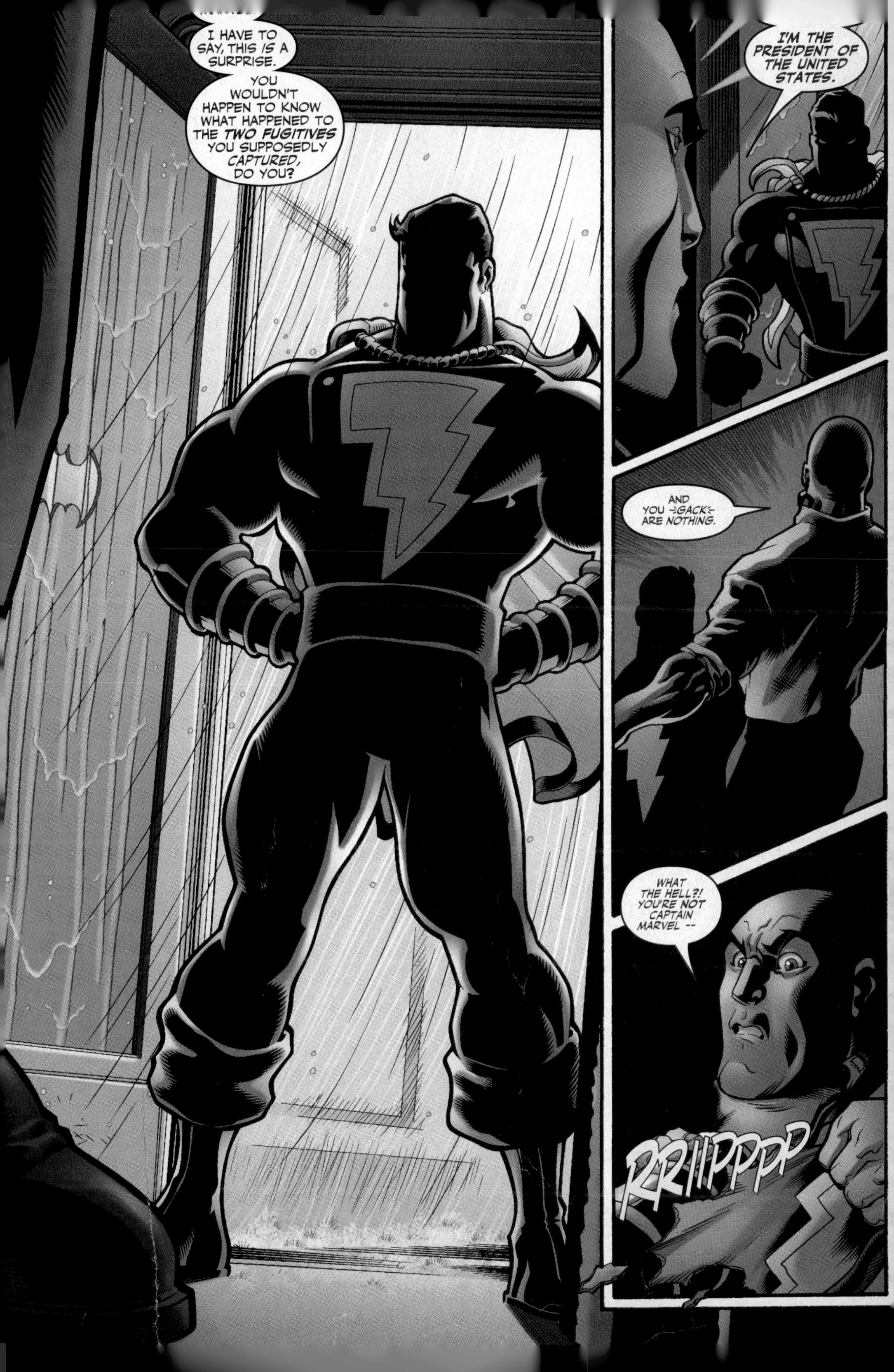
I HAVE TO SAY, THIS *IS* A SURPRISE.
YOU WOULDN'T HAPPEN TO KNOW WHAT HAPPENED TO THE **TWO FUGITIVES** YOU SUPPOSEDLY *CAPTURED*, DO YOU?
I'M THE PRESIDENT OF THE UNITED STATES.
AND YOU ~GACK~ ARE NOTHING.
WHAT THE HELL?! YOU'RE NOT CAPTAIN MARVEL --
RRIIPPPP

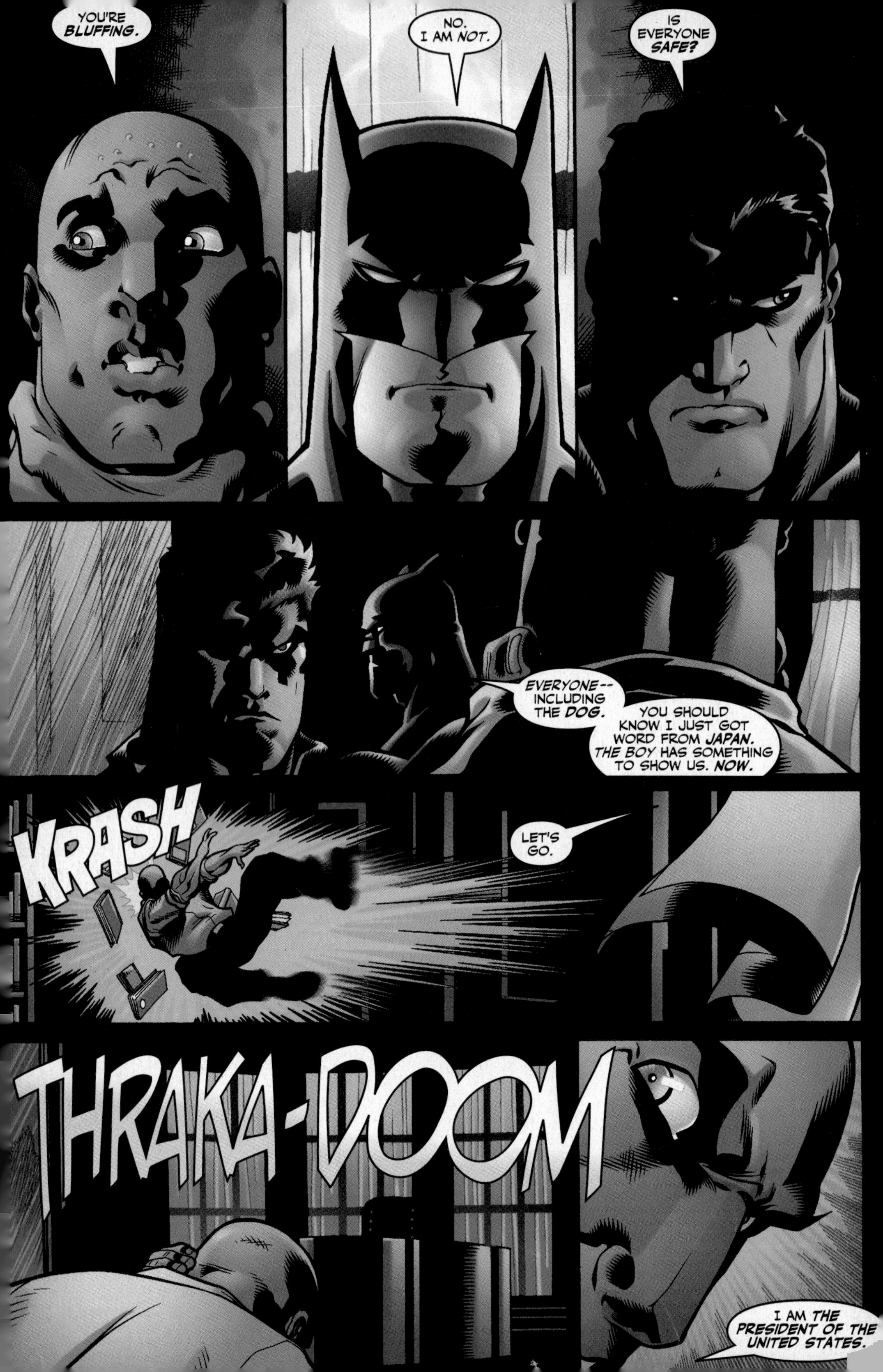
YOU'RE BLUFFING.
NO. I AM NOT.
IS EVERYONE SAFE?
EVERYONE-- INCLUDING THE DOG.
YOU SHOULD KNOW I JUST GOT WORD FROM JAPAN. THE BOY HAS SOMETHING TO SHOW US. NOW.
KRASH
LET'S GO.
THRAKA-DOOM
I AM THE PRESIDENT OF THE UNITED STATES.

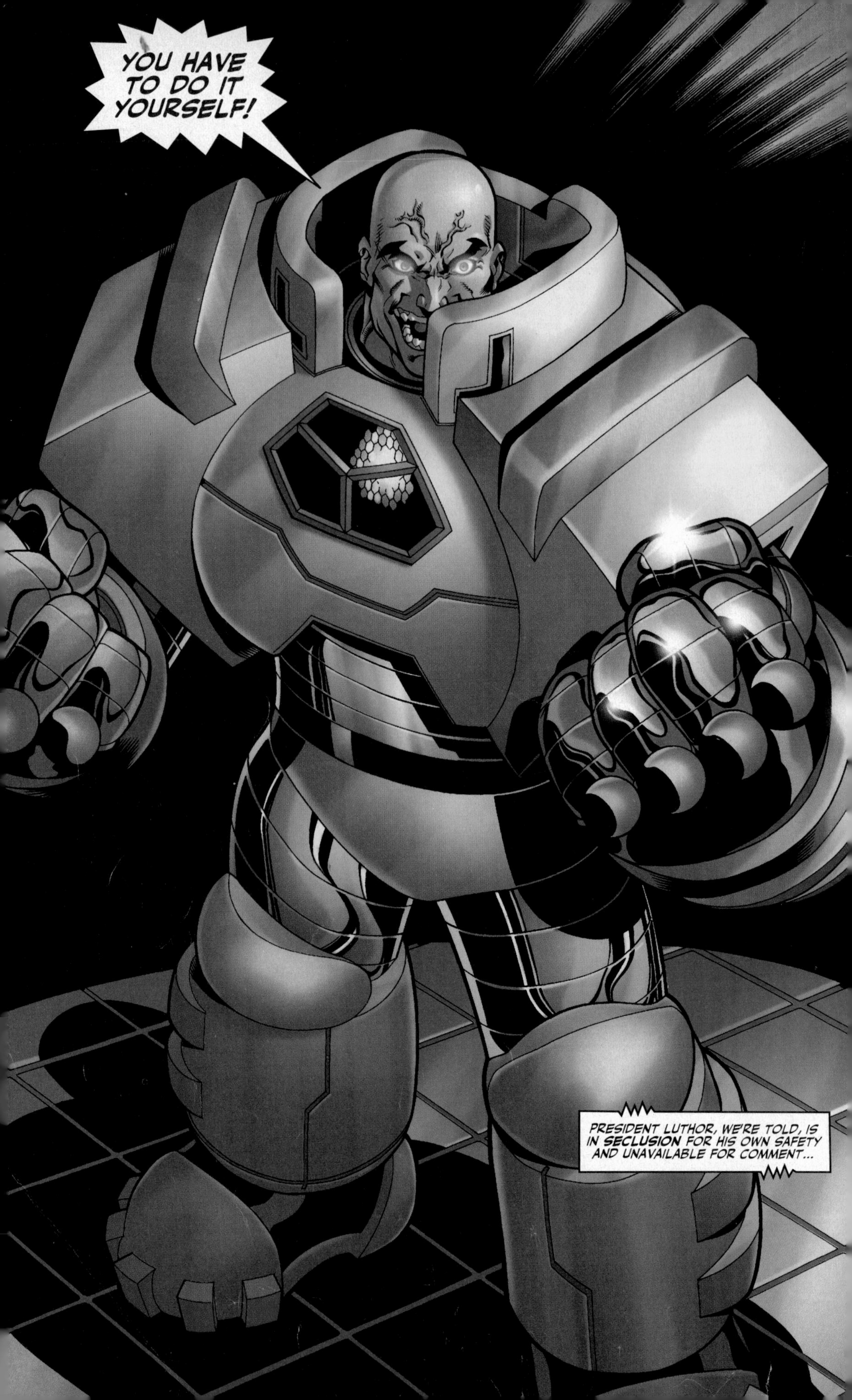
YOU HAVE TO DO IT YOURSELF!
PRESIDENT LUTHOR, WE'RE TOLD, IS IN SECLUSION FOR HIS OWN SAFETY AND UNAVAILABLE FOR COMMENT...

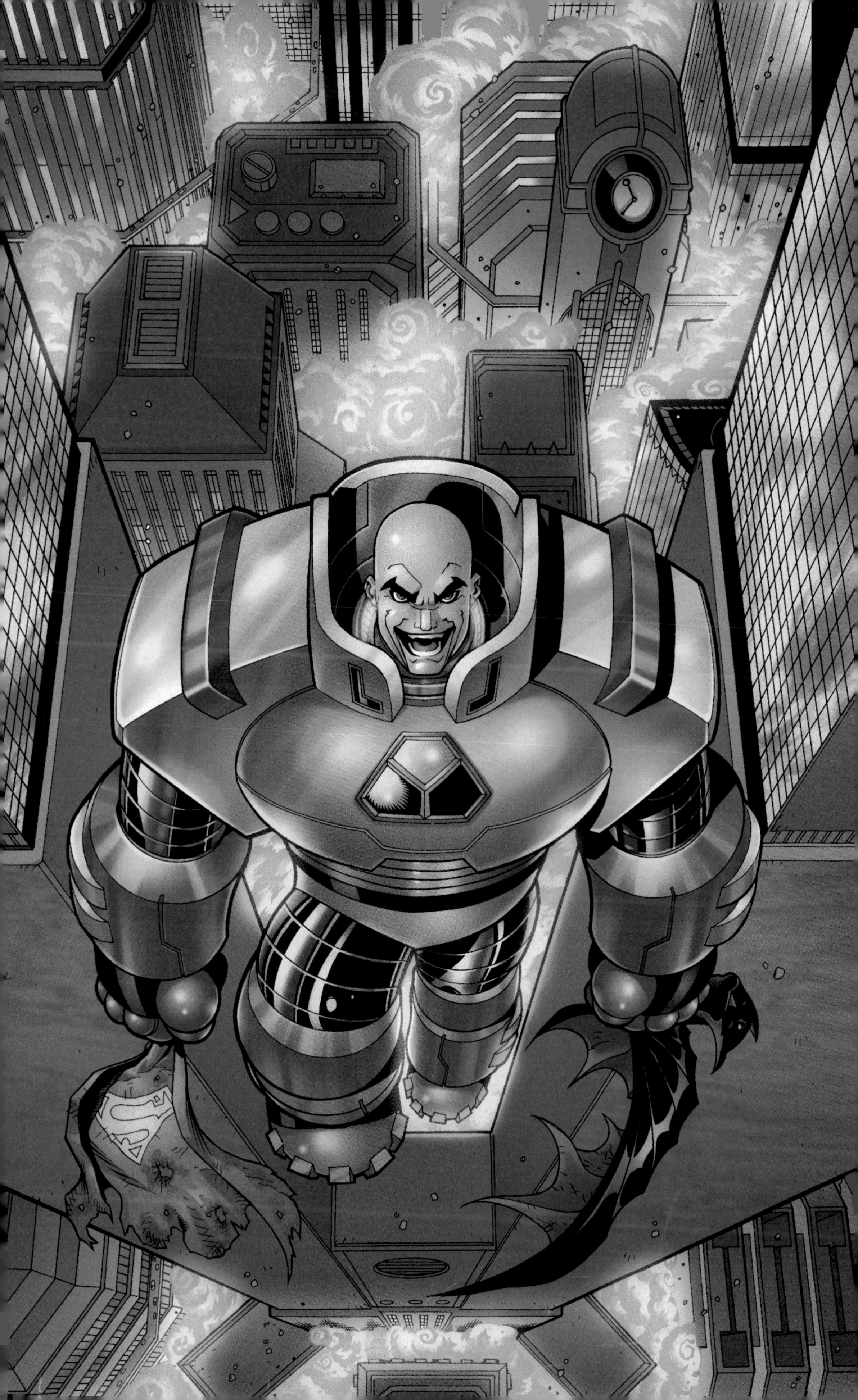

"When does it end, Luthor?"

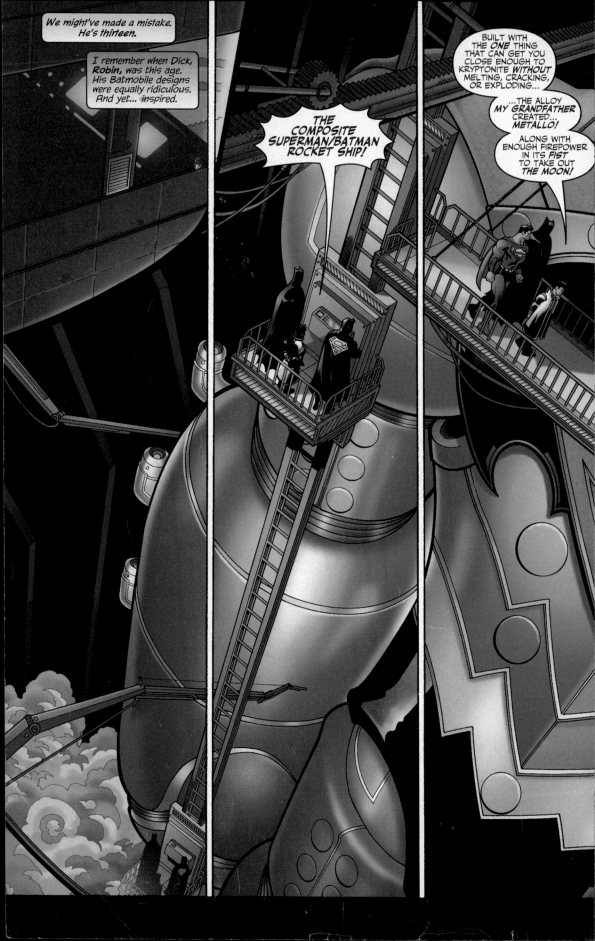

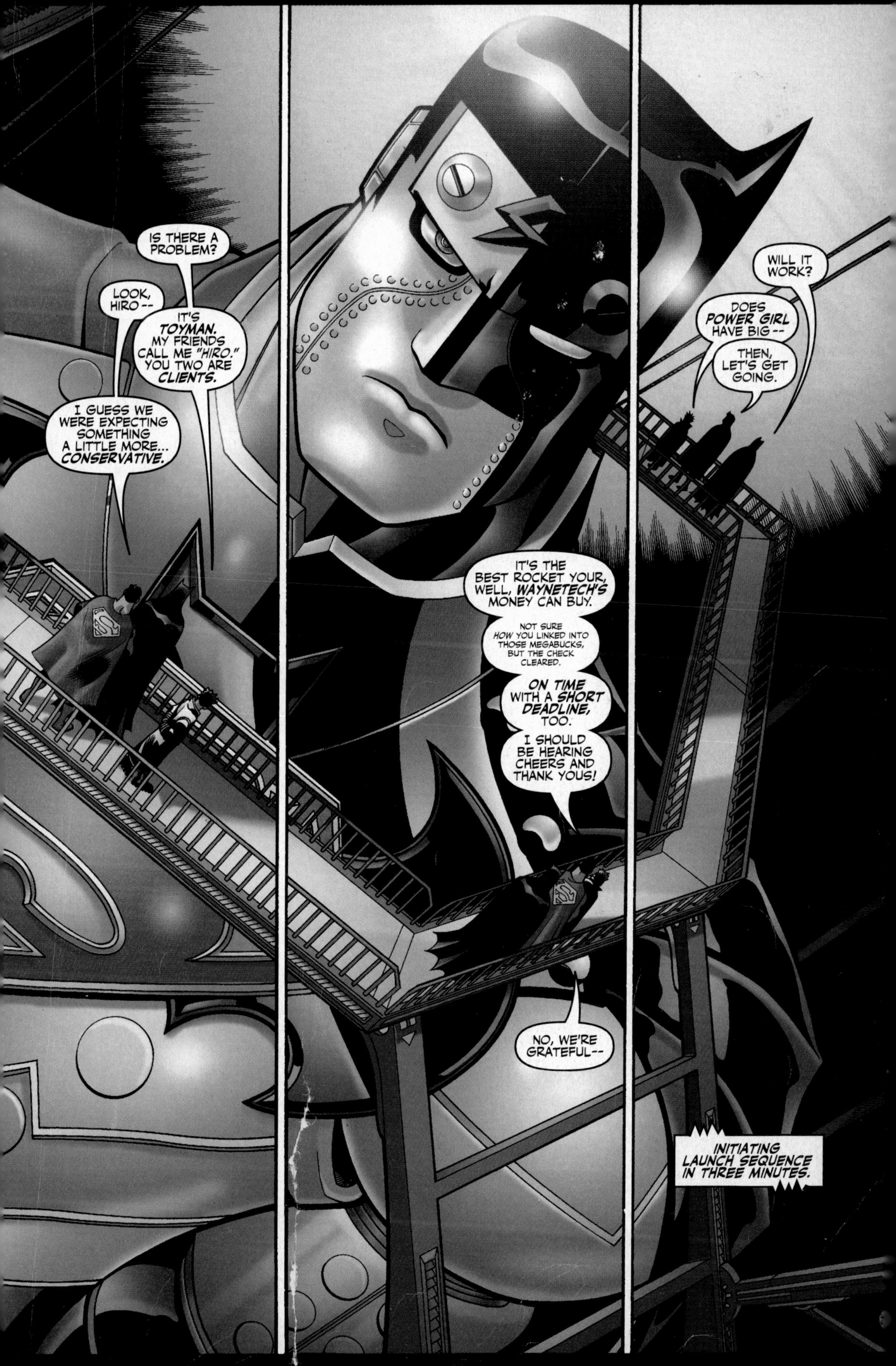
IS THERE A PROBLEM?
LOOK, HIRO--
IT'S TOYMAN. MY FRIENDS CALL ME "HIRO." YOU TWO ARE CLIENTS.
I GUESS WE WERE EXPECTING SOMETHING A LITTLE MORE... CONSERVATIVE.
IT'S THE BEST ROCKET YOUR, WELL, WAYNETECH'S MONEY CAN BUY.
NOT SURE HOW YOU LINKED INTO THOSE MEGABUCKS, BUT THE CHECK CLEARED.
ON TIME WITH A SHORT DEADLINE, TOO.
I SHOULD BE HEARING CHEERS AND THANK YOUS!
NO, WE'RE GRATEFUL--
WILL IT WORK?
DOES POWER GIRL HAVE BIG--
THEN, LET'S GET GOING.
INITIATING LAUNCH SEQUENCE IN THREE MINUTES.

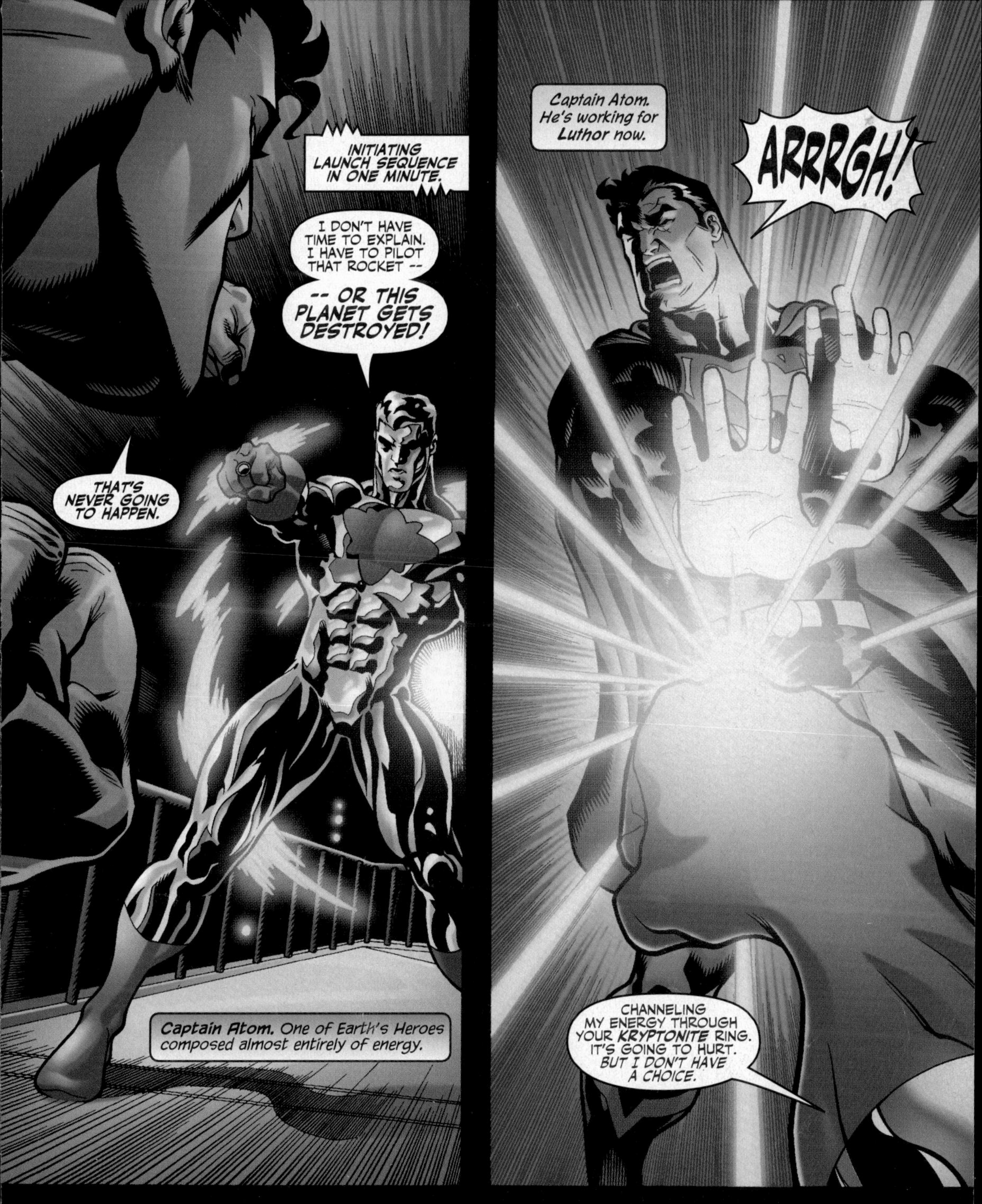
INITIATING LAUNCH SEQUENCE IN ONE MINUTE.
I DON'T HAVE TIME TO EXPLAIN. I HAVE TO PILOT THAT ROCKET --
-- OR THIS PLANET GETS DESTROYED!
THAT'S NEVER GOING TO HAPPEN.
Captain Atom. One of Earth's Heroes composed almost entirely of energy.
Captain Atom. He's working for Luthor now.
ARRRGH!
CHANNELING MY ENERGY THROUGH YOUR KRYPTONITE RING. IT'S GOING TO HURT. BUT I DON'T HAVE A CHOICE.

PART SIX: FINAL COUNTDOWN

TO THIS DAY I *STILL* CAN'T TELL IF YOU JUST *PLAY* NAIVE...

DARKSEID HAS *ALWAYS* BEEN MY ALLY. *TECHNOLOGY* IS WHAT MOVED THIS COUNTRY LEAGUES AHEAD OF THE REST OF THE WORLD -- THE UNIVERSE.

WHO DO YOU THINK FIRST ALERTED ME TO THE PRESENCE OF THE *ASTEROID?* WHO MADE ME *AWARE* OF ITS *ORIGINS* -- -- AND HOW AND WHY IT IS DRAWN TOWARD *YOU?!*

...OR FOR SOME REASON YOU SHOW NO MORE SENSE THAN IF YOU WERE RAISED IN A *BARN.*

If I am guilty of **one** *mistake, it was putting my faith in the American public* **not** *to vote for him.*

AND DARKSEID OFFERED *WHATEVER* I NEEDED AS PRESIDENT IN THAT REGARD.

The world will **never** *know how I struggled with the decision to* **stay out** *of the electoral process.*

Should I have gone on television and told the voters **not** *to elect this man? And what then?*

YOU REALLY ARE *DELUSIONAL.* YOU'RE TALKING ABOUT AN INANIMATE OBJECT -- A GIANT *ROCK.*

NO! IT'S FAR MORE THAN THAT. IT'S THE LIGHT THAT WILL OPEN THEIR EYES.

KRAX

IF MANKIND HAS ONE COMMON EMOTION -- IT'S *FEAR.* FEAR OF THE UNKNOWN. FEAR OF WHAT THEY CANNOT CONTROL.

AND LOOK HOW READY THEY ARE TO BELIEVE THAT YOU ARE THAT THING THEY FEAR THE MOST!

If I use my influence -- my character and my reputation -- to tell people how to vote, what does that make me?

EVEN IF IT *WAS* FOR LUTHOR. EVEN IF I HAD THE UGLY TASK OF BRINGING IN THE GREATEST HERO WHO EVER LIVED.

THIS WAS SOMETHING FOR *ME.* I BALANCED THE TEAM AS BEST I COULD. SADDLED WITH *MAJOR FORCE* -- I HAD *JOHN STEWART, THE GREEN LANTERN* TO WATCH HIM.

FOR ALL OF *STARFIRE'S* PASSION, *BLACK LIGHTNING* WAS LEVEL-HEADED.

AND I *GAMBLED* THAT *KATANA* AND *POWER GIRL'S* LOYALTY TO BATMAN AND SUPERMAN WOULD PROVE AN ASSET.

PERHAPS... IF NECESSARY... TO KEEP *ME* IN CHECK. AND IT DID.

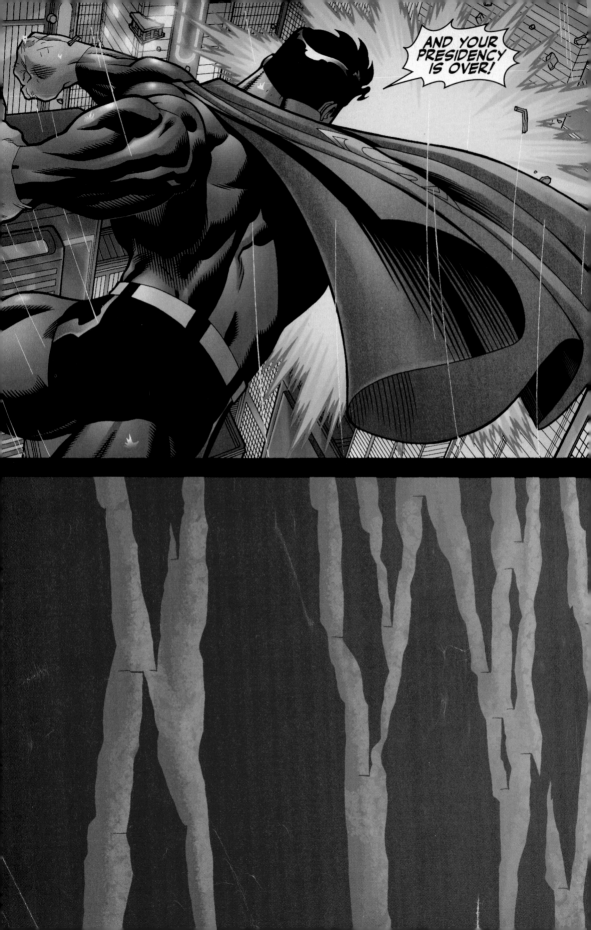

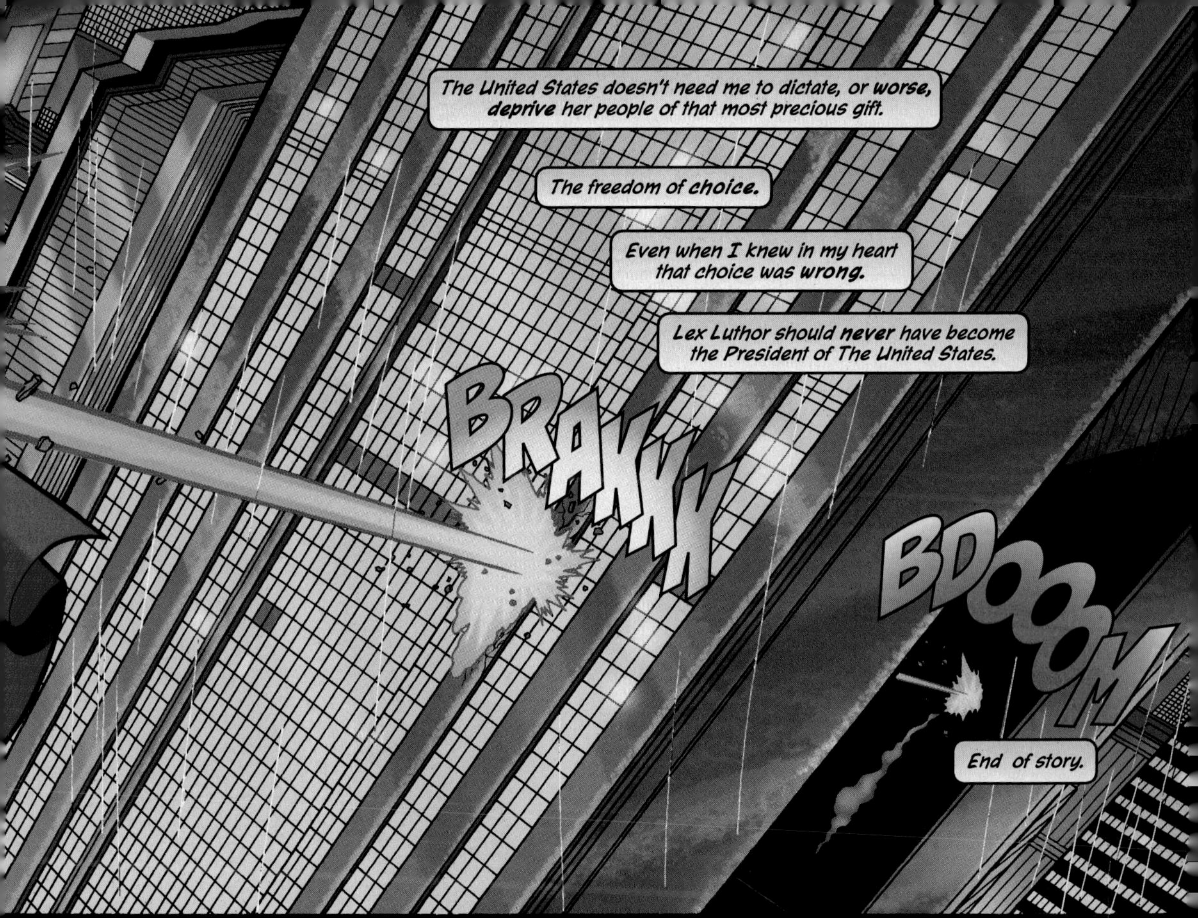
The United States doesn't need me to dictate, or worse, deprive her people of that most precious gift.
The freedom of choice.
Even when I knew in my heart that choice was wrong.
Lex Luthor should never have become the President of The United States.
BRAKKK
BDOOOM
End of story.

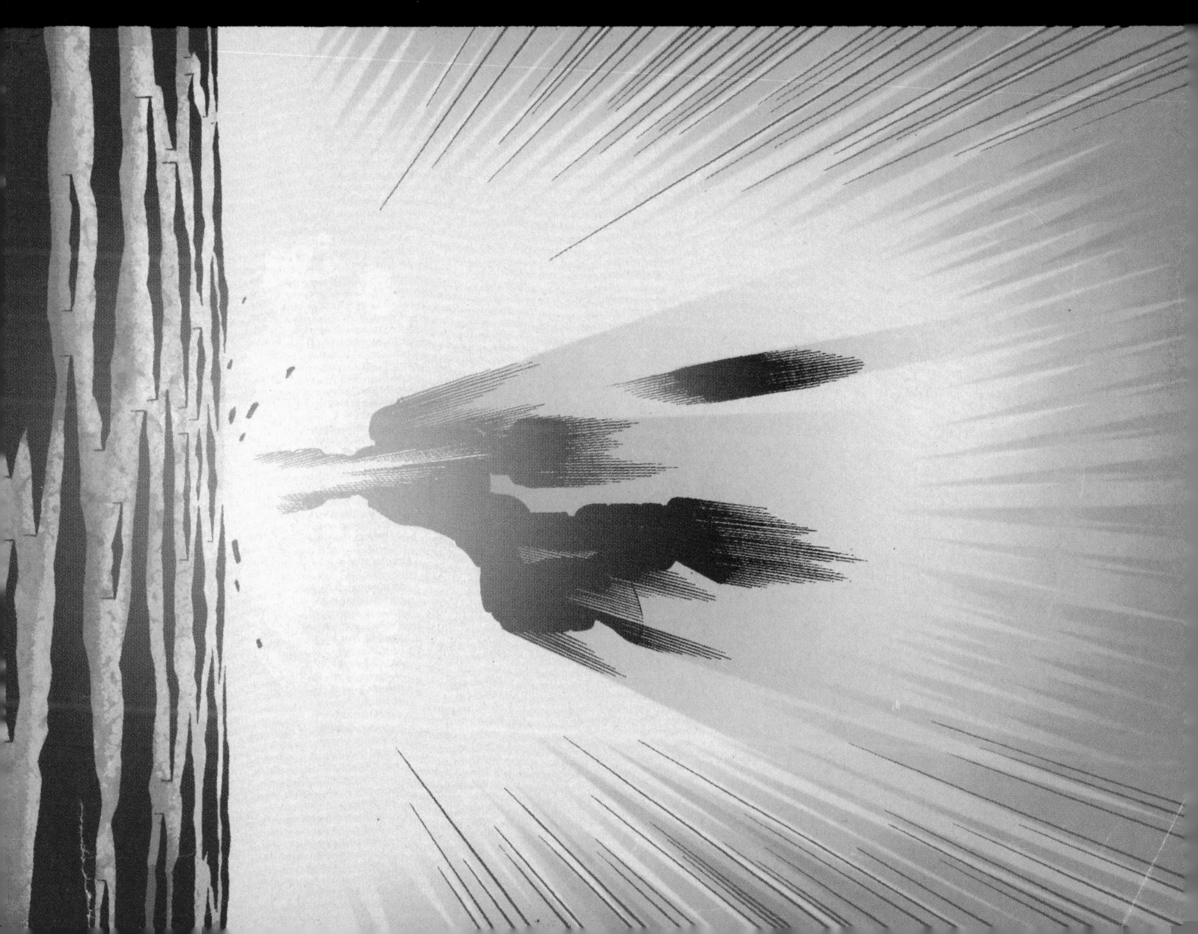

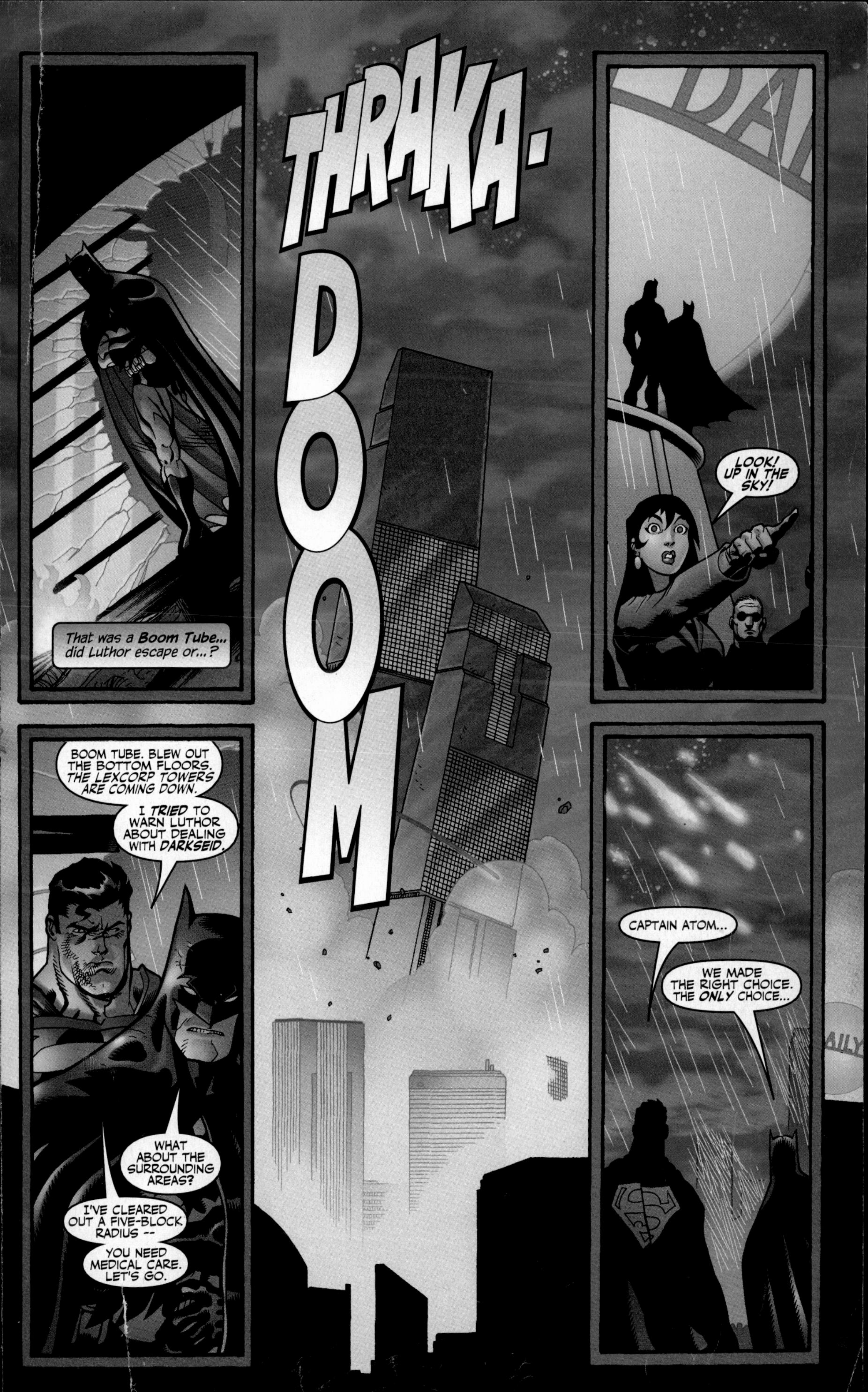

That was a Boom Tube... did Luthor escape or...?
THRAKA-DOOOM
LOOK! UP IN THE SKY!
BOOM TUBE. BLEW OUT THE BOTTOM FLOORS. THE LEXCORP TOWERS ARE COMING DOWN.
I TRIED TO WARN LUTHOR ABOUT DEALING WITH DARKSEID.
WHAT ABOUT THE SURROUNDING AREAS?
I'VE CLEARED OUT A FIVE-BLOCK RADIUS --
YOU NEED MEDICAL CARE. LET'S GO.
CAPTAIN ATOM...
WE MADE THE RIGHT CHOICE. THE ONLY CHOICE...

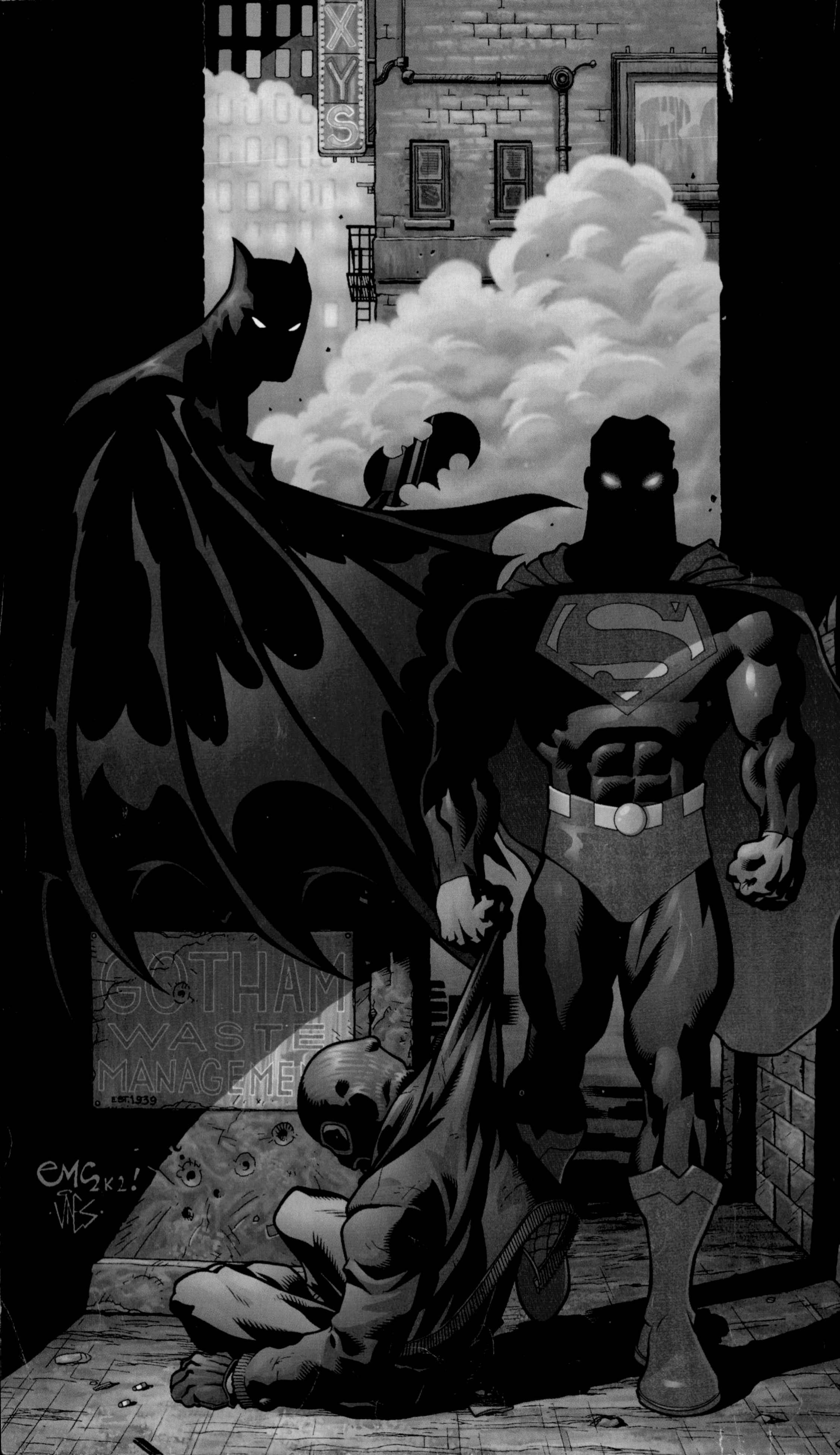
XYS
GOTHAM
WASTE
MANAGEMEN
EST. 1939

Cover to third printing of SUPERMAN/BATMAN #1.

BIOGRAPHIES

JEPH LOEB is the author of BATMAN: THE LONG HALLOWEEN, BATMAN: DARK VICTORY, SUPERMAN FOR ALL SEASONS, *Spider-Man: Blue*, *Daredevil: Yellow* and *Hulk: Gray*. Currently, Jeph is writing SUPERMAN/BATMAN and CATWOMAN: WHEN IN ROME. A writer/producer living in Los Angeles, his credits include *Teen Wolf, Commando,* and *Smallville.*

ED McGUINNESS first gained the notice of comic-book fans with his work on *Deadpool* and *Vampirella.* His short run on WildStorm's MR. MAJESTIC landed him a gig on the monthly SUPERMAN title with Jeph Loeb, which led to the THUNDERCATS: RECLAIMING THUNDERA miniseries and arcs on SUPERMAN/BATMAN. He lives in Maine with his wife and four kids.

DEXTER VINES has been an inker in the comics industry for nearly a decade, having worked on numerous titles for various publishers, including *Uncanny X-Men, Weapon X* and *Wolverine* for Marvel Comics, *Meridian* for CrossGen Entertainment, and BATMAN: TENSES for DC.

DAVE STEWART began his career as an intern at Dark Horse Comics, and then quickly moved into coloring comics. His credits include *Fray,* HUMAN TARGET: DIRECTOR'S CUT, SUPERMAN/BATMAN/WONDER WOMAN: TRINITY, H-E-R-O, and *Hellboy: The Third Wish* (for which he won an Eisner and Harvey Award). He lives in Portland, Oregon, and is currently working on DC: THE NEW FRONTIER, *B.P.R.D.* and *Ultimate Fantastic Four.*

RICHARD STARKINGS is best known as the creator of the Comicraft studio, purveyors of unique design and fine lettering — and a copious catalogue of comic-book fonts — since 1992. He is less well known as the creator and publisher of *Hip Flask* and his semi-autobiographical cartoon strip, *Hedge Backwards.* He never seems to get tired of reminding people that he lettered BATMAN: THE KILLING JOKE with a pen.

DAN DIDIO VP-Editorial EDDIE BERGANZA MATT IDELSON Editors-original series TOM PALMER, JR. Associate Editor-original series ANTON KAWASAKI Editor-collected edition
ROBBIN BROSTERMAN Senior Art Director PAUL LEVITZ President & Publisher GEORG BREWER VP-Design & Retail Product Development RICHARD BRUNING Senior VP-Creative Director
PATRICK CALDON Senior VP-Finance & Operations CHRIS CARAMALIS VP-Finance TERRI CUNNINGHAM VP-Managing Editor ALISON GILL VP-Manufacturing
LILLIAN LASERSON Senior VP & General Counsel JIM LEE Editorial Director-WildStorm DAVID MCKILLIPS VP-Advertising & Custom Publishing JOHN NEE VP-Business Development
GREGORY NOVECK Senior VP-Creative Affairs CHERYL RUBIN VP-Brand Management BOB WAYNE VP-Sales & Marketing

SUPERMAN/BATMAN: PUBLIC ENEMIES

DC Comics, 1700 Broadway, New York, NY 10019. A Warner Bros. Entertainment Company. Printed in Canada. First Printing. ISBN: 1 4012 0323 X.
Cover art by Ed McGuinness and Dexter Vines. All covers colored by Dave Stewart